Divided by Borders

Divided by Borders

MEXICAN MIGRANTS AND THEIR CHILDREN

JOANNA DREBY

UNIVERSITY OF CALIFORNIA PRESS

Berkeley Los Angeles London

University of California Press, one of the most distinguished university presses in the United States, enriches lives around the world by advancing scholarship in the humanities, social sciences, and natural sciences. Its activities are supported by the UC Press Foundation and by philanthropic contributions from individuals and institutions. For more information, visit www.ucpress.edu.

University of California Press
Berkeley and Los Angeles, California

University of California Press, Ltd.
London, England

Library of Congress Cataloging-in-Publication Data

Dreby, Joanna, 1976–
Divided by borders : Mexican migrants and their children / Joanna Dreby.
p. cm.
Includes bibliographical references and index.
ISBN 978-0-520-26660-5 (cloth : alk. paper)
ISBN 978-0-520-26090-0 (pbk. : alk. paper)
1. Mexico—Emigration and immigration. 2. Mexicans—Family relationships—United States—Case studies. 3. Emigrant remittances—Mexico. 4. Households—Mexico. 5. Marital conflict—Case studies. 6. Parent and child—Case studies. I. Title.

JV7402.D74 2010
306.874—dc22 200901865

Manufactured in the United States of America

19 18 17 16 15 14 13 12 11 10
10 9 8 7 6 5 4 3 2 1

This book is printed on Cascades Enviro 100, a 100% post consumer waste, recycled, de-inked fiber. FSC recycled certified and processed chlorine free. It is acid free, Ecologo certified, and manufactured by BioGas energy.

Dedico este libro a
Cristian y Raúl Mariscal
(quienes se encuentran en los dos lados de la frontera)

Contents

Preface

ORDINARY FAMILIES, EXTRAORDINARY FAMILIES

Mexican families divided by borders are both ordinary and extraordinary. Parents who live in the United States while their children remain in Mexico experience many of the difficulties faced by all families in meeting productive and consumptive needs. Family members struggle to balance pressures at work with those at home. Gender and generation battles are common. Men and women negotiate the division of labor. Parents and children negotiate authority. In this sense, this book is about rather ordinary tensions in families.

At the same time, migrant parents and their children live in vastly different environments. Parents live hurried lives, struggling to work hard, economize, and send much of their money back to children in Mexico. For them, the joys of life are found in Mexico. Children live in places where everyday consumption depends upon remittances from parents and other migrants. Contributions from *el norte* [the north] permeate their daily lives, and many children think that when the time is right, they too will end up migrating for work. Divided by borders and by the lifestyle differences involved in such separations, Mexican migrants and their children find ways to make their relationships with each other meaningful. These efforts are not easy. The difficulties parents and children endure make their stories both remarkable and unique.

Indeed, the stories in this book skip along a fine line between the extraordinary and the ordinary. Within the chapters that follow, I describe the social conditions that make it hard for parents to provide for their children in Mexico and spur their migration to the United States. I offer explanations for why some women and men make the heart-wrenching decision to leave their children behind. I discuss how their social status as transnational migrants shapes families' experiences.

Yet I also tell stories about fairly typical relationships between men, women, and children. Mothers anguish over their decisions to work. Fathers feel pressured to provide economically for their children. Teenagers complain that they need their parents while acting in ways that push parents away. Young children are jealous for their parents' attention. Parents struggling to understand their children's changing needs are unsure how to discipline them and worry about their children dating and becoming sexually active. Above all, parents hope their children will avoid their own mistakes and want to provide them with a better future. These themes are likely to sound strikingly familiar.

This was my experience as a researcher. I am not Mexican, nor Latina. I am not an immigrant. Yet I am a mother and a daughter. For a time, I was a wife. I often found during the four years that I conducted this study that my own life paralleled those of the families I was interviewing. My experiences are instructive about how I managed relationships with the more than 140 participants in this project, gaining access to what they often considered to be private aspects of their lives. They also illustrate the persistent tension between the ordinary and the extraordinary endemic in researching family relationships.

I ALWAYS THOUGHT YOU WERE NORMAL . . .

It was in January, after a day of sightseeing at the ruins of Monte Alban, in Oaxaca, and I was enjoying an evening of casual conversation with

Armando, a migrant father and a member of one of the twelve families with whom I did in-depth work for this study. I had met and interviewed Armando in New Jersey and then traveled to Mexico, where I interviewed his three children and his mother, who cared for them. While I was living in Mexico for nine months, Armando returned to live with his children. Later I visited and stayed with the family twice more. On this occasion, Armando and I had met up at a friend's house just a month after his arrival and spent three days touring the city and comparing notes on my time in Mexico and his return home.

That evening we drifted into a conversation about my research, how sociology differs from psychology, and how I planned to make my findings useful. We had previously talked about this in New Jersey, but Armando, who had already told me quite a bit about his life, was not the first to ask what I was "really" doing interviewing families like his in Mexico. He and I continued talking as the night wore on, moving into more personal topics long after the others had gone to sleep.

"You are always asking me all these questions about my life, but I never felt comfortable asking you before about yours," he commented.

"I am an open book," I responded. This was the attitude I took throughout the study. Separation was a sensitive topic for parents. When people I interviewed asked me about myself, my Mexican husband, or my son, I felt obligated to reciprocate with my own story. That night I elaborated.

Armando was a good listener. He quietly accepted the pieces of my story before responding, "I always thought you were normal, Joanna. But you are just like the rest of us."

A WIFE

Armando was referring primarily to my marriage and recent separation from Raúl. At the time, Raúl and I had been separated for about a year; we subsequently divorced. To Armando's surprise, I—who had served as a sounding board for his insecurities and concerns over his recent divorce—had similar skeletons in my own matrimonial closet.

In fact, there were a number of parallels in our experiences. Armando was twenty-nine when he married a woman ten years younger, and he felt that the age difference and her immaturity had caused problems in the marriage. Armando said he had very little in common with his ex-wife. "I fell in love with her smile," he once explained, emphasizing how they had lacked shared interests and goals. I met Raúl when I was just twenty-one, not long after I had graduated from college. Raúl, six years older than I, was an immigrant from Veracruz who had been out of school and working for years. We had met as activists. Before starting this research, I had worked for a number of years in three different social service agencies and as an ESL teacher in central New Jersey. Aside from our work in the Mexican immigrant community, however, Raúl and I were very different. Eventually our differences in age, education, background, and most crucially, experience became problematic.

Economic difficulties also plagued both our marriages. Armando's wife had pressured him to migrate, something he had not been eager to do, to help the family *sobresalir,* or get ahead. He felt she was more concerned with material goods and status items than he was. Raúl and I struggled to manage our finances as I pursued graduate school full time and he aspired to start his own business. Raúl's multiple obligations to family members in Mexico, particularly after the birth of our own child, further strained our resources. We disagreed on how to prioritize our family's needs.

Armando and I shared experiences common to many divorced couples. Economic difficulty, lack of common interests, and immaturity are typical sources of marital conflict. In fact, Armando's observation about me had missed the mark slightly: we were actually both normal.

Marital conflict is a central theme of this book and was common in all types of migrant families I interviewed. In some families, it was fathers who had migrated, leaving their wives and children in Mexico. For these fathers, physical separation presented a number of challenges in maintaining the marriage. Accusations of infidelity (by both wives and husbands) were particularly common. In other families I met, single mothers had migrated alone. Often their migration had been precipitated by difficulties with the children's father, which came either after an unintended pregnancy or after a divorce. Tensions in conjugal relationships were also evident in cases in which both parents were living together in the United States and had left their children in Mexico. I witnessed marriages breaking up in the United States or, in the case of one family I interviewed, after the couple had returned to Mexico. In the end, it was difficult to learn anything about parenting, the primary focus of this study, without first learning something about marriage. Men's and women's relationships with their children are inevitably intertwined with their relationships with each other.

A STEPMOTHER?

For Armando, it was the problems with his ex-wife that had prompted a deepening of his relationships with his children in Mexico and his return to live with them. I witnessed a similar dynamic while married to Raúl, who had two children in Mexico from a prior marriage. At the time, I did not know I would subsequently study families like his. At first I was primarily concerned with the plight of migrant mothers, and I had not considered Raúl's life to be particularly telling. Yet I came to view fathers' relationships with their children as key to understanding those of migrant mothers. I now see that my observations about Raúl's relationship with his children during the five years we lived together and afterward (we had a relatively amicable divorce) are consistent with the experiences of others in this study.

When we first met, I often listened to Raúl's phone conversations with his children, at that time ages four and six. Raúl maintained fairly regular contact with them and with his ex-wife, calling once a week and sending money once or twice a month. He would ask how the children were, if they needed anything, and what gifts they wanted him to send. At Christmas, Raúl sent money for bicycles. In the spring, we packed a box of toys and T-shirts that cost thirty dollars to send and took more than a month to arrive by mail. The following fall, when I visited Raúl's parents in Mexico, I left remote-control cars and clothes to be taken to the boys.

About a year later, Raúl's ex-wife, frustrated with her lack of work opportunities in Mexico, decided to come to the United States. Raúl was upset the day she called from Texas. He had no idea she had planned to leave the children with her mother, and he did not think this was good for them. After his ex-wife migrated, Raúl's communication with his children suffered, because the boys' grandmother did not let him talk to them.

Then there was an abrupt change. Raúl's ex-wife moved in with another man. Her mother, back with the children in Mexico, was angry. She complained to Raúl and allowed him greater access to the children. He called the children more frequently, sometimes twice a week; he visited the children and even spoke with his ex-mother-in-law about taking custody of them. Later, when I became pregnant, Raúl talked to the boys about their having a new sibling. They did not act angry or jealous. Initially they seemed ambivalent. Then they became excited. Raúl's oldest son gave us permission to name the baby after him (and my grandfather). When the baby was born, they wanted to talk to him over the phone. That December we traveled to Veracruz, and I met Raúl's children for the first time. The boys did not seem to hate me, as I had expected, but rather were curious. They played affectionately with their little half-brother.

Throughout this time, we learned of Raúl's ex-wife's life only through the grapevine. We were told that she too had another child with her new partner. The baby was born a month before our son, and fearing their reaction, she had not told the boys about it until after the fact. They were upset. Rumor had it that her attentions to her children in Mexico had waned because her new husband was *machista:* he did not want to accept her children from a prior marriage. Eventually, however, it was she, not Raúl, who returned to Mexico. After living with the boys in Veracruz for a time, she left them with her mother again and moved with her youngest child to her new husband's family home. After about a year of no communication, Raúl once again was able to communicate with his children freely. Later, Raúl's oldest son moved to his paternal grandparents' home to further his studies, and Raúl continues to visit his children in Mexico periodically.

Raúl's experiences in fathering from afar, I now see, are typical. Like that of other parents, Raúl's relationship with his children fluctuated greatly over a short period of time. It was dictated to some degree by his relationship with his ex-wife and also by gendered expectations of mothers and fathers. These two themes, gender and the passage of time, are central to understanding the extraordinary aspects of how family members' lives unfold while living apart.

A MOTHER

When Armando said, "I always thought you were normal," he was ribbing me for my complicated relationship with Raúl and his children in Mexico. But Armando's comment also points to another parallel in our experiences: we both worried greatly about how to provide our children with a stable and loving home environment. This was something that tormented Armando. He struggled over how his decision to migrate had affected his children. He felt guilty that his decisions and his difficulties with his ex-wife had adversely affected his children. He deliberated over how to explain his problems with his ex-wife to them. He considered his children carefully as he planned for the future.

That evening I shared with Armando my concerns regarding my son's adjustment to living in Mexico, so far from his father. Already separated from Raúl at the time, I was determined that two-year-old Temo would not lose touch with his father while we were away. I hoped that Temo would have an ongoing, positive relationship with his father, as I had with my own father after my parents divorced. Thus, during my first few months of living in a small community in Oaxaca, Mexico, I found myself anxiously anticipating Raúl's calls. I empathized with the women awaiting calls at the *caseta* (public phone) on the first floor of the house where I stayed for seven months. Though not economically dependent on such calls, as the other women were, I got frustrated when calls would not come through or when the phone card ran out of minutes, cutting off our conversations mid-sentence.

More strikingly, as I explained to Armando, I was surprised at how my son reacted to living without his father. Temo could not remember a time when he had lived with Raúl; the same was true of Armando's four-year-old daughter, who had never met him before he returned. For Temo, Daddy was someone who visited several times a week. Yet after we moved in with a couple in Mexico who had a three-year-old daughter, Temo was instantly interested in fathers. For a time he insisted that the taxi driver who accompanied us on a ten-day trip to visit families (including Armando's) was his father. At the beach, Temo requested that I draw pictures in the sand of not only the mommy and baby fish but the daddy fish as well. When we visited a woman who had a pet squirrel, he repeatedly questioned us as to where the squirrel's daddy was.

Even after his obsession with daddies wore off as the year progressed, Temo generally asked after his father several times a week. Here is one conversation we had before getting out of bed one morning, about a month before Temo turned three:

J. D.: Temo, what do you want to do today?
TEMO: With my daddy.
J. D.: You want to go with your dad?
TEMO: Yes [nods, smiling].
J. D.: But he is in the U.S.
TEMO: What is he doing?
J. D.: Hmmm. . . . Maybe he is clearing snow, or maybe he is resting.
TEMO: And "Sonido Tecos"? [Raúl's D.J. business]
J. D.: Well, since today is Tuesday, I don't think he is playing. He only does it on the weekends, like on Friday or Saturday. Maybe this weekend he will play.
TEMO: At parties? To dance?
J. D.: Yes.
TEMO: Hmmm. . . . And it is very far?
J. D.: Yes, your dad is far away.
TEMO: And that is why I can't go look for him?
J. D.: Yes.
TEMO: Hmmm . . .

Children's responses to parental absences and their ability to influence their parents is another topic of this book. For Temo, as for the children of migrants I interviewed in Mexico, the thousands of miles that separated us from Raúl did not diminish the importance of his father in his life. Unlike in New Jersey, where we lived with another single mother and her child, in Oaxaca, Temo was more aware of his father than he had ever been before. Reactions to separation are in part a function of a child's developmental stage. My second son, Dylan, for example, emerged, at age two, from his own "daddy" phase, a much shorter one than Temo's. But I also believe that Temo's heightened awareness of his father was related to our living in a small community where the roles of migrants, and particularly fathers, are celebrated. I found that children as young as five understood that their parents have migrated to *el norte* in order to provide for them. For children, physical separation does not diminish their expectations of their parents and, in some ways, augments them.

In turn, parents like Armando and me—and the migrants I interviewed—worried about our children's reactions to separation. We scrutinized little interactions—like Temo's requests for sand drawings of daddies or Armando's son's refusal to talk to his mother on the phone—for clues about how they were adjusting. While migrant parents may be the ones to decide where family members will live, they are preoccupied with the effects these decisions have on their children. Such concerns may be typical among all parents, but they are intensified when parents and children live apart.

THE ORDINARY AND EXTRAORDINARY

The themes central to this book are familiar ones. Marital conflict, gendered expectations of mothers and fathers, the changes brought on by the passage of time, and children's power in families have been evident in my own experiences as a mother and wife and may be familiar to you. Parents' social status as transnational migrants, however, creates unique dynamics in families. I turn now to the persistence of family ties in the transnational context and the hardships that make these families' experiences extraordinary.

Acknowledgments/Agradecimientos

I would not have been able to complete a project like this that looks at the very emotional aspects of family life and spans a number of years without ongoing support at both the personal and professional levels.

For excellent guidance in framing what I saw on the ground into a sociological story, I would like to thank Maria Eugenia D'Aubeterre, Mitchell Duneier, Phil Kasinitz, and especially Nancy Foner, Robert C. Smith, and Clare Stacey. For this as well as her ongoing interest in this project, insight and perspective on Mexican families' lives, and mentorship and guidance, my sincere thanks to Julia Wrigley. For comments on different pieces of the manuscript, thanks to Peter Brownell, Ernesto Castañeda-Tinoco, Amy Gottlieb, Annette Laureau, Cecilia Menjívar, Rich Ocejo, María Paredes, David Purcell, Susan Roxborough, and Vicente Ruíz. For their enthusiasm and research assistance at the end of this project, I thank Tim Adkins and Lindsay Stutz. At the institutional level, I am thankful for funding from the Fulbright Association, the Carole and Morton Olshan Dissertation Fellowship at the CUNY

Graduate Center, the CUNY Graduate Center's Research Travel Grant Program, and the Research Council at Kent State University. My thanks as well to the editorial team at the University of California Press.

As my family and friends know, I have needed quite a lot of help on the home front in completing this project. For their ongoing support in listening to my stories from the field and for help with child care and other personal matters, I thank my parents, Ed Dreby and Katie Dole, as well as Tim Dreby, Dick Dole, Margaret Mansfield, Vicky Tizón, Vanessa Colón, Silvia Navarro, Gregorio Félix, Efigenia Romero, and Raúl Mariscal. I thank my son Temo for his company throughout, for putting smiles on the faces of everyone we met wherever we went, and for ultimately making this project possible. I thank my son Dylan for giving Temo and me the gift of laughter while Mom was busy writing.

Varias personas me han apoyado con la parte más crítica de este proyecto: conocer a las personas cuyas historias se narran en este libro. Quiero expresar mi agradecimiento de forma especial a Vanessa Colón, Eugenia Cruz, Arturo Erasmo, Gregorio Félix, Gaudencio Ferrer, Ramón Hernández, Napoleón Mariscal, Raúl Mariscal, Efigenia Romero, Gregorio Romero, Juan Sierra Barbosa, Vicky Tizón, y a Teresa Vivar por ayudarme a ponerme en contacto con las personas entrevistadas en Nueva Jersey. Sin el apoyo, la confianza, y la fe de ustedes, este libro nunca se habría realizado. También le doy infinitas gracias a todos aquellos en México que me apoyaron durante mi estadía allá, entre las que se encuentran Victor Contreras, Margarita García, Adelaida Hernández, Elvira Méndez, Ramiro Ramírez, Macedonio Santiago, la familia Sierra-Barbosa, Crisanto Sierra, Eduardo Torres Rodríguez, Laura Vásquez, Diana, Agustina, y la familia Mariscal-Velasco.

Para mí, todo este lío empezó con aquella semilla de Unidad Cultural. Fue una idea pequeña de un grupo de personas jóvenes e idealistas que surgió de un trabajo comunitario que ha afectado a las vidas de muchas personas—el impacto que tuvo en la mía es evidente en este libro—y que ha madurado hasta convertirse en un grupo muy sólido de amigos. Agradezco el empeño que todos pusimos en esa idea, y a todas los que se involucraron a través de los años. Aparte de los que ya he mencionado, les doy las gracias a Alberto Aguilar, Massimo Bossachi,

Manny Domínguez, Elizabeth Erasmo, Walter Flores, Efrén García, Carmen Heredia, Francis Julián, Roberto Perea, y Norberto Reyes. Me han enseñado mucho.

Finalmente, mi agradecimiento sincero a aquellas personas que compartieron conmigo sus experiencias sobre la separación familiar. Reconozco que algunas han sido experiencias dolorosas y no tan fáciles de compartir. Les estoy agradecida por confiármelas y espero poder hacerles justicia a continuación.

For Mexican migrants, finding a job in a small city like this one in *el norte* gives them the means to provide for their children living back in Mexico. Photograph by Joanna Dreby

ONE Sacrifice

Paula is lucky.[1] Paula has worked seventy hours each week since 2001, when she arrived in New Jersey. Each morning at 9 A.M. she leaves the apartment she rents near the train tracks in a small suburban town for her first shift at a fast-food restaurant. In mid-afternoon she crosses the street to her second job, at another fast-food chain, returning home around 11 P.M. most nights. Unlike the other five Mexicans who share her apartment, Paula can walk to both jobs and has not been out of work since she arrived. Paula's housemates have schedules as busy as her own; in any given week they rarely interact. Even when they are home at the same time, they usually do not spend time together. Paula and the others typically use their little free time resting or watching TV in their bedrooms, behind closed doors (or behind the sheet of the makeshift bedroom in the living room). The only common area, the kitchen, sits largely unused. Paula eats most of her meals at work, and the men she lives with do not cook. When Paula lived in Oregon, she made extra money between shifts cooking for the family she lived with. But now, after working in kitchens all week long, cooking is the last thing Paula wants to do on her only day off.

Thousands of miles away, in Puebla, Mexico, the home where Paula's daughter, Cindy, lives with Paula's cousin and his family is quite different. The house is rarely unoccupied. In the morning, while Paula's cousin and his wife are at work as schoolteachers, fifteen-year-old Cindy is at home with her seventeen-year-old second cousin Lola. The two teenagers tend the family's storefront fruit and vegetable stand while doing homework. Around 2:30 in the afternoon, the adults return from work with their eight-year-old daughter in tow. Cindy sits down with the family to enjoy the midday meal before heading off to school in the afternoon. In the evening, Cindy watches TV with her "sisters" or talks on the phone with friends before going to bed. Though the three-story home is teeming with life, it is not overcrowded. Once the addition was added about five years ago, with the help of Paula's earnings, everyone got his or her own room. Cindy's weekend routine is also busy, but not hectic. She often helps shop for fresh food supplies for the store, and she attends Mass. Paula's cousin and his wife have many friends and often are invited to various social functions; Cindy attends most of these events with them as part of the family.[2]

The contrast between Paula's life and that of her family in Puebla may seem striking, but it is familiar to the nearly five hundred thousand Mexicans who migrated to the United States every year between 2003 and 2006.[3] Tens of thousands like Paula have voluntarily left their children in Mexico to come across the international border to work.[4] These migrants have made a remarkable but common parenting decision: they have chosen to move to places in the United States where they can earn more money for their labor while their children have remained behind in Mexico, where the cost of living is low. In this sense, migration is a gamble; by leaving their children, migrant parents hope to better provide for them. Their migration and hard work represent a sacrifice of everyday comforts for the sake of their children and their children's future.

Mexican migrant parents' commitments to their children may not be all that different from those of working parents in the United States. Like many others, Mexican migrants put in long hours on the job and entrust the care of their children to others.[5] They expect that through continued participation in the labor force, they will be able to enhance their children's opportunities. They feel conflicted about their decisions over how to reconcile the demands of work and family life.[6] But transnational parents work thousands of miles away from their children. They are unable to see their children at the end of every day, and the sacrifice involved in their work decisions is enormous.

How do migrant parents and children manage living apart? What are the costs of such a sacrifice? Drawing on interviews and fieldwork with more than 140 members of Mexican families and in schools in both central New Jersey and south-central Mexico, this book answers these questions. It is the first contemporaneous study of family members' experiences of separation that includes the perspectives of mothers, fathers, children, and children's caregivers. Although restrictive U.S. immigration policies and the rise in deportations at the turn of the twenty-first century may do their part to increase the forced separation of Mexican migrant families, this book focuses on the much more common experience of parents deciding, under such policies, that they must migrate without their children. I explore the lives of families in which married fathers and single mothers have migrated alone and those in which mothers and fathers have migrated together. I pay particular attention to the ways in which gender and family structure shape family members' experiences. I also include the perspectives of children, to evaluate the consequences such migration patterns have over a child's life course.

"International migration," asserts the social scientist Aristide Zolberg, "is an inherently political process."[7] In this book I look at the other end of the spectrum: migration as an inherently personal process.[8] By following the experiences of select families over a number of years, I provide an up close and personal account of private aspects of the lives of the Mexican men and women working in low-wage jobs in the continental United States, their hopes and aspirations, and those of their family members living in Mexico. Rather than in the workplace, street, or neighborhood,

I explore the migratory experience within the domains of family life, in what might be considered a "domestic ethnography."[9] In doing so, I reveal the impact that political processes of international migration have on the everyday experiences of families.

The interviews show the lives of parents and children divided by borders to be extremely difficult. Parents and children are tied to each other by the expectation that parents will make economic gains during their time abroad and that children will make their parents' sacrifices worthwhile.[10] Yet the lives of parents and children divided by borders are essentially unequal. Parents and children live in different worlds, with different daily routines, different opportunities, and different sources of tension. As their lives unfold in the United States, parents are unable to meet the expectations of migration as quickly as they had hoped. Unmet expectations, particularly of migrant mothers, cause tensions and hurt feelings in parent-child relationships. Meanwhile, children in Mexico feel resentful of parents' absences. They have a difficult time proving their parents' sacrifices worthwhile. The emotional fallout of parents' work decisions is a great source of hardship in families.

Over time, however, parents and children show remarkable resolve to overcome such hardships. Unmet expectations are not absolute. Parents cling to their parenting roles even when those roles are difficult to fulfill. They often adjust their goals and aspirations in reaction to their children's negative experiences of family separation, and children are able to influence their parents' subsequent migration decisions. Parent-child relationships at a distance are constantly in flux. The hardships arising from separation paradoxically reinforce family members' commitments to each other. A story of both adversity and the intensity of family ties, this book depicts the ways in which Mexican families struggle and persevere in a global economy.

TRANSNATIONAL FAMILIES

The dawn of the twenty-first century marks what some consider to be the third major wave of global migration.[11] Today, men, women, and their families are moving not from densely populated areas to frontiers, as was typical before the mid-twentieth century, but rather from less developed countries to highly industrialized nations, such as from Mexico to the United States.[12] Technological advances have enabled migrants to maintain more dense social and economic ties in home and host countries than in times past.[13] Migrants from Latin America, for example, sent more than 50 billion U.S. dollars back to their home countries in 2006, accounting for significant portions of many countries' gross domestic products.[14]

Contemporary researchers describe individual families who are divided by international borders and who maintain significant emotional and economic ties in two countries as "transnational families."[15] Transnational families are not new; international separations were also common in earlier periods.[16] Yet today this migration pattern is most common among those moving from less wealthy to more prosperous nations. When the most economically productive members of the family—men and women in the prime of their lives—move to areas of concentrated capital in industrialized nations, and children and the elderly remain in developing areas with few resources, inequalities between contemporary wealthy and poor nations are reproduced and reinforced in individual households.[17]

The inequalities experienced by today's migrant households are different in another way. It used to be that men were the primary movers in families. Although migrant mothers were not unheard of during earlier periods, these cases appear to have been unusual.[18] A study of family separation among U.S. immigrants in 1910 found that only 7 percent of mothers across ethnic groups had left their children in their home country when they came to the United States, compared to more than 50 percent of fathers.[19] Among Mexicans, the bracero program (1942–1964) institutionalized male-led migration patterns by providing men with temporary agricultural work visas but offered no provisions for the migration of their wives and children.[20] When men left women and children to work abroad, migration accentuated gender inequalities within families.[21]

Today, however, mothers who migrate without their children are increasingly common, suggesting a major shift in the ways families around the world fulfill individual and household needs. Transnational mothers have been reported around the globe: Turkish women in Germany; Sri Lankans in the Middle East; Ecuadorians, Colombians, and Peruvians in Spain; Filipinas in Canada, Hong Kong, and Italy.[22] In some cases, women migrate before their husbands and children, radically reversing migration patterns of times past.[23] Among the more than 11 million Mexicans currently living and working in the United States, estimates suggest that 38 percent of fathers and 15 percent of mothers have children living in Mexico.[24] Although rates of male migration still outpace those of females, Mexican women, especially those who are unmarried, widowed, or divorced, are migrating at higher rates than ever before.[25] A mother's choice to migrate is often reluctant, with deep emotional repercussions; such choices mark the pervasive impact of global inequalities on individual families.[26] At the same time, some suggest that migrant mothers are "actively, if not voluntarily, building alternative constructions of motherhood. . . . Transnational mothers and their families are blazing new terrain, spanning national borders, and improvising strategies for mothering."[27] Migrating mothers simultaneously replicate global disparities of wealth and—albeit inadvertently—challenge gender-based inequalities within families.

Scholarship on today's migrating mothers and others divided by international borders categorizes them, for the most part, as a new class of "transnational migrants" who can be distinguished both from nonmigrants in their home communities and from immigrants in receiving countries who have severed ties with family and community back home.[28] Researchers have found complex ideas of identity among this new class of citizens, who feel they belong to two or more nations.[29] Transnational migrants are often politically active in organizations from their hometown and support development projects there, and national policies and actions shape, and at times constrain, transnational migrants' activities.[30] Economic contributions of this new class of citizen may end up dividing communities of origin between those who have little or no access to remittances and those who have become the "remittance bourgeoisie."[31] Transnational migrants also may forge different types of social relationships, what some call "social remittances," because they negotiate gender in their families in new ways, reconfiguring the rituals and expectations associated with courtship and marriage in a binational context.[32]

Much of our understanding of the lives of transnational migrants comes from the experiences of Mexicans in the United States; perhaps no other immigrant group has as lengthy a history of transnational migration. Since the end of the Mexican-American War in 1848, migration of Mexicans to the United States has ebbed and flowed. During the upheaval of the Mexican Revolution (1913–1920), Mexicans moved north along the railroad lines to work both in agriculture and in the expanding industrial centers in the United States.[33] After the economic crisis of the Great Depression in the 1930s, Mexicans—U.S. citizens and immigrants alike—were rounded up and sent back to Mexico in deportation campaigns.[34] Between the 1940s and the 1960s, leaving their families, Mexican men moved north en masse to work seasonally on bracero contracts.[35] Many Mexican families, and even entire communities, became dependent on their laborers working abroad.[36] After the Mexican debt crisis of the 1980s, broader sectors of Mexican society, including urban dwellers and people from the middle class, have come to rely on migration to the United States.[37] Estimates suggest that today one in ten Mexicans lives in the United States, accounting for more than 30 percent of the U.S. foreign-born population.[38]

The Contemporary Legal Context

Over the past twenty-five years or so, the circular nature of Mexican migration has begun to decline for the first time.[39] After an amnesty program was passed in 1986, U.S. immigration policy became ever more punitive toward undocumented immigrants. There are currently no legal pathways to permanent residency for Mexicans who have entered the country illegally. In addition, the militarization of the U.S.-Mexican border has made it increasingly difficult and expensive to come to the United States.[40] The cost of an undocumented crossing tripled between 1995 and 2001.[41] Death rates on the border have also skyrocketed. Between 1994 and 2000, there was a 1,186 percent increase in deaths among unauthorized border-crossers in Arizona.[42] Although United States immigration policies are intended to deter Mexicans from working in the United States illegally, they have had the opposite effect. Mexicans continue to come north, and they are not returning home, as they used to.[43]

Meanwhile, labor demand has meant that Mexicans are moving to new destinations throughout the continental United States—to places such as Georgia, Nebraska, and New Jersey, where sizable Mexican communities did not exist prior to the 1990s.[44] Because of the difficulties in coming and going, Mexican immigrants are now settling in these communities at higher rates and in greater numbers than ever before. Family separation among Mexicans may have been the norm for years, but today separations are likely to be of a longer duration.[45] Mexicans in the United States have few opportunities to legalize their status and reunite their families. As they are also increasingly settling farther away from Mexico, return trips are even more difficult and costly. Prolonged family separations are common.[46]

Despite mounting evidence about the lives of transnational migrants, we actually have very little understanding of how these contemporary legal structures shape migrant parents' sacrifices. This is particularly important at a time when the lengths of family separations among Mexicans, the largest immigrant group in the United States, are rising. A research emphasis on transnational processes and on transnational migrants as a distinct social class has obscured the systemic differences in the experiences of family members who are divided by international borders. Pioneer social scientists W.I. Thomas and Florian Znaniecki recognized such differences in describing early immigrant families as internally divided between "new and old world values."[47] More recently, the sociologist Dalton Conley has proposed that "inequality starts at home" and that unequal outcomes within families are more pronounced among those who are racially or economically disadvantaged.[48] Even though contemporary transnational family members may move back and forth between two geographic spaces, the daily lives of family members residing in Mexico and the United States are fundamentally different.[49] At a time of increasingly rigid immigration policy, geographic separation—and the migratory status it entails—complicates gender and generational inequalities within families. A true assessment of the ways immigration as a political process shapes families' lives must move beyond the treatment of transnational migrants as a homogenous social class. It requires an in-depth study of the experiences, not the values, of different members of families while they are living apart.[50]

THE LIVES OF MIGRANT PARENTS

This book is based in part on fieldwork and interviews with twenty-three fathers and twenty-two mothers conducted between 2003 and 2006 in Central New Jersey.[51] I met most of these migrant parents in one new destination for Mexican migrants: a city of approximately fifty thousand residents where the proportion of Mexican foreign-born individuals grew 869 percent between 1990 and 2000.[52] It is also a city where I had lived and worked with Mexicans in numerous social service agencies, including as an ESL teacher, starting in 1997. I had developed lasting friendships with many Mexicans, some of whom helped me to locate parents to interview. Despite my community connections, I found the topic of family separation to be delicate. Many interviewees, for example, brought up issues of marital conflict or personal failures, such as problems of alcohol abuse. Snowball sampling did not work in the traditional sense; I generally gained parents' confidence one by one or via referrals from individuals without children in Mexico. Being accompanied by my young son, Temo, born in 2002, facilitated conversations about the sensitive topic of parenting from afar.[53] I ended up having multiple contacts with more than half of the parents, some of whom I have known for years.

The migrant parents in this study struggled economically before coming to the United States but were not living in abject poverty in Mexico. In fact, the poorest in Mexico usually cannot garner sufficient resources to move north for work.[54] The parents I interviewed came from a range of middle- to lower-class backgrounds. Five had some college-level training, ten had been to high school, fourteen had seven to nine years of schooling, and sixteen had been to school for less than six years. The high concentration of mothers in the latter group is consistent with findings from a Pew Hispanic Center survey that transnational mothering is more common among women with low levels of education.[55] Among my sample, parents' prior work experience in Mexico also varied. Fathers had previously worked as farmers (eight), government administrators (three), a baker (one), a police officer (one), electricians (two), and an accountant (one). Most of the mothers had not been regularly employed outside the home in Mexico; however, two were college educated and four were working professionals prior to migration.

The mixed socioeconomic status of migrant parents is not surprising. The majority of Mexicans in New Jersey had previously lived in the three-state region of Oaxaca, Puebla, and Guerrero, with many from a relatively arid region known as the Mixteca. Although internal migration is a long-standing practice in the region, it was not until after the Mexican debt crisis in the 1980s and again in the 1990s that U.S. migration rates from the Mixteca swelled.[56] It is an economically depressed area with low returns on education. Researchers have found that Mexican migrants from such areas are more likely to have heterogeneous educational backgrounds than are those from other regions where migrants may be less educated than nonmigrants.[57]

Once arriving in New Jersey, migrants of diverse class backgrounds find themselves on a relatively equal playing field. Legal status, in particular, prevents those with higher levels of education from gaining an edge. All but one of the forty-five parents I interviewed was undocumented at the time they first migrated without their children. Only three had obtained legal status by the time I interviewed them. Lack of legal status is a widespread problem among recent Mexican immigrants; it is estimated that between 80 and 85 percent of Mexicans arriving in the United States between 1995 and 2005 were undocumented, and that in 2008 nearly 55 percent of all Mexicans immigrants were undocumented.[58] Family separations are concentrated in this group.[59]

Above all else, the migrant mothers and fathers I interviewed, regardless of educational background, came to New Jersey to work.[60] Men who had been both government officials and farmers found themselves working side by side in landscaping, construction, factories, or private restaurants. Men typically earned between eight and twelve dollars per hour in such occupations. This is roughly ten times the typical rate of one hundred pesos per day that male laborers earned in the Mixteca at the time. The women I interviewed mostly worked in local fast-food restaurants and factories.[61] They earned less than men did, averaging between six and nine dollars per hour. Since most had not worked for pay prior to migrating, women viewed such salaries as quite productive. Migrant mothers complained that women in their hometowns simply could not find work, and this was one of their reasons for coming north. One mother explained: "The people are so poor. There isn't any work for women. Sometimes the women work helping to pick fruit, mostly lemons, and sometimes they make candies from coconuts to sell in other towns. Mostly they do not work at all."[62]

Work in New Jersey, however, is not always as easy to obtain as parents expect. Arising, perhaps, from the long-standing pattern of circular migration between Mexico and the United States, the impression that work is plentiful in the United States permeates many Mexican communities.[63] According to one migrant father, "I would say 75 percent of the people come fooled by this country. They are fooled by us immigrants who go back. We get a nice pair of shoes, good clothes and we say, 'I earn so much and I have a car.' . . . Everyone thinks that by coming they will make money quickly. They think coming here is living well."

Mexican parents may find it difficult to maintain a steady job. Most parents initially use temporary employment agencies that offer irregular jobs and deduct their services, including transportation, from workers' salaries.[64] Even once better established and able to obtain jobs directly with employers, migrants are frequently unemployed.[65] Many Mexican women work in factories that depend on a fluid labor force that fluctuates in size; the employers offer no benefits or job security. One mother I interviewed had worked for over two years at a factory, but she was fired when she took off too much time to care for a family member who had been diagnosed with AIDS. Ever since, she has moved from job to job, part of the temporary workforce. Work is also irregular in construction and landscaping, common jobs for Mexican men in central New Jersey. Work may be plentiful during the summer; some of the men I interviewed earned between six hundred and nine hundred dollars per week in cash. But when it rained and during the winter, they did not work at all.

Health problems, coupled with a lack of health insurance, also affect migrant parents' ability to work. One mother, for example, had to leave her job when she underwent an emergency kidney stone operation. Others stopped working during and after pregnancies. A father, Armando, had health problems when he first arrived in New Jersey and landed a job in landscaping with his brothers: "I didn't think it would be so hard here. . . . I first worked mowing lawns. But I didn't last because my health wasn't good when I got here. . . . I couldn't last at that job. Instead I went to work in a factory." As factory work pays less than landscaping, the move meant a lower salary than Armando had originally anticipated. Work-related accidents were also a problem for the fathers I interviewed. Mexican men have some of the most dangerous jobs in the United States.[66] Even when health care for such accidents could be covered under workers' compensation (regardless of immigrant status), they affect workers' ability to economize and send earnings back home.

The Mexican parents I interviewed were extremely busy, mostly because of irregular and long work schedules.[67] A migrant father explained: "When you come to this country, you have things to do; you have bills to pay, and responsibilities. It is not like your country where you work normally and you have time, because here you have to work to get what you want. You come home just to eat, in a bad mood and tired, to take a shower and go to bed." As Paula described in the opening vignette, migrant parents work hard to benefit from the wage differential between Mexico and the United States. They hope to work as many hours as possible to take advantage of the time spent away from their families and to make the sacrifice worthwhile.

Migrant parents do not spend a lot of time or money on leisure activities. Those I interviewed typically used their one day off to shop, clean, and go to the Laundromat. Some migrant fathers play soccer or basketball at community parks in their free time. Mothers and fathers occasionally attend baptism parties, weddings, and birthday parties. They also attend local festivals organized around Hispanic Heritage month,

Cinco de Mayo, and Mexican Independence Day. Some participate in church outings. Migrant parents rarely take vacations. Only one family I interviewed took an extended vacation to the beach; it was their first vacation in nine years. Spending little in New Jersey enables parents to save money more quickly. They hope this will decrease the total time spent away from their children.

Parents' primary strategy for economizing is to minimize their housing expenses.[68] Migrant parents share apartments with other Mexicans to save money. A few rent their own room in a house or apartment, usually spending about three hundred dollars per month. Most, however, split these costs further by sharing the room with someone else, often a spouse or romantic partner. Unattached fathers skimp even more. One man I interviewed occupied a shed at the nursery where he worked. Another slept on a mattress in the living room of a two-room apartment; a couple and their two daughters occupied the other room. Some fathers rented out space in unfinished, unheated basements (a safety hazard for them, because they slept so close to the homes' furnaces). The single women I interviewed had a hard time finding people with whom to share rooms. When Elsa separated from her husband, she rented an unheated basement room for a few months until she met a man and moved in with him. The few single mothers who remained unattached lived with their siblings. Overcrowded housing for migrant parents is the norm.[69]

THE LIVES OF CHILDREN IN MEXICO

The lives children lead in Mexico are quite different. Children may not have access to running water or a flush toilet as their parents typically do in New Jersey (regardless of the overcrowded housing). Children may even live in unfinished houses that are slowly added on to as parents send money for improvement projects. But children do not lack space. I visited the homes of the children of twelve parents whom I had interviewed in New Jersey. Some lived in urban centers, others in small cities, and yet others in small towns. I also interviewed an independent sample of thirty-five children of migrants and twenty-seven of their caregivers. These families lived in a small town of approximately twenty-five hundred residents in the lower Mixteca region of Oaxaca that I call San Ángel, where I lived for seven months. All of these children lived in homes with larger patio spaces than available in the homes of parents in New Jersey. Although most neighborhoods do not have multiple public parks like those in New Jersey, children frequent the streets and neighboring homes and patios. In San Ángel, children often play by the river and in the downtown plaza in the evenings. Neighbors typically keep an eye on other people's children. When my two-and-a-half-year-old son, Temo, and his three-year-old playmate decided to go out alone to buy candy at the corner store, I was quickly alerted to his whereabouts. All in all, the children I met in Mexico were less confined than were the children I met in New Jersey. In Mexico, children have greater freedom in what Roger Hart calls their "experiences of place."[70]

Children in Mexico most often live with caring family members, usually grandparents. Media portrayals of the plight of unaccompanied minors crossing the border suggest that they are the abandoned children of migrants and have experienced abuse prior to migration.[71] Although many children of migrants do end up migrating themselves, I found that most were not neglected or in physical danger in their homes in Mexico. Indeed, a 2008 study shows that 92 percent of unaccompanied migrants in U.S. custody lived with family members prior to migration and that none reported escaping abuse as their reason for leaving home.[72] Most of the children I met not only lived with family but also had a number of extended family members nearby, such as cousins, aunts, and uncles, who were a daily presence in their lives.

Although surrounded by family, children's caregivers in Mexico do not typically take in boarders as is so common in New Jersey. Families for the most part own their own homes. In fact, housing construction is one of the primary goals of migration.[73] They do not pay rent and do not have mortgage payments; therefore they do not depend on income from boarders to meet the costs of living in a given month. In 2003, only five of San Ángel's 510 houses were rented. I met only one family who took in a boarder; Doña María told me she deliberated for months before deciding

A main street in San Ángel, which stays relatively empty until the school day ends, when children are frequently seen outside playing. Photograph by Joanna Dreby

to let a young man rent one of the extra rooms in her house. "They keep asking me about the other two rooms in the back," she explained. "I tell them I don't want to rent them until the house is in better shape. People say they don't care. But, you have to be careful because, you know, we have things, and you don't know what someone might want to take."

In some ways, the children of migrants experience greater prosperity than do their friends without access to remittances. Studies have found, for example, that child and infant health in some Mexican communities is better among families with U.S. migrants than among those without migrants, presumably because of the overall economic benefits of migration.[74] I surveyed more than three thousand children in the Mixteca and other regional schools and found that in the Mixteca, 90 percent of children of migrants reported receiving money from abroad, compared to 77 percent among those with migrant relatives, but not parents.[75] The average amount of remittances reported by children of migrants was more than twice that reported by children without migrant parents (3,393 pesos per month compared to 1,478 pesos per month).[76] Access to remittances may give children of migrants greater social standing than their peers.[77]

Often, however, children of migrants told me they felt too embarrassed to show off the material advantages of having a parent working abroad. When I asked one fourteen-year-old who had just joined his father in New Jersey if he used to take things his dad sent him to school, he explained: "Some of the kids do that, but it is *mal visto* [looks bad]. The other kids make fun of them for it. When I was in grade school, I never took things from the U.S. to school and they never made fun of me." In reflecting back on her childhood, a young woman remembered a backpack her father had sent her. "Oh how I wanted this backpack for school. But once he sent it, I was too embarrassed to take it with me to school. It just hung there on the shelf." For children of humble backgrounds, displays of wealth from migration are perceived to be snobby and pretentious. Children do not want parents' migration to differentiate them from their peers.

If migrants' lives in the United States are organized around their busy workweek, children's lives revolve around school. To be sure, children's schooling is central to parents' sacrifices.[78] Parents hope their economic support from the United States will give their children the opportunity to have a good education in Mexico and not have the same economic difficulties as an adult that they have had. For example, single mother Paula, who had less than a sixth-grade education, dreamed her two children would become professionals in Mexico. She paid for private school with her remittances. Migrant father José explained: "My son wants to study at *Las Américas* [a prestigious private college in Mexico]. And that university is very expensive. I have to be here to pay for it. . . . And my daughter, she wants to be a military nurse. I have to send money there for that."

Providing children with educational opportunities in Mexico requires substantial economic resources.[79] Tuition for public schooling through the university level is free in Mexico, but parents often have difficulties with the costs associated with attendance past the ninth grade. Most of the younger children I met attended schools in their home communities for kindergarten (three years, starting at age three), grade school (grades one through six), and middle school (grades seven through nine). Parents of young children described regular contributions for fees, supplies, and uniforms. Migrants said they varied remittances according to the expenses related to their children's schooling. But because children attend schools near their homes, the cost of young children's schooling is manageable. Caregivers walk a midday snack to children at school during the recess period, and children are home a little after 2 P.M. for lunch. In contrast, most children who attend high school (grades ten through twelve) have to travel to other communities to do so. Siblings Cassandra and Fernando, for example, both studied in the city closest to San Ángel, which was a 3½-hour bus ride on an unpaved road at the time. They lived in the city during the week, returning home on weekends. Cassandra recalled: "I remember how uncomfortable it was to ask for money to go to school." By the time their younger brother Paulo attended high school, a new school had opened in the neighboring town. The expense for Paulo's education was less, but transportation costs to this school were still significant. One eighteen-year-old I met in San Ángel attended the same school and nearly dropped out because she worried that her attendance strained the family budget.

Indeed, a common complaint among the fifteen teachers and school administrators I interviewed in the Mixteca was school retention. In one middle school I visited, enrollment dropped from 220 in 1985 to 27 in 2005. Some students were lost because of the addition of schools in three nearby communities that used to send their young people to this school. But this development cannot explain all of the population decline, for I visited one of these new middle schools and found only fourteen students enrolled. The director attributed the school's severe drop-out rate to students' aspirations to migrate to the United States. At the beginning of the year, ten first-year students had preregistered; only two remained in December when I visited. Of the eight dropouts, the director reported that only three had subsequently migrated. The other five remained in town but told him they were planning to leave soon. Retention problems are not unique to middle schools. In this same town, 260 students were enrolled in the primary school in 2001. When I visited in 2005, only 70 remained.

In the Mixteca, children may simply not see any concrete benefits to staying in school. For students in rural areas, teachers are often the best-educated role models they have. Yet teachers' salaries have not recovered from losses in real income incurred after the Mexican debt crisis of the early 1980s, particularly in rural areas and in the southern state of Oaxaca. Although I was in rural Oaxaca before conflicts erupted in the teacher's strike of 2006, teachers said that skilled masons in their communities earned more than they did.[80] In fact, it is relatively common for these well-educated community members to migrate north, just as children's family members have done.[81] A social worker I interviewed told me: "My biggest illusion is to go there [to the United States]; the problem is I cannot." She then complained that the students had no aspirations other than migration. And a teacher in San Ángel explained that he earned approximately 250 dollars every two weeks:

> I don't know [how much that is per hour]. We are supposed to not work that much. But here I work as much as I did when I was in Texas, which is like forty hours a week. . . . And, it isn't enough. . . . Our president did it; he went north. So did Francisco [another teacher in town]. They took a year sabbatical to go north to pay off their debts. That is what happened to me. I did the same. I had a debt here to pay off, and I had to go and do it. And you know, on my salary here I could never buy a car. I had to go north in order to bring back a car.

Although migration to the United States from Mixtecan communities like San Ángel is not as long-standing as in other parts of Mexico, an undeniable orientation toward *el norte* permeates communities where many children's parents have migrated.[82] The economic contributions of migrants are vital to what some describe as a "culture of migration."[83] Aside from remittances to individual family members, migrants paid for fluorescent lights on the main thoroughfare in San Ángel. They paid for renovations of the central plaza. Migrants' financial contributions even change the pace of life. The year I was in San Ángel, a party or wedding was held nearly every weekend between December 12 (the celebration of the Virgin of Guadalupe) and the *feria,* or festival of the town's patron saint, in mid-February. Return migrants paid for these private parties, participated in them, and often took videos to share with town members living in the United States.[84]

Migration in this region of the Mixteca is so prevalent that even a local D.J. service refers to the other side of the border with its name "Luz y Sonido Manhattan." Photograph by Joanna Dreby

Children are aware of migrants' vast contributions to their communities. Ideas of the north pervade children's imaginations. Indeed, 81 percent of students I surveyed in the Mixteca said they would like to visit the United States: 72 percent were motivated by curiosity, saying they wanted to see the United States because they thought it would be a beautiful place, they wanted to learn about it, or they wanted to travel to a new place or meet new people. One fourteen-year-old girl explained that she wants to go "to see what it's like there. I would like to know if it is really nice there, because some of my friends told me it is, so I want to go see." A twelve-year-old boy wrote: "I want to discover new things not found in Mexico"; he also said he imagines the United States to be "like a city of gold."

Even young children have clear ideas about the United States. I had children in three primary schools draw pictures of their families and of the United States: many drawings depicted *el norte* as a place of tall buildings, elaborate roads, snow, and Christmas trees and presents.[85] Some students even included symbols of the United States in their drawings, such as the American flag and the Statue of Liberty.[86]

A game children played in San Ángel illustrates how U.S. migration shapes children's ideas of place. I often took my son, Temo, to the playground in town, always empty during the hot mornings. The seesaw

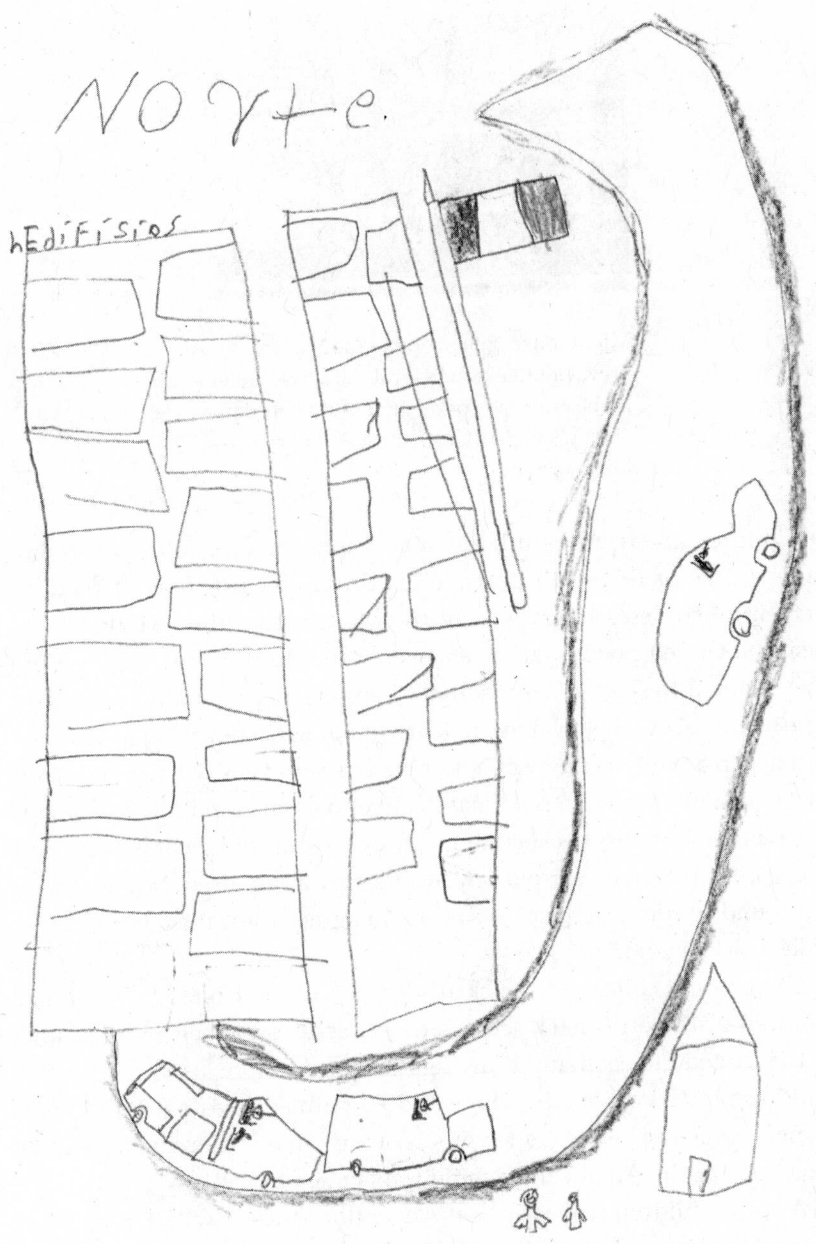

A third-grade boy's drawing of the United States.

The merry-go-round at the playground in San Ángel. Photograph by Joanna Dreby

was broken, as were parts of the metal swings, and a number of steps on the three slides were missing. Not until the sun began to set and the temperature cooled did other children come out to play. They rearranged the long metal bar of the former seesaw to climb the steep slides or balanced it between the steps of the monkey bars. The most popular game was always on the merry-go-round. Children as young as four years old positioned themselves on the circular seat while older siblings and friends pushed them round and round as if on a super-fast airplane. The children would say that spinning around a few times took them to the next nearest city. A little faster would transport them to the state capital of Oaxaca. The next stop was always—and I never heard it played differently—the United States. The young children on board would laugh and shout, "Spin it fast, real fast! Send us to *el norte*!" The older spinners interjected: "Wait, wait, wait! We have to stop in Tijuana first."

Children in the Mixteca grow up oriented toward the north. If for migrant parents opportunity lies in what they can do with their paycheck in Mexico, for their children, opportunities are unilaterally in the United States.

LEAVING CHILDREN

The vast difference in opportunities between Mexico and the United States are part of parents' rationale for leaving their children in the first place. Parents want to take advantage of employment opportunities abroad, but they anticipate that their lives as migrant workers will be difficult. They use a migration strategy that they hope will bring the greatest benefit and have the least impact on their children. Essentially, inequalities between parents' and children's lifestyles are at the heart of parents' sacrifices.

Yet such decisions are further complicated by parents' gender. Since mothers appear to be migrating without their children at higher rates than in the past, differences between mothers' and fathers' migrations are key. I find three types of family separation among those I interviewed: (1) migrant fathers who come alone, (2) migrant fathers who are subsequently joined by their wives (i.e., both parents are in the United States), and (3) single mothers who migrate alone.[87] Among the schoolchildren I surveyed in the Mixteca who had a parent in the United States, 73 percent had just a father abroad, 20 percent had both parents abroad, and 7 percent had only their mother abroad.[88] Parents' migration patterns are significant because each corresponds to a slightly different rationale for leaving children in Mexico.

Married Fathers

Nearly all the fathers I interviewed were married to the mothers of their children at the time of migration (although a handful had also migrated before getting married). One study estimates that male-only migration accounts for approximately 81 percent of migration events among Mexican couples.[89] Married fathers primarily view their labor migration as a straightforward path to fulfilling their role as economic provider for the family. Fathers come north after becoming unemployed in Mexico or when they see friends and family do better economically abroad. One father's description of migration as an escape from financial difficulties in Mexico is typical. The forty-year-old father was born in a very small town in the outskirts of a small city in Oaxaca. "We were very poor." Until the age of twenty-four, he worked as a farmer cultivating corn, chiles, and beans. When his three children were six, four, and two, he and his entire family moved into the city (including his parents, sisters, and brothers), where he worked unloading trucks. He earned about a hundred pesos a day (equivalent to ten dollars at the time of the interview), which was barely enough to feed his family. "I had no land or anything else in my name." Frustrated at his lack of opportunities, he decided to go north when a friend who had been once before offered to take him.

Many fathers described the pressure they felt from family and friends to migrate. Pedro said it was his brother who encouraged him to migrate. "I never wanted to come, but I was working in Mexico City in a factory, and I had a brother in California who sent me the money to migrate. Since he sent the money, I had to go." José, the first in his family to migrate, also felt compelled to leave owing to his relationship with his siblings: "I was a manager at the company, but it was a very stressful job, and I had a hard time working with my supervisors. But I also felt a lot of stress because I was not as successful as my brothers and sisters. We come from a humble background. They all have done well, and their houses were nicer than mine. I felt like the one most behind."

Wives also pressure their husbands to migrate.[90] Daniel, who had been to the United States before he was married, had wanted to stay in Mexico after he returned home. He agreed to migrate again as a newlywed only because his wife was adamant that she wanted to live in the United States. Armando said that he was reluctant to leave his family. Although many of his brothers were already working in New Jersey and he had been offered the opportunity to go north before, Armando decided to migrate at his wife's insistence.

Regardless of the source of pressure to work in the United States, fathers' decisions to leave children hinge upon the expectation that migration will lead to greater economic opportunity and that they will be able to better economize without their children present. Migrant fathers express qualms about the quality of life in the United States for their children. Many have strong opinions as to why it is better that their children be raised in Mexico. When I asked one father whether he thought about bringing his children to New Jersey, he said, "Definitely not, because here there is no family life." Another said he did not want his kids to be raised in the United States, because "here the kids forget they are Mexican." A father of two teenagers in Mexico explained: "I am not the kind of person who likes this life for my children. Here there is too much freedom for them. It is not really a safe environment." Married men plan to work hard and return to Mexico, where their children are raised by their wives, as soon as possible.

Married Mothers

Although also fundamentally related to work aspirations, mothers' motivations for leaving children are more complicated. Single mothers and married mothers often have different expectations of migration.

The married mothers I interviewed all joined their husbands who had already been working in the United States.[91] Married mothers described migration as affording them personal benefits in addition to being advantageous for the family unit. Many explained that their decision to migrate was prompted by curiosity. One mother said, "I wanted to know what it was like." Even husbands described their wives as being the primary movers behind family migration. A father living with his wife and U.S.-born daughter, with two more children in Mexico, told me: "It was her. She told me she wanted to come and see what it was like here." Another who lived with his wife and newborn son said, "I didn't want her to come, but she insisted."[92]

Married mothers may orchestrate their migration because of the negative effects their husband's migration has had on their marriage.[93] When husbands leave, women like Yolanda, who cultivated the family's peanut and bean crops on her own, may work harder performing both unpaid and paid labor.[94] Gabriela explained that when her husband is away, "When I lie down at night, I am exhausted. What is most tiring is having the responsibility for the children. It is much better when he [Angelo] is back visiting, because he takes over looking after the children. . . . I feel like it is a load off my back when he is here." The wives of migrants do find some benefits related to their husbands' absences. "At times," explained one woman in San Ángel, "there is a lot of freedom, because when he is here you cannot do anything. But if he isn't here, you can go out and come back whenever you want." However, their activities while husbands are away are closely monitored by their families and neighbors. Conflict with in-laws is common.[95] Accusations of women's infidelities while husbands are away are widespread.[96]

Aside from an increase in work and the intensified relationships with in-laws, the separation of wives and husbands during migration enhances the dependency of wives on their husbands, which may prompt women's migration to the United States. When a woman's husband migrates, she is disconnected from his daily life; she does not prepare his lunches, wash his work clothes, or relax with him after a long day, as she may do when living with him in Mexico. Her only link to her husband's work is via the money sent home. In Mexico, the wives of migrants anxiously await phone calls or other news of their husbands. Gossip about men's infidelities in the United States is common.[97] At a distance, phone communication becomes even more crucial to sustaining what would otherwise become a purely economic relationship. Yet because of the high cost of making international phone calls from many places in Mexico (eighty cents per minute where I lived in Oaxaca, as compared to the ten cents per minute for the same phone call from the United States), migrant husbands almost always initiate contact.[98] Physically divorced from their spouse's everyday activities and economically dependent on them, these women are less able to influence their husbands. For some, the separation means greater freedom of activity in Mexico. For others, it results in feelings of passivity. For married mothers, migration is not only a way to make money; it is a way to regain control over their family life.

Single Mothers

Single mothers who migrate to the United States do not experience the uncomfortable dependency on migrant husbands before leaving home. Their trouble with men came prior to migration. Yet, like married mothers, single women also migrate out of a combination of economic and personal motivations. In most cases, the economic situation of single mothers is more acute than that of married mothers. When marriages end, it is very difficult for women to provide for their children. One mother could not make ends meet after her husband left her for another woman. Her siblings in New Jersey offered to help and sent her the money for the border crossing. Zelia had to move in with her parents after she left her alcoholic husband, who "liked to go around with other women." Although she was able to work part time in town and had enough to eat, she lamented: "It is difficult because there isn't any work. The children ask for things, and we don't have anything to give them." Zelia's siblings helped her come to New Jersey. Migration places these single mothers in the position of family breadwinners.

Single mothers also find that migration gives them the opportunity to reinvent themselves. Young unwed mothers in particular feel they have few opportunities to get married in Mexico. In many Mexican rural towns, brides are quite young. In San Ángel, one nineteen-year-old daughter of a migrant mother told me that all her friends were already married with children. "I feel like I should already be married." Another nineteen-year-old woman, who had been married at age seventeen to a twenty-six-year-old man who had previously been in the United States, explained why she felt glad to be married to a migrant. "At my age, no one would even look at me. They all want young girls." The preference for young brides leaves single mothers out in the cold. Not only are they described as *masisa,* or overripe fruit, but since they are no longer virgins and have already been "eaten," they are no longer marriage material.[99] A twenty-year-old single mother I met in Mexico hoped to migrate within the year and eventually remarry. In Mexico, she explained, "They [men] don't think of you as a real thing; they see you as easy. And if they want me and love me, it has to be the whole package." In New Jersey, only one single mother I interviewed lived alone; the other seven, as well as the three mothers who divorced their husbands after migrating, lived with boyfriends. Migration offers single mothers a chance to start over.[100]

Mothers Leaving Children

As married and single mothers come to the United States expecting economic and lifestyle changes, they are typically more open to the idea of bringing their children to the United States than are fathers. Yet mothers feel they cannot do so immediately. For one, knowing they are migrating primarily to work, they worry about child care. One mother, for example, explained why she left her children: "Well, you also have to have a place to put them." Some married mothers are determined to take their children with them, until family members dissuade them. Ofelia said her mother reminded her that she did not know where she would live or who would be able to take care of her two-year-old son. Migration with children adds greater uncertainty not only about child care but also about health care and the educational system, particularly for the undocumented. Migrant parents are aware that U.S. immigration policy has become increasingly strict and punitive since the terrorist attacks of September 11, 2001.[101] Mothers believe they will be more prepared to bring their children into a new and potentially hostile environment once they have learned to navigate life abroad.

Mothers also worry greatly about the undocumented crossing.[102] One said, "I wouldn't risk taking them via the mountain." Crossing the U.S.-Mexican border without papers is considered to be more dangerous for women than for men.[103] When women's physical safety is entrusted to paid smugglers, the risk of rape, either by smugglers or by other men crossing with them, is omnipresent. The crossing is, however, even more dangerous and expensive for children.[104] Young children may be confined to small spaces, or even given medicines to make them sleep, in order to facilitate the crossing.[105] Risks for children at the border include experiencing human rights abuses, getting lost, sustaining injury or death, and being caught by officials.[106] Indeed, border enforcement policies have made the crossing even riskier for minor children, with the number of children returned to Mexico by border officials skyrocketing over the past few years.[107] As one mother summarized: "I didn't know what the crossing would be like. For me, I knew I could do it, but not for them."

Aside from the difficulties related to the border crossing and child care, technological advances may make Mexican mothers more willing to leave their children for a temporary period. The immediacy of communication means that mothers know they will be able to wire money via services like Western Union in response to minor crises, such as children's illnesses.[108] In addition, despite practical difficulties, most migrants can arrive home by air after a day of travel, and some do when their parents or children become seriously ill. New technologies foster migrant parents' ability to respond to family emergencies even from abroad. Satellite technology also makes communication possible for families living in even the remotest spots (without phone lines) through cellular phones.[109] Knowing that they can talk to their children over the phone at any time may make mothers more willing to endure a temporary separation, whether by reuniting with a spouse already abroad or, for single mothers, by becoming the primary family breadwinner.[110]

Migrant mothers and fathers who leave their children in Mexico are not acting impulsively out of desperation. They are proactive. They weigh the economic opportunities available in the United States, as well as the personal benefits they may gain from migration, with the costs of bringing children with them. But mothers and fathers arrive at the decision to leave their children in different ways. Men reason they can best fulfill their economic roles by migrating. Knowing their lives will be all about work is enough reason to leave their children in Mexico. For mothers, the decision to migrate arises out of a combination of economic and family considerations; a busy work schedule, the border crossing, and the insecurity of living in the United States without legal documents is not enough to deter migrating with their children except temporarily. Mothers make the choice knowing they will be able to communicate regularly with their children in Mexico for what they expect to be the short time before they are reunited.[111]

UNEQUAL LIVES

When parents move to the land of opportunity without their children, they purposely divide their families with the idea that doing so is the best economic strategy for the family as a unit. It would be a mistake, however, to consider the family as a discrete unit of analysis during the time parents and children live apart. Parents' and children's day-to-day experiences are not equal. Inequalities within families are not straightforward.[112] Geography complicates families already stratified by gender and age distinctions.

On the one hand, parents live difficult lives; they have busy schedules and live in uncomfortable, overcrowded places. Many parents reside in unsafe neighborhoods where their movements, and particularly those of children, are restricted. Working all the time, parents have little time to enjoy themselves or spend time with their families and friends, as is common in Mexico. Because of their legal status, they lose everyday privileges they had enjoyed in Mexico. They cannot easily drive and obtain car insurance. They cannot take a trip on an airplane. Men, in particular, may feel less free to frequent public spaces than they were in Mexico.[113] Migrants' lives are constrained. In this sense, as low-wage, undocumented workers in the United States, parents experience a drop in social standing and in quality of life when they migrate.[114]

On the other hand, when parents migrate, they have access to resources not available to their children who remain in Mexico. At a very rudimentary level, parents enjoy amenities associated with life in an industrialized nation, even if to a much lesser degree than enjoyed by U.S. citizens. No one I interviewed, for example, washed clothes by hand in New Jersey; they used Laundromats. In San Ángel, most families washed by hand, or—if they were able to purchase a washing machine with remittances—rinsed by hand and hung the clothes out to dry. Parents I interviewed also had access to hot water, something few families in San Ángel enjoy. Most parents lived in heated homes and had room air conditioners in the summer months. While heaters are not necessary in San Ángel, where temperatures in the summer months often exceed 100 degrees Fahrenheit, when I was in town no one had air conditioners. Parents also have access to employment opportunities that are nonexistent in Mexico (even if the opportunities can bear fruit only in Mexico). At the lower rungs of the social ladder in New Jersey, parents are optimistic that improvements in their lives are possible. They feel, for example, that by working hard and learning English, they may find a sympathetic employer or a job with benefits. They are hopeful that Americans will recognize their contributions to the economy and that eventually immigration laws will change, allowing them to regularize their legal status. Parents feel that with time, opportunities will increase. Children, in contrast, feel that their lives in Mexico are stagnant. Benefits from their parents' remittances are ultimately limited. In this sense, parents' prospects are more optimistic than those of their children living in communities whose economies are dependent on those working in the United States.

Such differences in the lives of migrants and their nonmigrant children are not surprising, particularly in Mexico, where patterns of labor migration to the United States are long-standing.[115] Yet there are reasons to suspect that disparities between the lives of migrants and nonmigrants have increased over the past twenty years or so, now that so many Mexican migrants live in urban and suburban areas of the United States, as in central New Jersey. In the past, when Mexican migrants were farmworkers or lived in border communities in the Southwest, their living conditions may not have differed so much from those of their communities of origin. Compare my descriptions of parents' lives above to the comment of a Oaxacan woman, also from the Mixteca region, whom Leo Chavez interviewed in a canyon campsite in San Diego in the early 1980s: "I had imagined the United States very differently. I thought it was one big city. I never imagined it was the same as there [Oaxaca]. In Oaxaca we live in a small village, and we live the same here. In our house there is no electricity, no water. We must haul water to the house the same as here. We use candles instead of electricity the same as here. There is no stove. . . . Our house is wood like these. It is the same. The same living there as it is here."[116]

The Mexican migrant parents I interviewed work in a service economy and live in urban and suburban areas near their employers; their children remain in places that depend on an ever-shrinking agricultural base. Consequently, parents' and children's daily lives are drastically different. Moreover, because family separations are of longer duration than even just twenty years ago, inequalities between migrants and their children are likely to have more long-term consequences.

The rest of this book focuses on precisely this question: what are the consequences of divided lives for Mexican families at the start of the twenty-first century? Drawing on a combination of the stories of specific families and my larger sample of interviews, each subsequent chapter focuses on one aspect of the inequalities between parents' and children's lives that affect family members' relationships over time. While chapters draw primarily on interpersonal experiences, social structures including the labor markets in the United States and in Mexico, immigration policy, public programs such as Social Security, and the Mexican educational system contribute to the context in which these relationships develop.

I start in chapter 2 with one of the most devastating consequences of parents' decisions to migrate without their children: separations are almost always longer than originally anticipated. Drawing extensively on the experiences of migrant mother Ofelia Cruz and her son, Germán,

I describe how such prolonged separations unfold and are more often than not the product of the temporal mismatch between the structure and pace of migrants' lives in the United States and those of their children in Mexico.

In chapter 3, I turn to a discussion of how prolonged separations are managed by both mothers and fathers who live apart from their children. Comparing mothers' and fathers' experiences as low-wage workers in New Jersey, I examine how gendered expectations subsequently shape parent-child relationships from afar. I show that in the transnational context, families "do gender," or ascribe meaning to their interactions, according to rather traditional gender role expectations. This is not always the case. As I show in chapter 4, when parents divorce after migration, fathers may seek new roles in the lives of their children during periods of separation. Drawing on the experiences of one father, Armando López, I describe the conditions under which men may redefine fatherhood.

In chapter 5, I shift the focus to how children react to parental migration at different ages and how parents attempt to be responsive to their children's changing needs. I describe young children's expressions of loss after a parent leaves, and parents' redoubled efforts to show young children they care. I describe teenagers' outward displays of resentment and their lack of social support not only at home but also at school. Although parents send money home to pay for children's schooling with the hope that their sacrifices will result in intergenerational mobility, teenagers struggle in school while parents are away. This is one of the most disturbing aspects of the separation. Thus, by the time children reach young adulthood, their prospects of financial security in Mexico still seem limited. At this stage, many children decide to join their parents working in the United States, and parents must change their migration strategies accordingly. Family reunifications rarely come, however, when parents or children originally plan. Although not the ones to initially divide the family across borders, children are afforded power in their relationships with the adults in their lives as a result of the separation.

In chapter 6, I move to the roles of Mexican caregivers, whom I call "middlewomen," in mediating relationships between parents and children. Most often grandmothers whose access to migrants' remittances is secured by caring for children, middlewomen have their own financial and emotional stakes in the caregiving arrangement. They are thus generally supportive of migrant parents' sacrifices. Prolonged separation does not diminish expectations of parents to provide emotionally and financially for their children in Mexico. With the support of caregivers, parents' and children's reunifications are possible—and increasingly likely—as children, and their caregivers, age. When divided by borders, family members "do family," or socially construct their families, in ways that reinforce parent-child obligation. In chapter 7, I narrate the story of Cindy Rodríguez, which illustrates the unintended consequences of family separation for young women and men. Children like Cindy experience instability even when living in stable home environments. They end up feeling caught between two families, not belonging to either, when families stress parent-child obligation during periods of separation.

Ultimately, the experiences of parents and children divided by borders result from a combination of family members' relative participation in migration and their relative position in their families. As I summarize in chapter 8, in a legal environment that promotes and necessitates prolonged periods of family separation, the emotional aspects of separation are extremely difficult for family members. Women are critiqued more for migrating without their children than men are. And the emotional consequences of separation are concentrated among the least powerful members of the family: children. At the same time, children are not powerless. They are able to influence their parents' decisions about migration. Likewise women show great resolve to affirm maternal ties to children despite the critiques of other family members and their neighbors. When both women and men are faced with economic difficulties in the United States, parents' ties to their children back home become even more important. Separation is a source of great hardship. Yet separation, and the sacrifice it entails, also reinforces parents' and children's commitments to each other, at the very least during the time that parents and children live apart.

Exemplifying the mismatch between the lives of migrants and their nonmigrant children, this family portrait superimposes an image of the child living in Mexico on a painting of the family members living in New Jersey. Photograph by Joanna Dreby

TWO Ofelia and Germán Cruz

MIGRANT TIME VERSUS CHILD TIME

November 2007. I finally caught up with Ofelia. It had been six months since I had last seen her, before I moved to Ohio from New Jersey. When we had spoken that past spring, Ofelia had once again changed her plans to send for her thirteen-year-old son, Germán. In April, she had made arrangements to bring Germán to the United States over the summer, after he had graduated from the sixth grade. Ofelia had hoped that by the time school started in the fall, he would be living with her and her husband, Ricardo, and their six-year-old daughter, Stacy, born in New Jersey. As I sat on Ofelia's sofa in May, just a few weeks after hearing these plans for the family reunification, Ofelia had announced: "Germán doesn't want to come anymore."

"What happened?" I had asked.

"Well, I finally had him convinced. Everything was in place. But then, you see, he went to these soccer tryouts in Puerto [Puerto Escondido] and was picked to play for Pachuca [a youth team for one of Mexico's professional leagues]. So now he doesn't want to come anymore."

"Wow, what an honor! He must be very good at soccer."

"He loves it," Ofelia said. She added: "He said, 'Mom, please, just let me play for a year and then I'll come over there with you guys. Just let me try for a year.' So he doesn't want to come anymore."

Ofelia had been disappointed. I later learned that Germán's soccer gig had not lasted. Because he had anticipated joining his parents in New Jersey as soon as possible, Germán had not started middle school that September. Indeed, he had made one attempt to cross the border, but he was caught by the border patrol and, since he was a minor, was sent all the way back to his grandmother's home in Oaxaca. Germán did not try to cross again that fall. In November, Ofelia told me that she and Ricardo were too worried about his safety and, having lost two thousand dollars in their first attempt to bring him to New Jersey, they did not want to waste any more money on another failed attempt. Instead, Ofelia told me, Ricardo would go back for Germán in December.

Four years earlier, when I had first met Ofelia, she had told me of a similar plan for a holiday reunion. At the time, Germán was nine years old. She had left him seven years before, when Germán was just two. By November 2007, it had been eleven years since Ofelia had seen her son.

PROLONGED SEPARATIONS

Most family separations are not as long as that of Ofelia and Germán. In fact, in seven of the twelve families I followed over a period of four years, parents and children have since been reunited. Although their case was unique, the difficulties that Ofelia and Germán encountered in their attempts to reunite exemplify a dynamic common in all the families I interviewed: periods of separation last much longer than originally anticipated. At times reunification came just a year or two later than expected; for most it was longer. The extreme of eleven years illustrates how such a dynamic unfolds even when parents and children long to be reunited.

A number of factors contribute to the prolongation of family separations. As low-wage, undocumented workers, parents have a difficult time meeting their economic goals in the United States; their limited resources make reunifications difficult. Over time, parents' resources are strapped even further by new commitments in the United States. Children, for their part, have conflicting emotions about seeing their parents, whom they may barely remember. Children sometimes resist reunification, and parents do not want to coerce them. Children are also loyal to their caregivers in Mexico. Caregivers, who enjoy certain economic and emotional benefits from caring for children, may also act in ways that extend periods of separation. I address the nuances of each of these dynamics—the difficulties migrant parents face, children's conflicting emotions, and caregivers' stakes in the arrangement—in subsequent chapters.

More deeply, prolonged family separations reflect the mismatch between the time needed for parents to reach their goals in the United States and the pace of their children's growth in Mexico. Families divided by borders lack what Eviatar Zerubavel has called "temporal coordination."[1] Parents' time in the United States is structured around irregular work schedules of forty to sixty hours per week.[2] I was often told by those I interviewed that "my life in the U.S. is all work."[3] Oriented toward future goals, parents are constantly scrambling to feel productive in low-wage, unstable jobs. "I did not do anything," explained Armando, describing his first two years in the United States. "I just paid off [my debts]. Another year went by, and not until then could I start to make plans to bring my family here." Parents do not want to give up their goals, because they want their sacrifices to be worthwhile; in the meantime, periods of separation grow longer. One father explained: "The problem is that we immigrants end up here a long time."

While parents feel caught, spinning their wheels in the United States, their children are changing at a pace parents can barely keep up with. Children, particularly those living in small communities like San Ángel, live in places where the pace of life follows agricultural work patterns, seasonal celebrations, and the school calendar and is marked by various holidays.[4] The slowness and even boredom of daily life in the Mixteca are also evident in Victoria Malkin's description of her fieldwork site in western Mexico: "Residents often sat on their stoops labeling different aspects of their surroundings as 'ugly,' 'boring,' 'backward,' and 'closed.' They contrasted this reality with the idea of an elsewhere drawn from the trips they have made to larger cities nearby, the soap operas they follow on television, or the migrants' stories about clean streets, shopping malls, escalators, planes, dishwashers and cleaning products."[5] As the pace of small-town life moves cyclically around them, children's growth and development stand out.

Parents and children experience the passage of time at different paces in different social locations. For parents, harried work schedules make time fly, while the time it takes them to meet their goals is drawn out. For children, daily life is slow, but their developmental changes are rapid. No case better illustrates how a lack of temporal coordination affects parent-child relationships than that of Ofelia and Germán. When the son knows little about his parents' life in the United States and the mother cannot keep up with her son's development in Mexico, parent-child relationships are not only elusive, but also they are constantly changing.[6] As a result, family reunification is unpredictable and may take longer to realize than expected.

A MOTHER'S CONSTRAINTS DURING MIGRATION

November 2003. I had arranged to meet Ofelia at her home at six o'clock on a November evening. I had known one of Ofelia's brothers and her husband, Ricardo, for years. Among other things, they had both been students in one of my ESL classes. I had never met Ofelia, however, and did not know that she and Ricardo had a son in the coastal town of Las Cruces, Mexico, until I started interviews for this project. On this particular evening, I arrived at Ofelia's house to find that she was out shopping. I sat in the narrow living room making small talk with Ofelia's brother over the cartoons blasting from the TV as a number of family members came and went from the room. Later I learned they were all relatives who shared the small home and that Ricardo had been upstairs the whole time. Throughout this project, most of my contact with his family has occurred through Ofelia and her kin.

After a bit, Ofelia's brother left for his class at the local community college. His wife, Chavela, politely waited with me and told me about what it was like to live in Las Cruces. Chavela was from the northern state of Jalisco but had moved in with Ofelia's mother when she married Ofelia's brother. "I grew up in the city. We weren't rich, but we weren't poor either. There was always enough to eat, and all I had to do as a child was worry about getting up, going to school, and doing my homework. . . . [Ofelia's] family is of a much more humble background. When I first got married, they all said it wouldn't last. But when I went to live in his town, I got along very well with his mother. She is a really patient person. I learned how to cook, make tortillas, and do other things around the house. It was hard, but I learned. And I learned that my husband's family is much more united than my own."

Chavela's description was cut short when Ofelia arrived, lugging Wal-Mart shopping bags. She giggled nervously upon finding me in the living room, excusing herself by saying she had thought the interview was to have been an hour earlier. When I had not appeared, she had gone out to pick up some diapers for her three-year-old daughter. As if in proof, a chubby toddler with messy pigtails trailed in behind her. Ofelia went upstairs to leave her bags. Within minutes of her return, everyone cleared the room to give us privacy.

Ofelia smiled and giggled again. "I have been asking everyone what they think you will ask me about." The laughter seemed a sign of her anxiety about being interviewed. It resurfaced every time we broached an emotionally charged topic. I tried to reassure her and asked simply that she tell me a little bit about how she had come to the United States and about her son who lives in Mexico.

"I came like everyone else," she said, "because there is no work in Mexico. The economic situation is very bad, and I wanted my family to get ahead." She explained that her husband was the first to leave. He worked in Los Angeles for about a year, and Ofelia stayed with her own mother and newborn son in Las Cruces. This was a hard time for Ofelia. "It was really difficult not knowing where he was, since it was the first time we had ever been apart. In Mexico, when the women are washing clothes, they say, 'Watch out, you could be using your husband to wash your clothes.'" She laughed. "You see, since we don't know anything about them when they leave, we joke that they come back as [laundry] soap."

Within a year, Ricardo asked Ofelia to join him. Ofelia was eager to migrate to New Jersey to see the place where her father and brothers had worked for a number of years when she was a teenager. "You see, my father left when I was thirteen. He was in the United States for nine years before he went back. While he was away [and after I married], it was my husband who was really the man of the house there in Mexico, helping out with the work. But just my luck, once I came to the United States, my father returned to Mexico. We crossed paths. I am the only one who doesn't know him. It has been fifteen years now. Oh, how I want to see my father."

According to Ofelia, Ricardo had wanted her to migrate with their only child, Germán. But Ofelia was concerned about where she would live when she got to the United States and who would take care of the two-year-old boy. At the urging of her mother, she left Germán behind and planned to send for him once she settled in the United States.

After Ofelia's arrival in California, the couple moved to central New Jersey to live with Ofelia's siblings. She started working at a factory; it was the first job she had ever had outside her home. "I felt really bad at first, it was like . . . " Ofelia struggled to find the words and instead laughed drily. "But then at the factory where I worked I found out that so many women had their children in Mexico, and then I didn't quite feel so bad, although I still really missed him, especially at the beginning."

"Do you like working?" I asked.

Ofelia answered: "No. If I could, I wouldn't work. I never worked in Mexico except in the house helping my mother out with things. But, you know, when you get older and get married, you need to do things for yourself, for your own family. So, that is why I came to work in the United States."

"Do you think you will miss working if you ever go back to Mexico?"

Again, Ofelia said that the work is not important to her. "It is not the work that people miss back there. It is that [in Mexico] no one pays you to sit around eating all day long. That is what everyone misses when they go back to Mexico, getting a check at the end of the week."

"Every day, everything in Mexico is more and more expensive," she continued. Recently, one of her brothers had returned from visiting Mexico and had told Ofelia that a pair of pants costs between 250 and 300 pesos (roughly twenty-five to thirty U.S. dollars). She was shocked. For this reason, Ofelia explained, she feels satisfied that her earnings in the United States are helping provide for her son's needs. "I know my son is missing the love of a mother. But I also know that he eats well, that he doesn't suffer from hunger, that he has clothes, and that he can study. I know that he is okay."

At the time of the interview, Ofelia had not seen nine-year-old Germán in more than seven years. "I don't have any recent pictures," she explained, "but when I first left, my mother sent me pictures all the time. I watched my son grow up through photographs."

Ofelia said she calls home about once a week. Her son is the only grandchild living with her mother and father, and although she wants to bring him to the United States, she is making no progress toward this goal. She said that Germán did not want to migrate and added that she was reluctant to take him away from her parents. "When I call him, he asks me to come home. But he says he doesn't want to come here, because he doesn't want to leave his mama in Mexico. You see, he calls my mother "Mama.' But he does know that I am his mother, because he says so. He says, 'I know you are my mother, but I don't want to leave my mother here.' And I don't want to force him to do something he doesn't want to do, even though I know there are more opportunities here in the United States than in Mexico."

When I interviewed Ofelia, she had recently lost her job at the factory because of a downturn in production. Even though a trip to Mexico would mean a risky border crossing on her return, Ofelia explained that if she did not find another job soon, she wanted to go home for the holidays. If not in December, she would travel back home in May. "Ricardo doesn't want to go home at all, but I do. I cannot wait to go back. But I would just stay for three months or so. This way I would have time to warm up to my son again so I can bring him back with me."

LIFE WITH GRANDMA AND GRANDPA

October 2004. Ofelia did not go back that year or the next. I first met Germán and his grandparents in 2004, when I visited their family home in Oaxaca. I had vague directions from Ofelia's brother, who had told me I should look for the house across from the basketball court. We first drove by the ice-cream shop and arcade, where a skinny, shirtless boy was hanging out with four older men, and then doubled back after realizing that we had been in the right place and that the young boy must have been Germán. His grandmother, whom I had talked to the day before to confirm my visit, was not there, Germán told us brusquely.

Germán's grandfather, also shirtless and in grubby pants, lay on a *petate* (a woven straw mat) on the dusty floor of the arcade. He instructed Germán to bring us chairs. Once seated, I was uncomfortable, feeling evaluated by these men and unsure what to say. Germán's wary eyes monitored me closely as well. I struggled through the awkward silences in conversation with Germán's grandfather, Don Francisco, who had worked in New Jersey for a number of years.

It was not until my second visit that I fully appreciated Don Francisco's gold-tooth smile when we spoke more comfortably. He described himself as a homebody, explaining that he had spent most of his eight years in the United States either working at an industrial factory job or holed up in his room watching TV. Don Francisco also explained that he was the first in the family to leave for *el norte.* He had been quite successful working abroad. The family used the money he sent home to move from a house in a nearby *rancho* to one he built in the town of Las Cruces. He and his wife were also later able to purchase the store where they currently live. They owned a number of cattle and also a palm tree grove. "I like life in the United States better than here, because here it is so hot. And there, things are more orderly, and they are cleaner," Don Francisco told me. He came back only because his sons migrated, and once they were no longer in Las Cruces to work his land, it began losing value.

Doña María was more outgoing than the reserved Don Francisco. On subsequent visits she admitted that it had been hard living with Don Francisco again after he came back from the United States. "I didn't get used to it, and I'm still not," she said, laughing. Doña María, a woman filled with an often-contagious exuberance and energy, was well respected in town. She introduced me to the directors at the local schools, all of whom she knew personally, facilitating my research in the schools. On my visit during the town *feria,* a number of indigenous women in town who did not speak Spanish were selling their wares. They all frequented Doña María's shop, because she was one of the few who readily allowed them access to the bathroom and to water.

On that first visit, I learned little directly from Germán, who was then ten years old. He did, however, scoff when I jokingly mentioned expecting to see him in New Jersey in a few years, which suggested he did not expect to join his parents there. He also seemed suspicious of me. On the last day of our visit, when we went to the beach, I mentioned to Doña María that Germán looked more like his father than his mother. Germán looked up from his soda at me warily. "So you really know my dad in the United States?"

"Yeah," I answered. "He was once in my English class and played soccer with some of my friends there."

"And what is his name?" Germán challenged me. He looked rather surprised when I successfully answered "Ricardo."

March 2005. Five months later when I visited, I learned more directly from Germán, who was still playing it cool but was noticeably excited when we arrived. On this visit he warmed up to us considerably, playing affectionately with my son, Temo, and talking more openly with me. He agreed to an interview. When I asked Germán if he remembered living with his parents, he answered, "No, because I was two when they left me."

"Do you remember anything about them?"

"Just from pictures."

"Why do you think they left?" I asked.

"To go where the money is," Germán explained.

Germán said he spoke with his parents often, usually once a week, and that he liked talking with them on the phone. "I mostly [talk] with my mom, not so much with my dad because he works."

"How do you feel when you hang up the phone?"

"Sad . . . because they are on the other side."

Germán told me he wanted his parents to come back to Mexico. When I asked, "Would you like to go over there to be with them?" he answered decidedly, "No, I don't want to go."

"Why not?" I wondered.

"Because it is cold."

"What's that about? When it's cold, you wear gloves, a hat . . . "

"It's just that I am used to living here," Germán explained.

"So you prefer that they come back?"

"Yes."

"And you don't want to go there?"

"Nah, I am all right here with my grandma."

I asked Germán about his sister; other children had complained about their U.S.-born siblings. Germán denied feeling jealous, said he loves his sister, and even talks with her on the phone. He could not tell me how old she was, however, and called in to his grandmother for an answer. I asked him, "Do you feel closer to your mother or your father?"

"Both the same."

"Do you feel like you need your parents, or are you okay the way you are?"

Germán did not hesitate in answering, "I feel like I need them."

"Why?"

"Yes, I need them because they are my parents."

Doña María told me later that Germán did feel uncomfortable about his U.S.-born sister and that this was one reason he did not let his parents send for him and insisted that they come back to Mexico if they wanted to see him. "Once he said to me, Gram, I think my parents love Stacy more than they love me." Doña María confirmed repeatedly on both my visits that Germán did not want to join his parents in the United States.

"[Germán] talks to his mother about once a week. You know, they want to take him there. His father says they are ready to send for him. But he doesn't want to go."

I was not sure if Doña María was holding on to Germán. After all, Germán seemed highly affectionate with his grandmother, especially given his rather independent manner. Moreover, Germán seemed to enjoy being the only child in his grandparents' home. Clinging to Germán, however, did not seem to be Doña María's style. Doña María had many friends in town and a clear identity independent of caring for her grandson. She often chatted and joked with those who passed her store and was frequently out doing errands. On a day-to-day basis, she often acted indifferent to Germán, going about her daily routine with little oversight of Germán's activities. For example, during the town *feria,* Doña María was not concerned that the ten-year-old went to the rodeo with some friends. And on the evening of the dance, Germán meticulously ironed his own pants and shirt to get ready to go out on the town. Doña María's hands-off style did not seem to match Ofelia's concerns that her mother would feel lonely and abandoned if Germán left for the states. Wondering about this, I asked Doña María how long she thought the current arrangement would continue. "Of course I will be sad for him to go," she answered. "But I cannot stop it, because they are his parents, and they should be with the boy. I know it is not the same to be [raised] by grandparents as to be with your parents. I am always conscious of this."

STANDING STILL

July 2005. Back in New Jersey months later, Ofelia stopped at my house to pick up some pictures of Germán I had brought her from Mexico. She sat at the edge of my sofa that afternoon, shaking her head with a nostalgic smile while looking at her son playing on the beach. "You know, he doesn't want to come," she said abruptly while flipping through the pictures yet again. "We tell him to come, but he doesn't want to. I have wanted to bring him since the first year we were here, but he never wanted to. He is like resentful that we left him. Sometimes on the phone he says, 'Mom, why did you leave me?'"

I asked, "What do you tell him?"

"I tell him, so that we could have more things, that he wants us to buy him lots of things, and this way we can buy him whatever he wants. I tell him that if I hadn't come, maybe he wouldn't have the things that he has and that he likes his things."

"And what does he say to you?" I asked.

"He says it is okay. Then I tell him that if he comes here, I am going to buy him lots of things too. But he tells me that it is better that I send the money there to buy things there. He says that I should go back there to get him."

"Maybe you can win him over if you go."

"Yes, that is why I tell Ricardo to go. He was going to go this month to get him. But since they say it is really dangerous, he couldn't go."

"Is that why you don't go, because it is dangerous?"

"Yes, you see, when I came, it was with papers. I didn't cross like the others. I went to Tijuana and they gave me some visitor's papers to cross with. And you see, because of the cost and everything [of the crossing], I can't go back."

OF STAGNATION AND CHANGE

January 2006. The next time I went to Las Cruces, the standoff between Germán, Ofelia, and Ricardo persisted. Although I had spoken with Doña María a few times since the previous visit, I had not seen Ofelia or Ricardo again. I did, however, occasionally talk to Ofelia's brother and learned that his family life had radically changed as his wife Chavela had returned to Las Cruces with their children to permanently resettle the family in Mexico. Ofelia's brother planned to join Chavela and their children after he worked a few more years in New Jersey to help save money to finish and furnish their house and store in Las Cruces. So while Ricardo, Ofelia, and Germán's relationships remained in a deadlock, other family members were making changes in their lives.

On the first evening of my visit, Doña María showed me to Germán's room, which I would use temporarily. After admiring changes in the house since my last visit, including the new computer Ofelia and Ricardo had bought for Germán, I sat with Doña María out front in the humid evening. While Doña María sold tacos of *carne asada* [steak], I sharpened two boxes of three hundred colored pencils I was using for a project at the local schools. When my hands grew sore, I convinced Chavela's son to help me. Germán joined us at the table to have a dinner of his grandmother's tacos. He listened warily as his younger cousin told me in a mixture of Spanish and English that he missed almost everything about his life in New Jersey. Germán's face showed that he disagreed with his cousin's opinions about the virtues of life in the United States. After a customer moved on with his order of tacos, Doña María idly told me about her taco sales and how much she made during the last town dance in December. Germán finished his tacos, wiped his mouth, and declared, "That is just how I like it: a poor and humble house but with lots of money." Doña María scoffed at his comment, aimed at his "Americanized" younger cousin. Germán laughed drily and left the table, making clear his resistance to the materialistic influences of the United States and his preference for the more modest way of life in Mexico.

The next afternoon, I spent time in Germán's school asking students to draw pictures of their families and how they imagined the United States. Germán's class was small, just twelve students on the day of my visit. Now eleven years old, he was in the fifth grade, and though I knew he had been held back a year, he was not markedly older than the others. Later, during recess, Germán's teacher described him as being extremely popular with the girls, quite a flirt, and also a bit uncontrollable in the classroom. During the drawing exercise, Germán sat sectioned off with three other boys; they appeared to be the unruly students of the classroom. But Germán was respectful during the exercise, and the others followed suit. While students drew their families, I went one by one to their desks, asking whom they lived with and who in their family lived in the United States. The other three boys in Germán's group of friends all had parents in the United States. When I came to Germán, I noticed he had drawn two figures: one he labeled "papa" and the other he labeled with the name of his young sister (whom he had never met). I was struck that he had not drawn his mother. Later when he turned in his pictures, I saw that Germán had scratched out the name of his sister and replaced it with the label "mama."

That evening, Doña María sold tacos once again. We sat and chatted as on the previous evening. This time, when Germán came out and declared he was hungry and wanted a cheese sandwich for dinner, Doña María snapped at him: "You are way too young to be demanding things like that." Germán retreated inside to prepare his own sandwich.

Although at Germán's urging we had originally planned another beach trip that Saturday, at lunch on Friday, Doña María told me that she had not been able to change the catechism class for Germán's Communion the next morning, so we would not be able to go to the beach. "Since his mother is not here," she explained, "I am the one who has to be there for him." When I told Germán that we would not be able to go to the beach after all, he looked disappointed. I left the next morning. As Doña María accompanied me to the bus stop, Don Fernando and Germán were busy washing the truck. Don Fernando mockingly faked wailing at my departure: "When are we going to see her again," he cried, and we laughed. I called out a good-bye to Germán, but he concentrated on cleaning the tires in the back of the truck, completely ignoring me. Doña María shook her head as we walked away. "You should have called out to him, 'See you in New Jersey'," she said. "Then he would have responded."

THE LONG ROAD TO REUNIFICATION

April 2006. As had been the case since I first met with Ofelia in the fall of 2003, talk of Germán's reunification with his parents continued. Once, when I called Doña María a few months after returning from my visit, Germán answered and chatted away about the party his family threw for his First Communion. "It was a big party. There was a D.J.," he reported eagerly. "My dad said that he would either put [money up] for a D.J. or a cow [to provide the meat for the party], but then my dad put [money] for the D.J. and my grandfather put the cow so I had both." After a bit, Germán asked, "So when are you going to come again so we can go to the beach?"

"I don't know," I explained. "Probably not for a little bit. When are you coming here? I bet you'll come here before I go there."

I was surprised when Germán answered decisively, "April 30th."

"Really?" I asked.

"Yeah, my dad says he is going to send for me. I am going to go with my cousin Trini. Antonio [Chavela's young son and Germán's cousin] is going to go back also."

"Wow."

"But I don't want to go," Germán added, although the excitement in his voice seemed to belie his reluctance.

After we spoke for a bit, Doña María came on the line. We exchanged news, again of the party and also reports on who in the family had been ill. I then added, "So are they really going to send for Germán?"

"His father says that he is going to come back for Germán and take him to the United States. But I don't know. I tell them to wait until he finishes school. You see, now he is in fifth grade, and he just has one more year left to graduate, so I think they should wait until he is done with school."

"Oh. Well, Germán said he is going to come in April," I explained.

Doña María simply laughed and changed the subject.

April came and went. Germán remained with his grandparents. Germán's cousin Trini, a single mother, did migrate to New Jersey and left her three children, then ages four, six, and seven, with Doña María. Although talk of Germán's migration still hung in the air, the next year he went on to the sixth grade in Las Cruces.

May 2007. Exactly one year later, I visited Ofelia, who spoke of her plans to return for Germán over the summer. Although this was only one of many conversations I had had with her about Germán's migration, this time it seemed that a number of factors had converged to make the reunification more likely.

First, Germán would now graduate from the sixth grade, which was the benchmark his grandmother had set for his migration. Second, according to Ofelia, Doña María was overwhelmed with the care of Trini's three children. Trini, now pregnant and living with a new boyfriend in the United States, was not sending enough money to provide for the children properly. Ofelia was providing most of the economic support for their care and had hired a girl locally to help her mother, much to Ricardo's chagrin. "My mother is getting too old to look after these kids; they are all young, not like Germán. And when I left Germán, she wanted me to. That was one of the reasons I left him, to give her company. But these three, they need a lot of work. My mother is getting too tired to look after them."

Not only did the changed circumstances in Las Cruces make Germán's migration seem likely, but Ofelia and Ricardo's economic situation seemed to have improved markedly since I had last seen them. They now rented a three-bedroom apartment on the outskirts of the city, which they shared with just one young woman. The living room was furnished with a new white sofa and love seat (covered in plastic to protect against spills), a large TV, and a bookshelf displaying pictures of the family. I looked over the framed pictures of Germán as a little boy, and Ofelia pointed out the pictures of her, Ricardo, and their daughter, Stacy, from their vacation the summer before. Ofelia had a new job with benefits, including a yearly two-week vacation, which they used for the first time to go away to Virginia Beach. Both Ofelia and Ricardo owned vans they drove to work, providing rides for coworkers at the going rate of twenty-five dollars per week per person, which augmented the family income. When I asked if they planned to have more children, Ofelia gave a decisive no. "When they are little, it is so hard economically. I didn't work for two years to stay with Stacy, and we only had Ricardo's [income]. But now she is in school, and I can work too. We are much better off. No, it is too hard when they are little. Two are enough for me."

Aside from the improvements in Ofelia and Ricardo's economic situation, Ofelia explained that she now had a concrete plan for bringing Germán back with her to the United States. She had finally caught up with the woman who had helped the family cross the first time. The expense would be great, two thousand dollars more than it would have cost ten years earlier, but she and Ricardo felt it was worth it. Over the summer they hoped to take Stacy back to Mexico, so she could meet her grandparents for the first time. If all went according to plan, the family would be living together in New Jersey by September.

As I was leaving Ofelia's house that afternoon, I admired a wall hanging I had overlooked earlier. It was a painted family portrait, depicting Ofelia and Ricardo at the center and Stacy just below them. Never forgotten, Germán was in the portrait as well. Ofelia explained that they had had a photograph sent so the artist could add him to the painting. Although recognizable, it showed Germán as he must have looked years before I had met him. The two siblings looked at most a year apart in age, while there is actually seven years between them. The wall-hanging captured the time disparities that governed the families' memories and realities: American-born Stacy had an up-to-date portrait, as did the parents who stood with her, while Germán was incorporated into the family as he had been years before.

PARALYSIS

What accounts for the dynamic between Germán and Ofelia, which led to indefinite postponement of their reunion? It is possible that caregivers in Mexico, in this case Doña María, resist family reunification so they can continue to garner economic support from parents' migration. Grandparents do rely on the remittances of their migrant children and develop close emotional bonds with their grandchildren while parents are away. Yet caregivers are not responsible for preventing the reunification of parents and children. Caregivers, in fact, respect the priority of parent-child bonds. They often reinforce these ties, and the obligations they entail, as did Doña María when she told me in front of Germán that she had to go to his Communion class because his mother was not there to go. If the prolonged separation of mother and child did not result from the grandparents' wishes, why did it occur?

Ofelia and Germán's standoff arose in part from differences in how family members perceived each other over the passage of time. For Ofelia, Germán remained a young boy bonded with his grandmother, even while her own life changed radically with the birth of another child and the work required of her and her husband to create an economic foothold in New Jersey. For the grandmother, another year or two in her care were worth it if Germán could reach a more natural stopping point at his local school. And for Germán himself, time brought big changes in both his feelings and his understanding of his situation.

From Germán's perspective, and that of other children like him, migrant parents are a presence even when physically absent. Germán felt that his parents were important to him, and he knew that they should provide and care for him. He felt resentful that they left him and now gave more attention to his U.S.-born sister. At the same time, Germán understood that they had migrated out of economic necessity and, in part, to support him. He liked living with his grandparents and in Las Cruces; in fact, that was the only life he knew. In essence, he did not want his life to change drastically, except that he would like his parents to return to show they care. With each passing year, the ways Germán communicated these mixed emotions to the adults in his life changed. Germán's jeers at my suggestions that I would soon see him in New Jersey gave way, within a little more than a year, to his boasts that he would soon be in the United States, even if against his will. More recently, Germán left school in Mexico and more wholeheartedly accepted the idea of coming north. As for children anywhere, each year brought developmental and emotional changes, and those changes affected his interpretation of his parents' sacrifice.

But for parents, the gains won each year as a migrant come painfully slowly. Stability in housing and employment may take years to achieve. Migrants invest huge amounts of energy and resources to carve out successful lives in U.S. cities. These investments made it hard for Ofelia and Ricardo to return for Germán, as he wanted them to do. They had to weigh the cost and the risk of doing so. They had to consider that Ofelia's family in Mexico depended on remittances from the United States and that their standard of living would fall if Ofelia went back. Moreover, Ofelia had a strong link to New Jersey through her U.S.-born daughter.

If she returned to Las Cruces and had trouble crossing the border on her return, who would look after Stacy during her absence? What would happen if she could not return? Ofelia reasoned that she might convince Germán to join them if she could spend some time with him, but the danger of the border crossing made a short return visit a great risk. It would also be extremely costly and would require economic stability that Ofelia and Ricardo were unable to achieve until Stacy started kindergarten and they both were working full time and did not have to pay for child care. Like Germán, Ofelia felt conflicted in deciding on her best course of action. As a migrant father explained to me, "Sometimes, Joanna, you simply cannot have everything you want at once."

Over time, parents become more engrossed—and invested—in their lives in the United States and even more conscious of the rising price of having left their children. Trapped by the lifestyle they adopt in the United States, scheduled almost entirely around the workweek, parents worry about their relationships with their children. Being absorbed by work at the expense of the family is not a novel concept. Working parents in the United States may have similar reactions of being in a "time bind."[7] Yet the physical distance considerably increases the dissonance between the pace of parents' lives at work and the pace of the lives of their children at home.[8] One migrant father's comment summarizes the effects of migrant parents' unique time bind on relationships with children whom they do not get to see at the end of each day:

> For a time, the phone works wonders. It is like your weapon, your love, your everything, because you talk, you listen; it's everything. But after a time, you lose that passion of talking. You lose that dream of waiting for Sunday to call your kids and talk to them. Why? Because you realize that it starts becoming ordinary. . . . Instead of seeing it as [a means of] affection, love for your children and to your family in Mexico, it becomes ordinary, like a line you have to follow. And you just don't feel the same anymore. . . .
>
> The distance makes you forget, it makes you lose something, it makes you . . . How can I explain? It makes it so that the affection, that which was love, becomes almost ordinary. It becomes commercial. Why? Because you only think about working, sending money, and that they [the kids] are okay over there. . . . [It is routine] because you

> cannot enjoy what you sent and take your child out to eat, take him on an outing, or buy him some clothes. All of this makes it so that you forget what the love of your child is like.

Conflicting emotions that result from the passage of time at different paces in different places often prolong periods of separation. Ironically, it is also the passage of time that can resolve standoffs between parents and children, like the one between Ofelia and Germán. Because parents and children have few opportunities for interaction, they do not have the ability to negotiate small solutions to their difficulties. They must wait for a combination of factors to converge, including economic stability, opportunity, and the willingness of children to migrate, in order to plan a reunification. In some cases, parents and children are reunited within a few years. In other cases, as for Ofelia and Germán, reunification is delayed for most or all of a child's childhood. I now turn to what happens to families from the perspectives of parents, children, and caregivers during these periods.

Regular phone calls home help fathers like this one maintain contact with family members in Mexico. Photograph by Joanna Dreby

THREE Gender and Parenting from Afar

It was mid-February 2005, and the atmosphere in San Ángel and the region was lively. Since the New Year, there had been at least two private parties per week. A number of couples had planned their weddings for this time of the year, which were open events that anyone could attend, since most of San Ángel's twenty-five hundred residents knew one another. Live bands played in the central plaza; these nights *ranchera* music rang throughout the town until the early morning hours. Many from nearby towns attended these events, and residents of San Ángel joined in the celebrations of neighboring towns. The festivities were even more exciting because the U.S. migrants who had come home for the holiday season had not yet returned north. With the arrival of migrants, there were new, even if familiar, faces in the crowds. Efrén, father of four, was one of them.[1]

I had first met Efrén in New Jersey. At that time, he had not been back to see his wife and children, who lived in a town just ten minutes from San Ángel, for more than three years. Although money was still tight, in December 2004 he had decided to go home for an extended vacation because his father was quite ill. Before his return, I had visited frequently with Efrén's wife, Claudia. Claudia was a schoolteacher and fun to talk with. We occasionally walked together for exercise and took our children on outings to the nearby river. I saw Claudia much less after Efrén returned. Understandably, they were spending more time together as a family. The couple's four children did not come to San Ángel to play in the street with their cousins and my son Temo nearly so often. They spent the evenings at home, watching TV and playing with their father.

Although Efrén spent much time with his wife, children, and ailing father, on occasion he took on the role of host, showing me around his town. He had, for example, invited me along with his wife to a New Year's Eve party. The night of the dance for the town *feria,* he invited me once again. That evening I joined Claudia, Efrén, Efrén's adult cousins, and an aunt visiting from Mexico City at the dance. By the time the band stopped playing at 3 A.M., we had finished a bottle of tequila and Efrén invited us to continue the party at his house. As three of us had lived in New Jersey, we sat in their living room listening and dancing to *merengue* and *bachata* songs typical among Latino crowds in the United States but almost foreign in the region.

Our informal party was interrupted shortly thereafter by some commotion outside. Two drunken men were upset because a car had blocked their truck and they were not able to get out. Claudia had gone to the door and was trying to explain to them that it was not their car and there was nothing they could do about it. Efrén got up and joined her, speaking more forcefully. I was not listening to the conversation until Claudia's loud voice, now directed at her husband inside the house, caught everyone's attention. "Don't be so stupid," she spit out. "You are not going to start a fight over something like this. You don't live here. I do, and I don't want problems." To this, Efrén erupted: "A woman doesn't tell me what to do in my own house." Before I fully figured out what was going on, he took a swing at her in front of us all. Claudia proceeded to run from him through the living room and into another room; Efrén followed and hit her once again.

Claudia wailed. The other family members followed and separated the couple. I sat shocked at the ugly face of violence and how it had caught me unawares. Then a small figure came out of the bedroom, rubbing his eyes to see what had happened. This got me to my feet, and I took the eleven-year-old boy—Efrén and Claudia's oldest son—back to bed. I sat with the boy in the dark until the voices outside seemed more subdued.

Feeling out of place in this family affair, I eventually emerged from the bedroom and spoke to both Claudia, who was being pampered by the female relatives in one room, and Efrén, calming down with a beer and his cousin in the outer room. I briefly gave Claudia a supportive hug while she dabbed her eyes. With a nasty resolve she told me this was not the first time he had picked a fight and left her with problems. "*Nunca le voy a perdonar* [I will never forgive him]." When I apologized for being a part of the situation, Claudia shook her head and replied bitterly, "*Nadie tiene la culpa menos él* [No one is at fault but him]."

I spoke at greater length with Efrén. I said that he should not worry and that I would forget about the whole incident for my book. Efrén disagreed.

> But—and you can write this in your book—that I, if right or not, will not accept that *my woman* intervene in *my house.* I try to be a little educated, and really I am a pretty tranquil man. Everyone can tell you this. It is rare that I get agitated like this. And I know I am being the typical *machista* man. *Pero, simplemente es mi casa, y soy yo en frente, y no acepto que mi mujer intervenga en eses asuntos.* [But, it is simply my house, and I am at its head, and I do not accept that my woman intervenes in these affairs.]

Eventually, I left with Claudia's "*Nunca le voy a perdonar*" and Efrén's "*No acepto que mi mujer intervenga en eses asuntos*" pounding in my head.

GENDER ROLES IN MIGRANT FAMILIES

Efrén and Claudia's relationship was not as one-dimensional as this incident suggests. In fact, Efrén and Claudia reconciled the next day and noticeably enjoyed each other's company every time I saw them together afterward. Unlike other couples who frequently complained about their partners, Efrén and Claudia quite often expressed their great love for each other over the four years I knew them. And although Efrén was "*machista*" in some ways, he supported Claudia's work as a schoolteacher in a town where it was unusual for women to work outside the home. Yet this dramatic incident between them illustrates how complicated family relationships can be, involving feelings of deep pain and hurt alongside those of profound love and support, when they are strained during periods of separation. In Mexico, as in the United States, approximately one in four women have experienced physical violence from an intimate partner, as did Claudia.[2] Although a painful feature of family life, domestic violence is not the focus of this book. Rather, I highlight the confrontation between Claudia and Efrén because it illustrates one of the major sources of tension in migrant couples that in this case erupted in an incident of physical violence. Mexican families have been characterized as highly valuing family unity, or familism [*familismo*], and as adhering to rather clearly defined gender roles, with men as providers and women as caregivers.[3] These roles must be renegotiated during periods of migration.[4]

Specifically, when married couples live apart, men's and women's authority in their families may come into conflict. Men's power in families is achieved mostly via honorable economic provision.[5] As evident in Efrén's comments, Mexican men, even when they are loving fathers, feel their masculinity is tied to some degree to their ability to be *macho*.[6] When fathers migrate, they act honorably in the face of economic adversity, sacrificing their own comforts for the sake of their family. For men like Efrén, migration legitimizes their power as head of the household.

In contrast, women's authority in Mexican families is related to their morality as the primary family caregiver. Women's roles as caregivers are celebrated and likened to the self-sacrificing characteristics of the Virgin of Guadalupe—Mexico's incarnation of the Virgin Mary.[7] Latin American scholars describe this culturally specific version of maternity as *marianismo*. According to this ideal, a woman should be self-negating and a martyr for her children, because she is spiritually and morally superior to men.[8] When men migrate alone, women must adjust to their husband's absence by assuming full responsibility for the family and home, which involves a great deal of sacrifice. One mother explained how she achieved moral superiority while her husband was away: "I learned how to earn respect from men. . . . I learned how important it is to defend oneself and one's honor as a woman." Women like Claudia feel it is a slap in the face for their husband not to recognize this sacrifice and respect the authority they must assume at home and in the wider community while the husband is away.

It thus seems inevitable that fathers' migrations cause some conflict in marital relationships as women and men must reconcile gender role expectations with the realities of living apart.[9] Indeed, gendered adaptations to male-led migration patterns are well documented, as are incidents of marital conflict resulting from migration.[10] While it is understandable that migration causes conflicts between women and men, the way gendered expectations influence mothers' and fathers' relationships with children has been largely disregarded. Too often children like Efrén and Claudia's son hiding under his covers in the back bedroom are depicted as a sidebar to the marital drama that arises during migration. Although child rearing is a crucial phase in the process by which gender differences are constructed and maintained, gendered expectations in parenting when women join men abroad as family breadwinners have yet to be fully explored.[11]

In this chapter I bring one dimension of inequality in families divided by borders to the fore: that which results from the differences between Mexican mothers' and fathers' migrations. The comparison of motherhood and fatherhood shows that differences in gender roles diminish when parents and children are separated due to migration. In analyzing migrant parents' efforts to maintain contact with their children over time, I show that mothers' and fathers' interactions with children are quite similar.[12] Yet parenting from afar is not equal for mothers and fathers. Mothers and fathers differ in their processes of leaving and returning home, affecting their relationships with the children who remain in Mexico. Moreover, family members' evaluations of migrant mothers and fathers are colored by conventional gendered expectations. In other words, although gender role differences diminish during periods of separation, gender continues to shape parent-child relationships.

While parents and children live apart, family members ascribe meanings to their interactions, what sociologists have called "doing gender," in a way that reinforces the expectations that mothers be family caregivers and fathers be family providers.[13] Ultimately, migrant mothers bear the moral burdens of family separation to a much greater degree than fathers do.

MANAGING SEPARATION

Given descriptions of conventional gender roles in Mexican families, I was surprised to find that migrant mothers' and fathers' experiences converge in parenting their children across borders.[14] Their methods for staying in touch with children are remarkably similar. Separated from their children, mothers and fathers rely on the same three techniques to communicate with their children: weekly phone conversations, the sending of gifts, and regular remittances. Physical separation results in standardized mechanisms of transnational parenting. Mothers and fathers also perceive similar risks associated with changes in their family life abroad to potentially erode their relationships with children in Mexico.

Phone Calls

Although seemingly straightforward, regular phone conversations are not always easy to arrange. Not all parents have easy access to a phone in the United States. Many do not have land lines and either use cell phones or public pay phones. Nearly all use calling cards, which offer the best rates to Mexico, but numbers often ring busy during peak calling times.[15] Also, parents have to ensure that their children have a place to receive their calls. Many do not have a home phone in Mexico and call their children at a neighbor's home or at a local *caseta*. (A *caseta* is a small business in Mexico where people can receive phone calls from abroad for a minimal fee.) Despite technical difficulties, most parents interviewed, regardless of gender, reported calling home once a week, fitting calls around work schedules. Likewise, 61 percent of the children of migrants I surveyed in the Mixteca reported talking to their parents in the United States once a week or more. Children of migrants report more frequent phone communication with relatives in the United States than do children without migrant parents.[16] There is no significant difference between children's frequency of communication with migrant mothers and migrant fathers, nor in the frequency of phone calls reported by daughters and sons.[17]

Both mothers and fathers gave a similar checklist of things they discussed with their children over the phone. They ask about school, how siblings are behaving, and what things children want sent from the United States. School progress is particularly important to parents, and many offer material rewards to children who work hard in school. I listened to José, father to fifteen-year-old Brian, when he called home one Saturday. Brian answered the phone. José said hello and asked how Brian was doing. Then he asked when Brian would have his high school entrance exam. I assume he learned the date of the exam, because José next asked, "What do you want me to get you, a stereo or a tape player?" They discussed the benefits of each, and José concluded that a stereo was better and he would send that. He asked what else Brian would like as a gift before asking to speak to the boy's grandmother.

Typical conversations also focus on the economic aspects of the parenting relationship and future migration plans. A migrant mother of four said her children "tell me they are good, and they ask me when I am going back there. . . . They ask me for shoes, clothes, toys and money." A migrant father told me: "My son asks me when I am going back and asks me to send him money." A migrant mother said her six-year-old says, "Take me north. I want to go north with you."

Children's versions of conversations with parents are surprisingly similar; differences in conversations are not dictated by the parent's or the child's gender, but rather by the child's age. The youngest children talk mostly about material goods and migration. A six-year-old boy said that when his mother calls, "I ask when she is coming and she says she is coming soon." A six-year old girl explained that her mother says "she is going to send clothes, a dresser, a bed and a mirror." As children grow older, they talk with their parents about school performance and behavior. For example, an eleven-year-old girl who lives with her maternal grandmother and siblings said, "My mom asks if I want something—I say yes—clothes, shoes, and school supplies. Then she tells me not to hit my little sisters because my sister tells her that I hit her. But I hit her because she hits the youngest one." The oldest children are concerned about parents' emotional well-being, saying they talk about the family news and give and receive advice from their parents. Fifteen-year-old Brian described conversations with father José as follows: "[We talk about] how he is, that he works harder there because there are a lot of things to do. I tell him to work harder because he has been there a long time and hasn't done much, and I tell him not to get discouraged, that he can trust us and tell me anything."

Gifts

Although phone conversations are filled with talk of gifts, parents said they preferred to send money, as it is expensive to send goods either through mail services or via courier businesses. Most only sporadically send gifts with friends or relatives or bring things back on their own trips home. A father who had been migrating seasonally for seven years gave me the following list of items he takes to his wife and four children whenever he returns: one pair of shoes each, two to three sets of clothing for each child, toys (almost always remote control cars for the boys), and an electronic item, once a TV, another time a VCR, and most recently a video camera. Another migrant father said he collected random toys throughout the year to send to his four-year-old son. As proof, he disappeared into his basement bedroom to retrieve a small teddy bear from his collection to give to my son, Temo.

The most common gifts from parents are photographs, school supplies, clothing, and shoes. Among the students I surveyed in the Mixteca, 74 percent of those with migrant parents reported receiving emotional-type gifts (like photographs or home videos) from the United States, 80 percent reported receiving clothing or shoes, and 59 percent reported receiving school supplies.[18] There is no significant difference in the types of gifts they reported receiving from their migrant mothers and their migrant fathers.[19] Daughters of U.S. migrants in the Mixteca more often reported receiving all types of gifts than did sons.[20]

Despite parents' intentions to provide for their children by sending things from the states, children and grandparents said parents often get sizes wrong since they have been away so long. One grandmother gave me a pair of her grandson's almost new shoes for Temo; her daughter had sent them two sizes too small. Tina said her father sends "clothes, shoes, toys, because he still thinks I am a little girl and I like them." The twelve-year-old rolled her eyes, pointing to a row of Barbie dolls on a shelf in the room. "But," she added, "my cousin likes to play with them." Age-inappropriate gifts exemplify the ways parents lose track of their children's development over time, signaling the time dislocations characteristic of parent-child separations.

Children may also feel embarrassed about the material aspect of their relationship with their parents. When I asked what kinds of things they want their parents to send them, many children grew shy and simply answered "I don't know." Tina said that she does not ask her father for much: "What I ask for, he sends. But I try not to ask for much." When I asked a six-year-old if he asked his mom for toys, he answered defensively, "Not me," causing his five-year-old sister to object and call him a liar. Children seem aware that material objects are not equivalent to parental affection, and some are wary of parents' use of gifts as replacements for time together.

At the same time, children recognize parents' gifts as markers of love. One fourteen-year-old girl, for example, told me she does not love either her mother or her father. Her parents are divorced, and both have remarried and live in the United States. She said she was most uncomfortable with her father, who recently had tried to reestablish a relationship. Her maternal grandmother, the girl's caregiver, told me a story of a small jewelry box with a gold locket inside that the girl's father had recently sent: "It was a small box. And we had just read in a book about a father who gave his daughter a small box, like that one, but it had nothing inside. Supposedly every time the girl opened the box, she would receive a kiss from her father. So [she] joked that the box her father sent her was like that; she would keep it in her dresser and open it when she wanted a kiss." As this grandmother eloquently concluded, gifts "make them [children] feel special and loved. But the gifts don't inspire love from children for their parents. They cannot bring trust and affection."

Remittances

Gifts are symbolically significant.[21] But money is the most important item both mothers and fathers send home. In New Jersey, mothers and fathers reported similar frequency of remittances: once or twice a month. However, parents were reluctant to disclose the amount of remittances and were more sensitive about financial matters than about their undocumented status, which other scholars of Mexican migration have also noted.[22] Most mothers and fathers were vague or dismissed my questions about the amount of remittances by giving what seemed to be generic answers. While other research suggests that women send less money home than men do but send a larger proportion of their income, among the parents I interviewed, variations in reported remittances were greater among mothers and among fathers than between them.[23]

Among the children I surveyed in the Mixteca, 96 percent of those with migrant mothers and 89 percent of those with migrant fathers reported receiving money from their parents. Children who had only their father in the United States reported higher amounts of remittances per month as compared to those of single migrant mothers and those with both parents abroad, although differences are not statistically significant.[24] There is no statistically significant difference in amount of remittances reported by sons and daughters.

In interviews children, like their parents, were vague in discussing monetary remittances. All children, however, even those of very young ages, understood the economic nature of their parents' migrations. A five-year-old girl said her parents went to the United States "because they are earning money there." An eight-year-old told me his mother migrated after his parents split up, "because there we were going to have a different life and she was going to earn more money." A nine-year-old boy explained: "My dad is there so that he can send us money." I asked, "How much does he send?" The boy replied, "I don't know." Virtually all children responded similarly; they understood that their parents had migrated to support them, but few told me how much money their parents sent home and how often. Interestingly, 77 percent of students of migrant parents in the Mixteca reported specific details about how much money parents sent home and how often. It is not necessarily that children do not know details about parents' remittances; it is that they do not want to talk about them.

Given the importance of money to parents' sacrifices—that parents leave home in order to provide for their children financially—and children's ability to answer survey questions about monetary matters, the reluctance of children and parents to describe the financial aspects of their relationship during periods of separation is interesting. It suggests their unwillingness to use remittances as a measure of the quality of their relationship once away. For children of divorce, suggests Gry Mette Haugen, "money may symbolize a currency for both love and care."[25] Yet for transnational families, money risks replacing love and care. While money matters perhaps more than anything else, parents and children resist defining their relationship as purely economic in nature.

Changing Families over Time

Because of their status as low-wage, undocumented workers, both mothers and fathers have difficulties in meeting their economic goals of migration. The longer it takes to meet these objectives, the more likely it is for parents' relationships with children in Mexico to be affected by changing family dynamics. For both mothers and fathers, new marital relationships and additional children challenge relationships with children back home.

Marital discord frequently arises in immigrant families as couples find they must adjust their relationships to the U.S. context.[26] For fathers who migrate without wives, accusations of infidelities affect relationships with children in Mexico.[27] One migrant father said his relationship with his oldest daughter was damaged by false rumors that he had had a baby with his sister-in-law. When this daughter migrated as a young adult, she refused to live with him; he complained that to this day she does not trust or respect his fatherly advice. A migrant father of four teens told me that his wife suspected he had another wife in the United States. He said this about his most recent trip home: "My two older boys came to me together and they said, 'Dad, if you have another wife, we don't want you here. You can leave.'" At times, such accusations were based on rumors; at other times, men I interviewed did have a new partner in the United States, although they still maintained ties to their wife and children in Mexico.

For women who migrate on their own, it is fairly common to remarry once in the United States. Relationships with stepfathers can be very difficult for children in Mexico to accept.[28] Moreover, a new partner may not recognize a woman's children back in Mexico as part of their new family. Neighbors criticize mothers who have lost touch with their children in Mexico, saying these women have remarried and that the new husband is unwilling to provide for another man's children. One woman I interviewed praised her husband for not being like others; he had accepted her two daughters back home as his own. "My girls even call him *papi*." Couples migrating together are not immune from marital problems.[29] Many divorce or separate once in the United States. For these couples, relationships with new partners are a source of tension with children in Mexico.

It is also hard for children in Mexico to share their parents with siblings born abroad. A consistent theme in interviews with parents was how the birth of children in the United States threatened their relationships with children in Mexico. One migrant father, for example, wondered whether his two children in Mexico would accept his newborn son, but then he decided, "they are young enough to grow attached to him." Another explained that his daughters in Mexico are jealous of his U.S.-born child: "Once one of the girls asked me to go home because [she worries that] if I don't I am going to love the one that was born here more than them." A mother who joined her husband two years earlier left her daughters in Mexico and subsequently had a baby boy in the United States. She complained that on the phone "the girls reproach me. They are jealous, extremely jealous, the younger one more than the older one."

Children in Mexico view U.S.-born children as a potential threat.

Younger children, in particular, fear that U.S.-born siblings or half-siblings will compete more successfully for their parents' love and attention because they live with the parents. Fatima's mother, for example, had a baby in New York City, brought the baby back to Mexico to live with Fatima and her grandmother in San Ángel, and then returned north. Fatima—age eleven at the time—said, "Sometimes I think my mom loves my little sister more because she was born there with her. I feel like she gives her more love. When she [the sister] arrived, I didn't like her." A sixteen-year-old told me, "I don't understand—it is so ignorant [that his father has a child in the United States]. If he [father] cannot make it with us, how can he with another one?" In effect, U.S.-born children not only compete with children in Mexico for scarce parental resources, but also undermine parents' statements that migration to the United States was undertaken for the sake of their children back in Mexico.

Children's fears are not entirely unfounded. For mothers, the pain of separation is so great that having a new child in the United States may make them feel better. According to one mother, who had a daughter in Mexico and two U.S.-born children, "It is like you carry the weight of all the love that you have been holding in and then you put it on them," that is, the U.S.-born children. Fathers are often much more involved with the care of U.S.-born children than they had been with children in Mexico; when both partners work in the United States, they tend to share child care, and many men migrated while their Mexican-born children were still infants.[30] In fact, a surprising number of fathers (ten) left a pregnant wife and did not get to meet their youngest child until they returned home to visit. One father explained: "In fact, she didn't even tell me about the baby until I had arrived here, because she didn't want me to worry." A father who returned to San Ángel with his U.S.-born daughter and his wife to reunite with the couple's son said that his son is not close to him and that the son thinks that the father loves his daughter more. The father insisted that he loves his son but admitted it is not the same. "I also feel different [toward him]. I raised my daughter since she was born. I bathed her, I changed her diapers, I prepared her bottles. I never did that for my son, because I was away working in the north when he was little."

Of course, conflicts related to step-parents and new siblings are common in the general U.S. population.[31] Yet for families living together, the passage of time helps parents and children adjust to the changes in family composition and eventually accept new routines and new family members.[32] In contrast, for Mexican transnational families, parents and children have few (sometimes not even any) opportunities to work out their differences in daily interactions. Over time, the likelihood of marital conflict, new partners, and U.S.-born children increases. The strains that the changes in family composition cause are likely to intensify or remain unresolved.

The physical constraints of living in the United States mean mothers and fathers have similar experiences in managing separation from their children. To be sure, there are some important differences in mothers' and fathers' experiences. For example, fathers reported helping children with homework over the phone, whereas mothers did not. Fathers also often had romantic relationships in the United States without disrupting their relationships with their wife and children in Mexico, a pattern I did not find among mothers. Families also described alcoholism to be a more common risk of migration for Mexican fathers than for Mexican mothers.[33] Yet these differences pale compared to the mundane routines of parenting children from a distance. Geographic separation, in many ways, diminishes gender role differences in Mexican families.

DEPARTURES AND VISITS HOME

Migrant mothers' and fathers' experiences as transnational parents, however, are not the same. Mothers and fathers leave different types of families when they migrate, and they manage the process of leaving and returning home in different ways. Particularly important for children adjusting to changes in their family is a sense of stability in the household.[34] Children of migrant fathers, migrant couples, and single migrant mothers experience instability during parents' migration to markedly different degrees.

Migrant Fathers

When fathers migrate alone, adjustments in the household are generally minimal. In many cases, children continue to live in the same home, go to the same school, and live with the same family members as before, with the exception of their absent fathers. In some families, a father's departure does lead to a change in the household, as a woman may move in with other relatives after her husband migrates. Yet children continue to live with their mother, who can help to mitigate the effects of these changes. More important, since mothers generally do most of the caregiving for children in Mexico, daily routines such as the timing and type of meals change very little. According to one fifteen-year-old girl who described herself as extremely distraught by her father's absence, the only major difference in her family life since her father left six years before (aside from longing for his return home) had to do with family economics. "Before, they administered the money together, my mom and my dad, and we didn't know anything about it. And now she tells me about the economic problems. Now I know more about my mother's problems." If anything, these adjustments in routine and structure when a father leaves result in stronger bonds between mothers and children.[35]

Fathers are often evasive in managing their departures and visits home to their children, which is difficult for children. The fathers I interviewed reported that they left home without saying good-bye to their children so as not to upset them. One father told me, "This time I had to hide in order to leave. I left really early when the kids were sleeping, because my oldest girl didn't want me to leave." Another never told his children he was leaving. The first time he called from the United States, five months after leaving, his daughter still did not know he was abroad. "She said 'where are you?' I answered, 'Working really far away.' She asked 'When will you be back?' I said, 'I am far away. I don't know.'"

Fathers avoid discussing their departures to make it easier for them to leave. According to one father who had periodically been away from his nineteen- and seventeen-year-olds for eighteen years, departures were easier when the children were younger. "The last two times I left, it has been really hard. Before, when the kids were little, they would go to bed at night and were sleeping when I left. This time, my son asked to take me to the bus terminal. . . . I didn't want him to, because it made me feel bad about leaving. And my daughter said to me, 'Dad, you don't care that you are leaving us.' I said to her, 'I know you see my smiling face, but you don't know what is inside, what I am thinking and feeling.'"

Migrant fathers may not want to talk about their imminent migration because they do not want to get emotional in front of their children. It is also possible that they do not feel that an explanation is necessary. Since fathers leave children with their mother, they know someone is around to explain their departure after the fact. Moreover, they may not feel that their labor migration requires an extensive explanation because it does not deviate from the expectation that fathers be the primary economic provider for the family.

Fathers also typically engage in temporary, or seasonal, migration, making regular trips to see their children in Mexico, a historically common pattern since the years of the bracero program.[36] Thirteen of the fathers I interviewed had returned to visit their family more than once. Fathers prefer to return home every winter, when work is slow. However, because of legal complications, return trips often vary according to fathers' economic situations. Some fathers wait until they have saved enough to take money home and to finance the return trip. One father said, "I like to go home with a lot of money to enjoy there." They stay in Mexico until money runs out, making the return north also unpredictable. A conversation I had with Angelo and Gabriela illustrates this unpredictability. When I arrived at their house, Angelo was absorbed in a card game with three of his children, while Gabriela sat watching TV with the youngest child asleep against her. When the game ended and laughter died down, I asked Angelo if he planned to go back north soon. "Not yet," he said. "I don't know when I will be leaving."

"Not tired of vacation yet?" I joked.

He laughed. "No, not yet," he said, adding, "Soon I might up and go. But not yet."

Gabriela directed her comment to me: "This is the way he always does it. Just one day to the next he decides that it is time to go back."

Fathers, as a result, float in and out of the lives of their children in Mexico depending on their work schedule and economic situation. This is a source of anxiety for children. Some children grow to resent fathers who are not around. Trinided, twenty-five, in looking back on her father's perpetual absences commented, "I felt like *el norte* robbed my father from me." Others nervously await their father's return or departure. Angelo and Gabriela's ten-year-old son, Gilberto, told me that it felt good to have his father back in town: "It is better with him here . . . because he drinks less here than he does there." Gilberto said he liked living with his mother and that his life was the same whether or not his father was in San Ángel. But clearly Gilberto worried about his father; knowing that his father was okay physically made him feel better. Children who are apprehensive about their father's migration may grow closer to their mother while their father is away.

When Both Parents Migrate

When married women join their husbands in the United States, the mother's departure leaves children without either parent. For the most part, children stay in fairly stable home environments, almost always with grandparents. In some cases, children had lived with these caregivers prior to their mother's departure, whether with paternal grandparents or, if their mother had moved back home when their father left, with maternal grandparents.[37] While married couples are away, changes in family structure may not be as great as changes in children's daily routines. When their mother leaves, other family members prepare children's food, get them ready for school, and bathe them. Children, especially daughters, also may be expected to contribute more to housework.[38] For example, when the mother of one seventeen-year-old girl joined her husband in the United States, the girl and her three siblings moved to their grandmother's house. Having dropped out of school after ninth grade, she was the one to clean the house, take her younger siblings their lunches, wash their clothes, and do the dishes for the entire family. Not surprisingly, this young woman preferred living with her mother. She explained: "It isn't the same [living with her grandparents].

We have small problems. . . . It isn't the same type of affection. We don't feel the same as with our mother."

When both the mother and father live in the United States, children often feel their mother's absence more acutely than their father's. This disparity arises in part because of the gendered expectations children have of their mother. But it also arises because the father leaves home first. During this initial period, children grow more attached to their mother. Fifteen-year-old Brian, for example, said at first he was glad that his father had migrated. "He was very strict, and I thought that here [with my mother] and *sin golpes* (without being hit), I would do better." When the mother subsequently leaves, children have a heightened sense of abandonment. Moreover, after a mother leaves, it is more likely that a father will make the trip back to see the children owing to greater dangers women face during the border crossing. Children may feel more resentful of their mother for failing to visit. One migrant mother in New Jersey, for example, said her relationship with her eight-year-old daughter in Mexico deteriorated after her husband went home. "She is closer to her father than she is to me. You see, he went back three years ago to visit. He was only there for three weeks, but this was enough for her to get to know her father. But she doesn't know me. She doesn't remember me. She was little when I left." Children of migrant couples often feel closer to their father, whom they may see more frequently.

Unlike fathers, mothers, whether single or married, rarely leave children without preparing them for their departure. A number of the mothers I interviewed had introduced the idea of migration to children well in advance, and they talked about how their children had supported their decision to migrate. When Nicandra returned home after her mother died, she included her children in the decision to return to the United States. "I said, 'Okay, now what do we do?' They said it was okay (to go back), because we needed the money." Another mother said, "I told them a few months ahead of time that I was going to the United States to work with their father. The youngest boy said, 'It's okay, Mommy. Go and work so that when you come back you can bring us a pizza.'" And, when one mother decided to join her husband abroad after he had been away for a year, she carefully explained her decision to her then four-year-old son.

"What was it that he said? . . . Oh, he said that is was okay because I had been with him for a year already, and he said, 'You should go now to be with my daddy because he is also very lonely over there.' " Whether because they leave home after the father does, because they have better communication with children, or because in leaving they deviate from cultural expectations of mothers as children's primary caregivers, mothers carefully explain migration plans to children.

Single Mothers

Children's consent was particularly important in allaying the concerns single mothers had about their migration decisions. Many children of single mothers understand quite clearly their mother's reasons for leaving. This is because single mothers experience desperate economic situations prior to migration, something that children, even at very young ages, are able to understand. For example, an eight-year-old girl explained that her mother went to *el norte* "because she was going to go work because my brother is sick and so that she can cure him and because my dad died." Nicandra's nineteen-year-old son, Tony, recalled: "The economic situation was terrible. I remember how she used to wring her hands and crack her knuckles because she was always so nervous." Nicandra explained: "Sometimes I didn't know where to get the next meal."

In cases where children are very young and do not remember their usually unwed mother, they almost always live with maternal grandparents, who are quick to explain maternal absences to children. For example, Zelia's mother, Doña Adelaida, lauded her daughter's hard work in the United States. "She has always been very responsible, and she works two jobs. . . . She used to work three jobs but stopped. I think she works in a factory or something like that. She usually sends money twice a month, like fourteen hundred or sixteen hundred pesos [140 to 160 U.S. dollars]. And she always sends clothes for the boy. When she came to visit, she had a whole suitcase full of underpants and socks of different sizes for him." Because single mothers are careful to prepare children for their absences, and children who do not remember their mother live with supportive maternal kin, children of single migrant mothers understand the rationale behind their mother's absence.

Nonetheless, children of single mothers often live in more volatile family environments. Many young mothers have the support of their parents, but others feel partially blamed by some of their family members for ending up alone. Single mothers have only one family as a resource, as opposed to the two kinship networks available to couples. For example, when Nicandra's mother died, she had no recourse other than to allow her boys to live alone. Eventually she recruited a cousin to move into her apartment and keep an eye on them, but since he was only a few years older than her sons, the arrangement caused a lot of conflict.

Divorce may also cause great instability for the children of single mothers, because it often prompts a mother's migration.[39] At times children are caught in custody battles between their parents. Some single mothers I interviewed described extremely adversarial relationships with their ex-husbands who had custody of their children. One mother, for example, decided to migrate when she found out her husband was living with another woman. For three years she had little contact with her three boys; she only occasionally spoke to the oldest when a neighbor helped arrange it. Another was not able to talk to her two children living with her ex-husband, who was remarried, and he would not accept the gifts that she sent them. She was infuriated when she learned that the children were selling candy. "When I was there we were poor, but at least they weren't out on the streets." One mother whose fourteen-year-old lived with her ex-husband, was at first excited that I would be going to Mexico; I could take a ring for her daughter's *quinceañera,* the traditional Mexican coming-out party for young women when they turn fifteen. A month later, I went to arrange the visit, but she scowled when I mentioned her daughter. "I am not going to send her anything," she told me. "She doesn't deserve it. She is rebelling." When I asked what she meant, she explained: "She won't talk to me when I call. She is too close to her father. When she gets on the phone, she says she has to go because her father doesn't like her talking to me."

Children's experiences when parents migrate can vary greatly because of individual circumstances. Yet fathers and mothers leave their children in different types of homes, and they manage the process of coming and going in different ways. When fathers migrate alone, children remain in fairly stable home environments but experience a high degree of insecurity regarding their father's comings and goings. They feel more attached to their mother. Children are often better prepared for migration when both mother and father migrate; they experience changes in their daily routines but usually live in stable home environments. Over time, however, they feel most resentful of a mother who is not able to visit. Children of single-mother migrants also are well prepared for their mother's departure, particularly if caregivers support the mother's migration. At the same time, home environments may be volatile, particularly over time. These children experience the greatest instability while their mother is away.

EVALUATING MOTHERS' AND FATHERS' SACRIFICES

Mothers and fathers have different relationships with their children because of the different types of families they leave in Mexico. Moreover, even though the mechanics of transnational parenting are similar for all parents, parents' activities after migration are interpreted both by children and by parents themselves through a gendered lens. Anthropologist Cati Coe has suggested that parents and children's differential feelings about separation structure their relationships.[40] I find, however, that both children's and parents' emotions are often affected by the evaluations of mothers' and fathers' sacrifices during migration, which hinge on the expectations that fathers should be family providers and mothers should be family caregivers. Similar actions by migrating mothers and fathers have unequal consequences insofar as their relationships with their children are concerned.

Children's Evaluations

If it were the case that Mexican children simply liked their mother more than their father, we might expect them to be more distraught by a mother's absence. Indeed, Rhacel Salazar Parreñas has reported Filipino children to be quite ambivalent about their father's migration, while greatly disturbed emotionally by their mother's absence.[41] The children I interviewed, however, were not ambivalent about their migrant father; most children wanted to live with their father and were eager for him to come home.[42] A fourteen-year-old said she felt sad when hanging up from her weekly calls to her father "because it isn't the same to talk on the phone than to have him close." What she missed most was "his personality. How he was with us. . . . He is very loving with us. He pays a lot of attention to us." A sixteen-year-old was one of only two children who cried during the interview when describing how she missed her father's love. Her message to migrant men abroad was "that they try to fight here in Mexico. That they don't go there. That the affection of their children is not something you can pay for with money."

Not all children I interviewed were so kind; some were quite resentful of their father's absence. Yet even children with mixed feelings about their father believed a father should be there for his children. One twelve-year-old boy, for example, told me that he does not like to talk on the phone to his father. "I remember that he gets angry a lot. . . . It is better that he is there. . . . It is better to live with my mom." Regardless, he said he missed his dad and admitted, "Well, yes, sometimes I do want him to come back. . . . [I miss him when I think] that he is far away and he cannot come back." Mexican children's distress, whether felt as resentment or longing that their father return, suggests that fathers are important to children.[43] Or perhaps it is the experience of living apart that makes children more appreciative of their father's role in the family—a classic case of absence making the heart grow fonder.

While most children miss their migrant fathers and want them to come home, they believe that mothers play a more central role in raising children. In the surveys I distributed to school students in the Mixteca, the majority of respondents, 61 percent, said that it is better for the father to migrate.[44] Of these, less than half cited qualities of fathers as their reasoning, including that they are physically stronger and that it is their role to work and maintain the family, but more students (51 percent) wrote that the father should leave because the relationship between mother and child is more important.[45] According to one fourteen-year-old girl: "The dad [should migrate], because the father doesn't know how to give advice to his child. He doesn't really know what his child likes. He doesn't know how to understand him. But the mother can give the love of both the father and the mother."

Male students agreed. A fourteen-year-old boy reasoned: "Because if the mom left, the father wouldn't be able to replace a mother's care." Another explained: "The father doesn't understand them [children] like the mother." Students described a mother's role in the family as more central and intimately tied to the care of children. In contrast, students considered fathers to be more suited for migration because of their obligation to provide for children economically.

Children's expectations that mothers care for them and that fathers provide financially for them color their interpretations of parents' communication. Many described greater *confianza* [trust] and *cariño* [affection] with their migrant mother than their father. This was true of children of all ages and of both girls and boys. Although at age eleven Germán explained that he felt the same amount of *cariño* for both his mother and his father, he said he was closer to his mother because she talked to him longer on the phone. Germán's logic illustrates how for children in Mexico love from each parent comes on different terms.

J. D.: Do you love your mom?
GERMAN: Yes.
J. D.: Do you feel that she loves you?
GERMAN: She says she loves me.
J. D.: And your dad, do you love him also?
GERMAN: Yes.
J. D.: So you feel that he loves you?
GERMAN: Yes, well, he is the one who sends more money.

For Germán and others like him, a mother's love is expressed in words and a father's love is expressed in dollars, or pesos.

Children also have higher expectations of migrant mothers than they do of migrant fathers. They feel more disappointed by their mothers who have U.S.-born children than they do of fathers. One eleven-year old girl, for example, did not feel like her U.S.-born sister jeopardized her relationship with her father, but she complained of feeling jealous for her mother's attention after her sibling was born in New York. Her parents had since divorced, and her father had recently returned to San Ángel and married another woman. Although prohibited from seeing her father by her grandmother, the eleven-year old did see him. "When I go by after school, he talks to me and he gives me money . . . fifteen or twenty pesos (one and a half to two dollars)." The small amount was enough to show the eleven-year-old that her father cared. Although her mother, who lived thousands of miles away, supported her economically and called once a week, it did not appear to be enough. She admitted that at times, "I want to go and live with him [her father]."

The gendered double standard toward migrant parents also means that children often feel more distraught about a migrant mother's new relationship than they do about a father's. Brian, age sixteen, told me that he felt like his mother had abandoned him after his migrant parents had divorced and then had acquired new partners in New Jersey. "Because if she loved us really, she would call. Or not even that she doesn't send [money], because that doesn't matter. But at least she has to call." What mattered to Brian was not the money, but "that she calls and says that she is okay." In contrast, Brian said he loved his father, who had not only remarried but had another child, which Brian was upset about. When I asked, "Do you feel like your dad loves you?" Brian answered, "Sometimes I say that no, but well, yes. He is the only one who supports us."

Children evaluate a father's sacrifice according to his financial responsibility and a mother's sacrifice by her ability to demonstrate emotional care from a distance.[46] If, over time, a migrant mother takes on a new partner and has more children in the United States, the children in Mexico feel disillusioned with their mother. Research in Mexico has found children to experience more negative outcomes, including greater levels of stress, when their primary caregivers, typically mothers, migrate than when fathers do.[47] Mothers' failures to live up to standards of care during periods of international separation, not children's ambivalence about their fathers, explain why mothers' migrations are so emotionally distressing for Mexican children.

Parents' Expectations

Children are not the only ones to evaluate mothers' and fathers' sacrifices unequally. Mothers' and fathers' expectations of themselves while living apart from their children are also highly gendered. Fathers evaluate their own successes and failures as migrants according to a "family breadwinner" criterion, while mothers describe emotional intimacy as key to their relationships with children from abroad and their personal success as migrants.

Fathers have extremely high expectations of what they can achieve economically from their labor migration.[48] When fathers perceive failure and feel they cannot fulfill their role as family provider in terms of sending money home, communication with their children wanes. One father, for example, said, "I only call when I have a number to give them [for the money order]." Another explained: "I call home more when I have money. Right now, since I am not really working much, I haven't sent any." A father may not send money because of lack of employment or because he drinks away his paycheck. However, what is important is not the act of drinking or the state of being unemployed; it is the act of sending money that matters most to him.

As long as fathers are able to provide financially for their family in Mexico, they feel that their role as father remains intact. One husband and father of two teenagers said he visits his family in Oaxaca every year and calls home weekly. This father first migrated to New York City when his oldest son, now nineteen, was a year old. On his second trip to New York, he got involved with a Puerto Rican woman and moved in with her, but he never told his family in Mexico about her. The relationship ended after six months, when he hit her and ended up in jail for three months. While in jail, he had a friend send money home in his place—two hundred dollars a month—and lied to his family, saying that there wasn't much work at that time of the year. He laughed as he recounted how his friend would call home for him, saying he couldn't call personally because he was working somewhere in the mountains where there was no phone line. To this day, his family doesn't know about his incarceration or the Puerto Rican woman behind it.

Another father said he continues to call his wife and four children whenever he has money, even after ten years of binge drinking in the United States and an alleged affair with his sister-in-law. Remarkably, he still considers himself the head of the household. Clearly fathers' relationships with family members are often troubled. Still, migrant fathers make it clear that when they send money home they feel their prerogatives as the head of the household are maintained. As Efrén mentioned in the opening vignette, financially responsible migrant men feel they continue to have rights over their home and family.

Mothers' relationships with children, in contrast, are not based on financial support. The emotional care they are able to provide from a distance matters most to them. Before one migrant single mother sent for her children, for example, she spoke with them weekly. Every time she called, her eight-year-old daughter would say, "Mommy, when are you coming back to be with us? I want you to be here with me already." This mother did not, however, send money home regularly. She explained the financial relationship she had with her sister, who cared for the children, this way: "I trust her because we help each other out. I send money when I can, but sometimes when I don't work for two or three weeks, I don't send any and she feeds the children. And sometimes if she doesn't have any money and needs it, she will call me and ask, and I try to send something." Whether or not she sent money home did not affect how she related to her children. In fact, I found that ten mothers were not working when I interviewed them, some because of new child care responsibilities and others because they were frequently out of work. All remained in touch with their children and did not consider lack of employment as an impediment to the relationship.

If financial support is not essential to mothers, emotional intimacy is. Migrant mothers expect themselves to call home regularly and to suffer greatly without their children. Fathers generally minimize the emotional costs of family separation despite evidence of substance abuse, depression, and feelings of loss living without their children, perhaps owing to men's efforts to distance themselves from what Catherine Riessman calls "direct manifestations of sadness."[49] In contrast, fourteen mothers detailed how they cried for months upon arrival in the United States, lacked appetite and became physically ill, or grew severely depressed. For example, one mother told me, "I cried for two months when I first arrived. . . . I was nervous all the time and made lots of mistakes when I first started to work." Another complained that before her husband went back for her son, "I didn't work well. I didn't sleep well. I didn't eat well." One mother in San Ángel told me she returned to Mexico because "I suffered a lot in the United States without my son, especially when we had first arrived. When we would go out to the stores and I saw the children with their parents, I would start to cry." These symptoms are similar to those reported in the general literature on mothers who are separated from their children for other reasons, including incarceration, institutionalization due to mental illness, or homelessness.[50]

Mothers often express guilt over leaving children, whereas fathers rarely do.[51] A father of three who calls and sends money weekly to his children living in three different households, one with his ex-wife, one with his mother, and one with his current spouse, explained when I asked whether he feels guilty for not living with his children: "No, it is not guilt. I think I would feel bad if I knew the children were suffering, and that they wouldn't suffer if I was there with them. But they aren't, so I don't." Compare his comment to that of Nicandra, whose teenage sons, Tony and Miguel, actually live in the same neighborhood as her ex-husband and are supported by her weekly remittances. "I often feel guilty. When things aren't going well, I feel guilty. When my son wasn't doing well, it was like I wasn't on top of things. I mean, one feels guilty for not giving them the attention they need." Nicandra feels her children's emotional well-being is her responsibility, even though their father lives nearby. The father of three, on the other hand, considers his responsibility to be for his children's economic well-being. His children suffer less, economically, because he works abroad and sends money home regularly, alleviating the guilt he might otherwise feel about his sacrifice.

GENDER AND PARENTING ACROSS BORDERS

Gender role differences alone cannot explain the differences in migrant mothers' and fathers' experiences. Migrant mothers and fathers actually engage in very similar parenting activities when separated from their children. Divided by borders, mothers' and fathers' roles in their families are more alike than they are dissimilar.

The sociologists Candace West, Don Zimmerman, and Sarah Fenstermaker have proposed that gender is a "routine, methodological and on-going accomplishment." What they call "doing gender" is a social interaction that "cast[s] particular pursuits as expressions of manly and womanly 'natures.'"[52] If we consider parenting across borders as a gender accomplishment, we can better explain why mothers' migration has unique consequences for families. Because of their different positions in their families, mothers and fathers leave home not only for different reasons but in different ways. The meanings ascribed to parental absences are informed by cultural constructs that women are the caregivers and men the providers. Mexican parents and children separated internationally accomplish gender in a very specific way.

Fathers are ultimately seen as economic providers. Fathers do not explain their absence to their children very carefully. Often they come in and out of their children's lives in Mexico according to their economic situation. Although children may resent such absences, they judge their father's success abroad according to economic indicators: that is, the remittances that are sent home. The same is true for fathers. Fathers feel they have a right to their children in Mexico as long as they are sending money home.

Migrant mothers, in contrast, are viewed as the children's primary caregivers. Mothers usually are the last to leave home. They carefully plan their departure, ensuring that children understand their motivations for leaving. While away, however, mothers are expected to continue to show they care for children from a distance. This is not always an easy feat. Mothers are not able to return to visit as easily as fathers are. When mothers have U.S.-born children or a new husband in the United States, children are wary of their mother's competing obligations. Mothers feel extremely guilty about leaving their children, independent of their economic solvency as migrants.

On the one hand, evaluations of migrant mothers as caregivers and fathers as providers are not surprising. We might not expect women and men to shed conventional parenting roles so easily. In fact, scholars suggest that women bear greater burdens of care in the transnational context.[53] On the other hand, women and men do renegotiate conjugal relationships during migration; courtship, concepts of sexuality, and child care duties of children born in the United States change.[54] Given the possibilities for gender relationships to change during migration, it is quite remarkable that women who migrate to work without their children continue to be defined as family caregivers when they are no longer the primary caregivers. Despite these mothers' bold moves away from their children, they and their families do not appear to be revolutionizing concepts of motherhood.[55] Like working mothers in the United States, transnational mothers continue to be responsible for family caregiving.[56]

The "doing of gender" in conventional ways when parenting from afar is crucial to understanding the ways parent-child relationships evolve during periods of separation. Indeed, gendered expectations help explain the tensions family members may experience over time.

Fathers have difficulties with their children when they have trouble providing for them financially. Because working conditions for Mexican migrants in the United States are often difficult, economic considerations are not inconsequential. None of the fathers I interviewed earned more than fifteen dollars per hour. Many worked two jobs or an average of sixty to seventy hours per week. Mexican fathers face significant pressures in supporting their families in Mexico and constantly compare themselves to other migrant men's achievements. Fathers expect to build a house, start a new business, and increase the family's standard of living through remittances. The emphasis on economic provision inherent in labor migration reinforces the expectation that men be the primary family provider, something they are not always able to accomplish. The economic relationship is paramount, for fathers communicate with children in Mexico only as long as they are sending money.

The emphasis on fathers' economic contributions has consequences even for men who are able to send money home. Historically, migrant men have been accused by their wives for being *"padres de cheque no más,"* or fathers by virtue of check only.[57] Moreover, I found that after not having communicated for years, some fathers may attempt to reassert themselves in their children's lives once they are gainfully employed. When fathers are able to send money home, they feel they have a claim as a father and a right to their children. These actions are not always well received by families in Mexico. One woman in San Ángel, for example, explained that her husband—whom she had not heard from in more than five years—recently resumed contact with her son. She had considered herself abandoned by him, and having formed a new relationship with a man in Mexico, did not welcome this effort.[58] "He has sent a little bit," she explained. "Maybe fifty dollars or something like this. What can I tell my son? I tell him that it's fine, but that he [the father] should have sent money when he [the son] was little, when we needed it more. Now I have already figured out a way on my own." This mother interpreted her husband's renewed contact as a threat. She worried that her husband would stake claim not only to her son's affection but also over his old family, herself included. Attempts to reestablish connections by fathers like this one show that emotional ties to children are important for fathers, as they are for children. It is significant that fathers feel they must establish an economic connection in order to facilitate an emotional one.

Mothers, in contrast, do not expect themselves, or other mothers, to perform economic miracles with remittances. Instead, they hope to find work either to put food on the table or to assist husbands in meeting their goals. Mothers do expect themselves to be able to maintain significant emotional bonds with their children despite the distance. When mothers have competing demands for their affections in the United States and lose touch with the pace of their children's lives in Mexico, they feel their relationships with their children suffer. One mother I met, for example, never sent money home regularly but spoke with her two boys in Mexico often, even after she divorced their father. However, once she remarried and started a new family, her regular phone calls stopped. Another had not reduced economic support for her eight-year-old daughter over the six years she lived with her husband in New Jersey. Her phone calls and intimacy with her daughter waned as her U.S.-born children began to occupy her time.

It is significant that mothers do use the giving of material objects as expressions of care, an act akin to a father's economic provision of goods. For this reason mothers, like fathers, send children gifts through friends and talk on the phone about what children want or need. However, when mothers do not send money or gifts, they do not necessarily feel they have damaged their relationships with their children. What matters is the expression of care rather than actual material goods. For fathers, in contrast, it is what is sent home that counts.

For mothers, intangible expressions of care more easily fade with time, as it is nearly impossible to reclaim the role of caring mother after long periods of inattention. This does not mean that mothers do not attempt to reestablish connections with their children. Indeed, mothers show great commitments to their children even after having been criticized for abandoning them. Mothers reestablish relationships with children, however, not when they are economically secure, but rather when they are emotionally stable. Silvia, for example, had been condemned by her own mother for her inattention to her children while going through a divorce. As soon as Silvia felt the turmoil with her ex-husband had subsided, she sent for her children. At the time, she had only a part-time job and relied on child care from her sister and child support from her ex-husband to provide for them.

There are clearly some ways in which physical separation is a gender equalizer in transnational families because it limits the type of activities mothers and fathers can engage in with their children. The conditions of migration may put women and men on similar playing fields and alter Mexican gender expectations within marital relationships.[59] Yet, while separated, family members act in ways to reinforce the notion that fathers' relationships with their children are directly related to their ability to honorably fulfill the role of economic provider for the family. Migration, in fact, magnifies the economic role of men in families, as monetary support becomes the most meaningful tie to their children in Mexico. In contrast, family members' evaluations of migrant mothers center on their ability to be caregivers from a distance, quite a difficult accomplishment.[60] Migrant mothers' and fathers' absences are not equal. In the end, mothers carry the moral burden of transnational parenting.

After migrant parents divorce in the United States, some fathers may redefine transnational fatherhood, taking a more active role in the lives of their children living in Mexico. Photograph by Joanna Dreby

FOUR Armando López on Fatherhood

> When I first came [to the United States], it was like they didn't miss me that much. I felt this, anyway, I think because their mother was there [in Mexico] and they felt secure with their mother. They didn't need anything. But when she recently came [to the United States], I saw that they got closer to me; it was as if—like they were very stuck to their mother. When she was there, they were attached to her. She was like their idol.
>
> Armando López

When mothers and fathers live apart from their children, the meanings they ascribe to parent-child interactions across borders recreate rather conventional definitions of parenthood. Yet, as Armando's comment suggests, there are some situations in which fathers' emotional roles in their children's lives expand. For Armando, this occurred after his wife joined him in the United States and then left him for another man. After her migration and the divorce, Armando's ex-wife violated the standard of care expected of mothers. Armando felt that his relationship with his children in Mexico actually improved. This was a source of pride for Armando, which gave him a sense of accomplishment during a difficult time in his life.

Indeed, I found that fathers often take a more active role in the lives of their children living in Mexico after migrant parents divorce in the

United States. Mothers, in contrast, fade from their children's lives, at least for a time. José talked to his two children, Brian and Tina, much more frequently than his wife, Elsa, did after they divorced in New Jersey, even though the children lived with Elsa's mother. The same was true for Daniel when he and Silvia went through a divorce and sent their children back to Oaxaca for a time. In another case in San Ángel, the father maintained custody of his children; he and his ex-wife divorced in Las Vegas, and he brought his eighteen-month-old twins and four-year-old son back to town to be cared for by his mother. According to the grandmother, "Recently she [the mother] just came back to Mexico. The younger boys don't know her. They don't remember her. But the older boy does remember her, since he was older when he stopped seeing her. He doesn't like to talk to her, though; none of the boys do." When parents divorce after they migrate, mothers' commitments to their families come into question and new opportunities arise for fathers to redefine their relationships with their children in Mexico.

What constitutes fatherhood, and masculinity more broadly, is not necessarily fixed.[1] As the anthropologist Matthew Gutmann has suggested, "Masculinity in Mexico, as elsewhere, is definitely more subtle, diverse, and malleable than is generally assumed."[2] Fathering activities may very well change under certain conditions and in specific social contexts. Mexican men raised in urban areas may participate more in child care than do those raised in rural areas.[3] Mexican men with lower socioeconomic status may be more involved in parenting activities than are those in higher income brackets.[4] However, they may discipline their children more frequently and be less nurturing than Mexican men of higher socioeconomic backgrounds.[5] "We need further understanding," writes Maxine Baca Zinn, "of larger societal conditions in which masculinity is embedded and expressed."[6]

What is the meaning of fatherhood when Mexican men engage in labor migration? I find that not only are migrant fathers' expressions of masculinity associated with their ability to provide for their children, but their relationships with their children are also in dynamic relationship with the moral evaluations of migrant mothers. The limited situations in which migrant men display alternate expressions of fatherhood show that men's relationships with their children are almost always mediated by women.[7] Mothers' failures to live up to the moral burdens of transnational motherhood create new possibilities for fatherhood.

This chapter explores through one in-depth case how marital conflict during migration can spill over into parents' relationships with their children in Mexico and create the space for fathers to expand their roles with their children. In some ways Armando is atypical. Unlike other fathers, Armando carefully explained his decision to migrate to his children. His wife, in contrast, did not prepare her children for her departure. Armando also felt that by living in New Jersey he could offer his children a more stable environment than where they lived in Mexico. Most migrant fathers preferred that their children be raised in Mexico.

Although unique, Armando's experiences illustrate a common pattern: after his migration and subsequent divorce, Armando expanded his emotional ties with his children. This pattern occurs only under specific circumstances. The fathers who do this—Armando included—are the primary economic contributors to the family; their success as family breadwinners gives them an opening with their children when mothers appear not to live up to caregiving expectations. It is also true that fathers' efforts in this regard are often short-lived. As I followed Armando and his family's experiences after he returned to live with his children in Mexico, it became clear that, despite Armando's initial resolve to radically deepen his emotional bonds with his children, over time his economic ties to them continued to be paramount. Although some divorced fathers may "do gender" in different ways while living apart from their children, with time, definitions of fathers as providers and mothers as caregivers may resurface.

MARITAL WOES

May 2004. A friend told me about Armando, who had children living in Mexico and had recently been separated from his wife. When I called, Armando immediately agreed to an interview. As he lived just blocks from my house, I walked over the next day and was greeted by a young woman holding a baby. The woman, I later learned, was Armando's only sister. She invited me in to the first-floor apartment, and the door opened into a sparely decorated, spotless living room. The rose-colored carpet had been recently vacuumed; the gray sofa and love seat set, as well as the coffee table, were free of clutter. Armando joined us immediately, dressed in baggy jeans, a stylish T-shirt, and a baseball cap.

Armando, I learned, is the second-oldest of six brothers and one sister. He was living with one of his brothers, his sister, her husband, and their newborn baby. Armando's three other brothers rented the second-floor apartment, where they lived with their respective partners. Only one brother still lived in the family at home in Guerrero, Mexico. I had entered a home filled with Armando's relatives.

Armando is a soft-spoken man, who was deliberate and thoughtful when he talked about his life. He was one of the few who agreed to being tape-recorded during our interview. At the time of our first conversation, Armando had been separated from his wife for six months. The couple had three children: nine-year-old Michael, five-year-old Mary, and three-year-old Lupe, who lived with Armando's mother outside of a major Mexican city.

Armando started by explaining that he had finished high school in Mexico and was licensed as an electrician. When he graduated and began to look for work, he found that the jobs paid less than a hundred dollars per week. "Since my family was very poor and my older brother had already married, I felt responsible for the family. And the money wasn't enough."

So Armando joined the marines, working as an electrician on naval ships traveling from port to port within Mexico. However, Armando did not like life at sea, and after four years he left his post and returned home. At age twenty-four, Armando started working as an electrician at local hotels, a booming industry. When he was twenty-nine, Armando decided it was time to get married. His bride was more than ten years younger, and, looking back, he considered the generation gap to be partly responsible for their separation. Armando had just turned forty when we met.

After a civil ceremony, Armando and his bride moved in with

Armando's mother. The couple's first son, Michael, was born in 1995. After two years, Armando bought a property just a few blocks from his mother's home. He built a wooden house and moved his small family into the new home. Mary was born in 1999. In 2001, Armando's brother invited him north.

Armando was reluctant to leave home. A few years earlier he had turned down an offer from another brother to help him migrate. "I thought about it a lot. I didn't want to leave my family. I was happy with my family. But my wife and I decided that I would come. The idea was to save money. To save. I didn't think I would stay for long, or that I would bring my family [here]. . . . I wasn't crazy about the idea, but I talked to my wife about it, and she convinced me it would be good idea so that we could fix up the house and save money as well. So I decided to go."

When Armando left, his wife was pregnant with their third child. In order not to worry him, she did not tell him she was pregnant until he had arrived in the United States. Little Lupe was born in 2001. Armando explained: "I have never met her, only in pictures and videos."

Armando did not expect that life would be difficult in the United States. "My brother gave me the impression that the money hung on the trees here." His brothers found him his first job cutting grass for a landscaping company. But Armando's health was not good when he arrived, and he found ten hours a day outside grueling. Instead he went to work at a factory. At the time of our interview, he still worked at a factory. Armando's health had improved. He worked the early morning shift and was home by 4:00 P.M. to go to another part-time job in the evenings.

After a year in the United States, Armando paid off the loan that had financed his migration. There were also a number of debts at home arising from the birth of his youngest daughter at the hospital (since he had been away when she was born and no longer had health insurance to cover the medical costs). He sent between eighty and a hundred dollars a week but felt like he was spinning his wheels, not making progress toward his initial goals. "By the second year, I thought about bringing my children here. I thought that here there would be a better future for them. . . . Children suffer in Mexico. There is a lot of insecurity [there].

People are bad over there. And nutrition is bad as well. There is less distrust [here]. There is less insecurity."

During Armando's second year away from home, he proposed the idea of coming to the United States to his family in Mexico. "My wife, she wanted to come. My son didn't want to come, because of his friends, his school, and his grandmother." Soon after he first raised the idea, he sent for his wife. Armando's children moved in with his mother, who still lived around the corner in Mexico. "They are fine with my mother. . . . She is a very responsible person. I trust her a lot." Armando's mother hired someone to help with the housework after his wife left. His mother was fifty-nine at the time and also cared for another six-year-old grandchild, whose parents lived in the United States with Armando.

"But here comes the saddest part of the story," Armando warned. After Armando's wife joined him in New Jersey, they lived together for just three months. Then she left him. "Now," Armando explained, "my wife lives with another man. She left me to go live with someone else."

After his wife left, Armando took over responsibility for the children. For a few months, his wife sent approximately fifty dollars a week for their care, as this was their arrangement upon separation. But then she stopped sending money and calling as frequently as she had before. One day, she called Armando and was very angry. "She said that when she calls, my mother won't let her talk to the children. It isn't true. It is that the phone at the house is a cell phone, which is sometimes hard to get through on. But since then, she hasn't been calling. But I try not to ask about her when I call." Armando said he wanted to know if his ex-wife talked to the children, but was afraid to ask. "[Once] he [Michael] said to me, 'She forgot about me.' I was hurting him by asking about her, so I stopped."

Armando said he generally calls home twice a week. When he talks to his son, they discuss "school, some goats he has, his homework, if he took his bath, if he brushed his teeth, if he combed his hair. I ask him to go around to the house and sweep it out. I ask him about his grandmother and about his sisters. . . . I see him as a friend aside from being my son. He tells me everything: what they want, what I should buy them, what they like, about school, about the girls." Armando said communication with his daughter Mary was not as easy. "She doesn't like to talk to me quite so much. When I call, she just asks me to come home. She wants me to take her to the plaza. She asks to see me." Lupe likes to talk a lot on the phone, but Armando felt that communication with her was superficial, as it was with Mary. "Of all of them, I speak most with my son, Michael."

Armando said he sends home a thousand dollars per month, and his mother puts what she does not use into his savings account. He complained that before his wife came to the United States, he used to send her a hundred dollars a week, but she did not spend the money wisely. Correcting himself, Armando said that they did fix up the bathroom and make some home improvements. But Armando felt his mother had done a better job of administering his meager resources, enabling him to save money for the first time.

In the six months since his wife had left him, Armando had hit a real low, both emotionally and economically. "I went really down. Because everything broke at the same time. I wanted to go back [to Mexico]. But my siblings gave me a lot of support. They told me I should stay so that I could return to Mexico with something, instead of nothing." At the time of our interview, Armando was working two jobs and planned to return to live with his children in Mexico before the holiday season.

Despite Armando's devotion to his children, he stated matter-of-factly, "I feel like the children need their mother." He thought they felt more vulnerable since their mother left home. "Right after I left for the United States, they were more distanced from me, like they didn't miss me much." He believed they felt secure because they lived with their mother. He also suspected that she said bad things to the children about him, telling them that he was irresponsible. Armando felt that this had changed after his wife came to the United States. "Things are different now, especially with my son, Michael. . . . I feel like he looks to me more and that he trusts me more."

"After the separation, I didn't know what to say to my children about their mother. My daughter Mary would ask to talk to her, and I would lie, saying that she was out at work." Armando said he had wanted to tell his son about what had happened but could not bring himself to do so, not knowing what to say to the boy. Finally, months later, he decided to break the news. "So one day I called on the phone and said, 'Michael, there is something I have to tell you. Your mother and I no longer live together.' And he said, 'Dad, I know already. The kids at school told me.'"

Armando went on to explain that he has a neighbor from Mexico who also lives in New Jersey. The neighbor had sent for his wife at the same time Armando had sent for his, and gossip about both women traveled back to his neighborhood.[8] "You see, she did the same thing my wife did." Armando had not suspected that his neighbors had marital problems. The couple visited Armando and his wife when the women arrived in New Jersey. At first, the other woman did not work. Once she started working, she and her husband began fighting. "One day they had a fight and he hit her, so she left. This is the same thing my wife did."

I asked tentatively, "Did you fight with your wife like they did?" Armando admitted that they fought the day she left. His family wanted to chip in to rent a new house together, he explained, and they needed to put up some money for the security deposit. Armando said his wife did not want to live with his family anymore. She left with a neighbor, saying she already had another place to go. Later he learned that she went to live with another man. "I loved her and was really upset when she left. I had this idea that we would work together and be able to give our children a better education. . . . It wasn't what I thought."

"How do you think your experiences as a father compare to those of your own father?" I asked. "They are completely different," Armando answered without hesitation. He went on to explain that his own father was very irresponsible. Armando's father never lived with Armando's mother but with another woman and their children nearby. Armando's father maintained two families for many years, continuing to have more children with each woman. "[In contrast], I consider myself responsible for my children."

ONE FAMILY'S MIGRATION CHAINS

October 2004. Given Armando's description of his father, I was slightly surprised on my first visit with Armando's family in Mexico that it was his father who spoke to me on the phone, offered us drinks and conversation when we visited the family home, and accompanied us to lunch the following day. Armando's mother, Doña Mica, a trim, handsome woman with shortly cropped curly hair dyed black and a spry body, said little about her role in taking care of Armando's children on that first visit. Instead, when I interviewed the couple together the next day at a formal lunch Armando had arranged, and I asked about how they had met, Armando's father did most of the talking.

When Armando's father was twenty-four, he met Doña Mica, who was fifteen. "*La robé*—I stole her," he explained, saying he took her to be his wife without asking for formal permission from her parents to do so. At the time, Armando's father was a day laborer without steady work. Later Armando's father got a job at a hotel where he worked for thirty years, until health problems prompted his retirement. Doña Mica sold lemons, coconuts, and other fruits from the house to make ends meet.

The first in the family to migrate was one of Armando's younger brothers, who left for New Jersey with a cousin at the age of seventeen. He financed the construction of the concrete house where Doña Mica lived with Armando's children. After five years, he returned for two months. At this point he took up with a girlfriend (one of Armando's sisters-in-law, whom I met, as she lived with Doña Mica), and shortly thereafter he returned to the United States. He visited again four years later, at which point his girlfriend got pregnant. They married and after a few months, he migrated again, leaving his pregnant wife with Doña Mica. Two years later, he came home to meet his daughter but stayed for just a month. I learned that day that although his Mexican wife desperately wanted to join him abroad, he is married and has children in New Jersey as well.

Armando's oldest brother was the next to leave. This brother was married when he first left and was away for three years before returning home for three years. The pattern of periodic migration continued until his children grew up, when they joined their father in the United States. Their mother had stayed behind because of health problems but hoped to be healthy enough in a few months to join her children and husband abroad. "I am the last of the family to be left behind," she explained.

Then a third brother migrated and had been in New Jersey for six years when I first met Doña Mica. Like his older brother, he left a wife and daughter in Mexico. However, after two years he sent for his wife while the couple's daughter remained in Doña Mica's care. Just three weeks prior to my visit, the couple had sent for their then six-year-old daughter.

Armando's sister and his youngest brother migrated next. Armando's sister had been married in Mexico before going to the United States, and Armando told me she was abused by her ex-husband. Her brothers helped her migrate to leave the bad marriage behind. "We didn't know that he hit her; she never told us until later. She asked his [her husband's] permission to leave, and we sent her [to the United States]. She said she would send for him, but it was a lie. After a year, she told him that it was over."

Armando was the last to leave Mexico. I asked Doña Mica how Armando's children had adapted to their parents' migration. "When she [their mother] first left, they cried a lot for her and got sick easily. The boy [Michael] not so much as the girls," she explained. "How long did it take for them to adjust to living with you?" I asked. "Maybe six months."

"Who decided that the children would stay with you?" I asked Doña Mica.

"Armando decided. They have another grandmother in another part of the city, but the kids didn't want to go with her when their mom left. They didn't know her well, and there was really no question that they would stay with me." I wondered aloud: "What does their mother say about them being with you?" According to Doña Mica, "She says she is going to come for them, but we don't really know. That is the gossip that we hear, but it is nothing more than that. . . . Their mother wants them to go to the United States and asked her son if he wants to go there with her, but he said no. He doesn't want to go to the United States; he wants to stay in Mexico."

When I asked what will happen to the children when Armando returns from the United States, Armando's father told me, "They will stay where they are because Armando will have to work and someone will need to watch them."

HOMECOMING

January 2005. True to plan, that December Armando returned to live with his children. We had the chance to meet a few months later, when Armando visited family members near where I was staying. On our visit, Armando told me about his reunion with his children. Even though before he told me he trusted his mother completely, he confessed: "I was scared when I arrived about how it would be to see my children. I imagined that they were not well cared for, but not nearly so much as when I saw them. I found them so skinny. . . . I had thought that they were better. And I saw my son so old, and I didn't recognize him really. He was so skinny, and the little one as well." I asked him to tell me about the moment he arrived at the house. "The little one came up right away and hugged me." This is the daughter who had never met her father. "Did they cry?" I asked Armando. "Not them. But I did. I felt so moved that tears came out—after four years to see them again so different, not well cared for either . . . much sadder than what I imagined."

Armando said he changed the rules when he arrived. "I had imagined how they were being raised because I know my mother. I know how she raised them. Not that she didn't care for them. More that she spoiled them . . . like she didn't prohibit all the bad things because, well, because she couldn't. So I imagined this. And I arrived, and it was true, just as I had imagined it. They were a little confused, and I arrived and I began to prohibit the things they shouldn't do. . . . Like not going to other people's homes. They used to go into other people's places to play." He also described having to change rules about food. "If they haven't eaten, I don't want them to have candy. If they haven't eaten, I don't want them to drink soda. . . . And also that they wash their hands always before they eat."

Armando also said that coming home he learned about his children's experiences when they had still been with their mother. "My son, Michael, told me that his mom hit him a lot. . . . I didn't know about any of this. I thought they were fine. . . . She hit all of them, even the little one when she was just a year old." I asked Armando if his mother had told him about this.

"No, just my son. He said she hit all three of them. And sometimes they wouldn't eat. Because their mother told them that I didn't send enough money, so she didn't buy them anything to eat. And she wouldn't let them go to their grandmother's house [to eat]. Once the neighbor tried to give them something to eat, but their mother wouldn't let them take it, and they were hungry. [Michael said] she would go out a lot for many hours. She wouldn't leave them with my mother, but instead with a neighbor who lived way up the hill. . . . And I felt sad [to learn about this], because they are children, and it isn't their fault. And I sent her money, enough to eat, and she didn't feed them. Sometimes I didn't send a lot, but I always sent something, enough for food. It was that she didn't spend the money wisely. Because I would send like eight hundred pesos, that is eighty dollars, and that is more than enough for food for a week. My mom never told me anything while I was away. Now that I am back, she has told me a lot of things. I don't know why she didn't tell me—she should have. But she told me that my ex-wife would go out a lot with other men."

Nonetheless, Armando continued to believe that his children needed a mother. "Mary—it is as if she loves her mother more. Yes, she is affectionate with me, and hugs me . . . but I know that when her mother arrives, that she is going to go more to her mother. Because I feel that she loves her mother more. The other day they talked on the phone. I told my mom that if she [the ex-wife] calls, to tell her to send money to their [children's] other grandmother—to her own mother, that is, that she shouldn't send it to my mother, that if she wants to send it, to send it to her own parents and they can bring it over. So she [Mary] comes out in defense of her mother—Mary always defends her mother. She says, 'it's better if she sends it here.' I know that if anyone speaks badly of her mother, Mary always defends her. Because she is her mother. She has to love her. You can't take away their love for their mother. It is stronger, I think, a mother's love than a father's love."

ADJUSTMENTS

April 2005. In April, I visited Armando's family again in Mexico. A number of things had changed since I had last seen them. First, the house seemed different. Armando explained: "It is cleaner than you remember. Everything was a mess when I arrived." Second, Armando's sister-in-law, who had lived at the house before with her daughter, had left and moved in with her own mother. She had gotten fed up waiting for her husband in the United States to send for her and decided to start a new life of her own. I ended up staying in the room where she had slept. Finally, there were two new members of the household: Doña Mica was now taking care of her three- and four-year old nephews, whose mother had left them while Doña Mica's brother was in jail.

During my visit, I spent most mornings with Armando and his children on outings. In the afternoons, Armando worked at a hotel as an electrician. "How much are you making at your new job?" I asked one day when we visited a nearby pool.

"Not a lot, but they just gave me a raise."

"How much?" I probed.

"Well, now I am earning 120 pesos [twelve dollars] a day. I just got a raise from 100 pesos [ten dollars]." Armando laughed when thinking back to salaries in the United States. "It is really nothing. But," he added more seriously, "I have benefits and insurance, so it is better than it sounds. Still, this is why I want to buy a *combi* [minivan used for public transport]. They make about three times what I do in a day."

On various outings to a nearby pool and Armando's soccer games, I witnessed how loving Armando was toward his children. Armando also told me about his plans for the future and how he hoped to marry soon. "Ideally I want someone who is in her thirties, someone who is mature and who can help me take care of my children." He told me how his daughters get jealous when he goes out on dates. "Sometimes I cannot find my cologne when I am getting ready to go out. I look everywhere, and it turns out that Mary has hidden it from me to keep me from going."

While Armando was at work, I chatted with Doña Mica and played with the children. Although on my first trip I learned little in interviews with Mary and Michael, this time each had more to say about what it was like to live with their father again. I had a conversation with six-year-old Mary:

J. D.: How do you feel now that your dad is here?

MARY: My dad was in the north and I missed him a lot.

J. D.: Do you feel happy that your dad is here?
MARY: My mom left.
J. D.: Do you feel sad that your mom left?
MARY: Yes.
J. D.: Do you talk to her on the phone?
MARY: She doesn't call anymore.
J. D.: Do you miss her?
MARY: Yes, a lot.
J. D.: What makes you miss her?
MARY: That she doesn't call anymore.
J. D.: Do you want your mom to come back?
MARY: Yes.
J. D.: Are you happy that your dad came back?
MARY: Yes.
J. D.: What do you want to do when you grow up?
MARY: I want my mom to come back.
J. D.: Do you want your mom to live with your dad again?
MARY: Yes.
J. D.: Do you think she is going to come back?
MARY: No.
J. D.: Do you love your mom?
MARY: Yes.
J. D.: And your dad, do you love him?
MARY: Yes.
J. D.: Who do you love more, your mom or your dad?
MARY: My dad.
J. D.: Why?
MARY: My mom said she was going to take me [to the United States] and she never did.

I also spoke with ten-year-old Michael:

J. D.: When your dad left, how old were you?
MICHAEL: I was six.

J. D.: What year were you in school?

MICHAEL: I was in my last year of kindergarten.

J. D.: And when you mom left?

MICHAEL: I was in second grade.

J. D.: Some other children have told me that when their parents left, they felt kind of sad and had a hard time keeping up in school. Did that happen to you?

MICHAEL: When my dad left.

J. D.: How was that?

MICHAEL: I felt really sad because before he used to take us out a lot and then he didn't.

J. D.: And your mom?

MICHAEL: She didn't tell us. I didn't know when she left. It was just like that, without telling me.

J. D.: And your dad told you he was going to leave?

MICHAEL: Yes, he told me he was going to go.

J. D.: Do you remember when he left?

MICHAEL: No, I don't remember.

J. D.: I don't mean the date, but do you remember what happened on that day?

MICHAEL: Yes.

J. D.: Tell me about it.

MICHAEL: I remember that my dad was with his brother and that they left together. They got into the bus; in the bus they left.

J. D.: And your mom?

MICHAEL: She didn't tell us she was leaving.

J. D.: Tell me about it.

MICHAEL: She left in the morning. I was in school, and she wasn't there when I got back home.

J. D.: Did you feel bad? Did you ask where she was?

MICHAEL: No, I didn't ask anything. . . . It was just like that.

J. D.: Do you talk to your mom now?

MICHAEL: No, she doesn't really call anymore.

J. D.: Do you wish she would call more?

MICHAEL: Yes.

J. D.: Do you miss her?

MICHAEL: A little.

J. D.: Did you miss her more when your dad wasn't here?

MICHAEL: The same.

J. D.: Do you love your mom?

MICHAEL: A little.

J. D.: Do you feel like she loves you?

MICHAEL: That I don't know.

J. D.: Do you love your dad?

MICHAEL: Yes.

J. D.: Do you feel that he loves you?

MICHAEL: Yes.

ROUTINES

January 2006. Nearly nine months later, when I visited Armando's family once again in Mexico, the house was just as I remembered it. More surprising was that the children all looked the same; none of the five children appeared to have grown much since my last visit. Of Armando's three children, Mary looked the most different. Her hair was long again (after her father arrived, he had cut it off, saying it was too long to take care of), and her face looked thinner. She looked more like her older brother, Michael, than she had before. As for little Lupe, she had grown considerably in personality, if not in size. Michael remained thin, lanky, quiet, and distant.

On this visit I spoke mostly with Doña Mica, who was more comfortable with me than on any of my previous visits. She told me about her nephews, now in her care for more than a year, and that their mother had come for them, but she refused to let them go without her brother's consent. At the moment, the DIF (the Mexican version of Child Protective Services) was involved in the case. Unlike Armando's children, who called Doña Mica *mamá*, the boys continued to call her *tía* [aunt]. The four- and six-year-old boys did not attend school, although Lupe and Mary at the same age were both in school that year.

Doña Mica told me, "Mary is jealous of her father. She doesn't want him to find another wife. But I tell her that someday she is going to get married, and then there will be no one to take care of her father. Who will make his food? I say. I tell her that he has to do it because her mother left him over there [United States]."

I asked about what news they had of Armando's ex-wife. Doña Mica said she called around the time I had last visited the family and then again over the holidays. For Christmas, she sent her own mother over to visit and to bring a doll and two hundred pesos (twenty dollars). One day, Doña Mica told me, she could not find Mary and Lupe. Although it turned out they were visiting a neighbor, Doña Mica grew terribly worried after looking up and down the streets and not finding them anywhere. The first thought that came to her mind was that their other grandmother had come and stolen them away.

Doña Mica also reported that when their mother called, Michael did not want to talk to her. His mother complained over the phone: "Why don't you want to talk? . . . You don't love me anymore?" Michael answered curtly: "That is just the way I am." Doña Mica confirmed that Michael was resentful of his mother for leaving them.

"His mother asked Michael, 'What do you want me to send you?' And he answered, 'Whatever.' And when she asked, 'What is wrong, son?' he answered, 'Nothing. This is who I am.' Lupe told her that she wants some sneakers. Michael was laughing at her for this, because she asked for something that her father had recently bought her. . . . See, there they are." Doña Mica pointed to a pair of shoes in the bedroom.

As for little Lupe, Doña Mica observed: "She says, 'She is not my mother.' She says that I am her mother. She says that she is no longer López Pérez, because [Pérez] is her mother's last name. She says that she is López Márquez, because I am a Márquez. She says that her sister, Mary, can be a López Pérez if she [Mary] wants, but not her. She is going to be a López Márquez."[9]

Later that afternoon Mary and Lupe braided my hair while we watched TV. Out of the blue, Mary blurted out, "I don't have a mother."

J. D.: What do you mean that you don't have a mother?

MARY: Because my mama Cici left my dad and she went with another [man].

J. D.: So that is why she isn't your mother anymore?

MARY: No, not anymore.

J. D.: And your grandmother?

MARY: Lupe calls her mama . . . [notable pause] . . . and me too.

For Mary, and perhaps also for her siblings to a lesser degree, feelings about her mother had shifted significantly over the past year. Uncomfortable with the idea of their father remarrying, but increasingly angry with their mother, Armando's girls looked now to their grandmother as the most important maternal figure in their lives.

CHANGES AND CONTINUITIES

Fall 2006. Armando's ex-wife returned to Mexico and took Armando to court for alimony. While Armando got his own lawyer to dispute her claims, a third of his weekly paycheck went to his ex-wife in alimony while he continued to financially support his three children. Then Armando remarried; he and his new wife had an infant boy. Unable to make ends meet with these new responsibilities, Armando quit his job and began to work informally so as to avoid the alimony payments. He and his new wife and infant moved into his old home, less than a block away. Michael, Mary, and Lupe remained in the care of Doña Mica.

June 2007. One day, Armando's ex-wife went to the children's school and took Mary away to live with her. Armando went to look for his daughter, who told him she now wanted to live with her mother. Armando conceded. A few months later, legal problems with his ex-wife stopped. Armando continued to work informally for a time and eventually got a job at a hotel again. He lived with his wife and new baby in one home, while Lupe and Michael stayed with Doña Mica. Armando frequented his mother's home in the evenings.

Spring 2008. After six months of living with her mother, Mary called Armando and said she wanted to go home. Armando went to the neighborhood where his ex-wife lived and brought Mary back to live with his mother. Armando continued to divide his time between his two families. He lamented: "Sometimes I just feel split in two, like I cannot do it anymore." Worried about his income, he began to think about returning to the north.

This family's experiences suggest that contrary to what might be expected given the conventional ways parents "do gender" during periods of separation, marital conflicts during migration create opportunities for fathers like Armando to grow closer to their children and expand their role in the family beyond that of economic provider. However, these changes are generally short-lived. After a period of turmoil has passed, families may return to gendered routines in which women, whether a grandmother or a new spouse, are the primary caretakers of children. The economic pressures fathers feel continue to be paramount.

What explains the role reversal that occurs after migration and divorce? Nonresidential fathers are typically less engaged in their children's lives than are nonresidential mothers and men who live with their children. Some suggest this emotional distance is related to fathers' tendency to view caregiving as a role related to marriage and coresidence.[10] Research in the United States also suggests that martial conflict reduces nonresidential fathers' contact with their children.[11] Why is it, then, that in the transnational context divorced fathers exert so much effort to reconnect with their children from a distance? And why, given that mothers are generally the primary caregivers in divorced families, do transnational mothers appear to retreat from the lives of their children living back in Mexico after a divorce?[12]

It is possible that mothers feel embarrassed about having left their husbands or that they simply want to wash their hands of their children to enjoy newfound freedoms abroad, but neither seems likely. First, there is a strong preference among Mexican families, as in the United States, for mothers to retain custody of children after marriages break up.[13] Of the six migrant mothers I interviewed who divorced in Mexico before coming to the United States, the three who did not have custody of their children had bitter fights with their ex-husbands over the children (which prompted their migration). In San Ángel, the only family I met in which a father had custody of the children was one in which the marriage broke up in the United States. Second, mothers who divorced in the United States expressed interest in their children and did not abandon them completely. In Armando's case, his ex-wife did eventually go back for Mary, the only child whose alliance she still commanded. Even migrant mothers who break social norms show interest in their children.

Mothers' transgressions, I believe, make fathers like Armando feel more entitled to develop greater emotional connections with their children as long as they are able to provide for them financially. This is because, unlike mothers, these fathers have not symbolically failed in their moral responsibilities as parents. These fathers are able to "do gender" in different ways.

Parents' relationships with their children are not rigid. Gendered expectations of parenthood are under negotiation during the changes that accompany migration. The conditions under which fathers embrace greater involvement in the care of their children, however, and the temporary duration of such shifts, shows that family members often negotiate relationships without fundamentally altering gendered expectations of parenthood. Men's caregiving in the transnational context, and perhaps any context, is contingent on the behavior of women.[14] Men substitute for mothers they perceive to be failures. When circumstances change and mothers—or other women—again become available to children, fathers cede to women as family caregivers once more.

Laundry hangs outside the apartment of two teenage boys living alone while their divorced mother works in the United States to support them. The teenagers had decorated the apartment inside and out with their graffiti tags. Photograph by Joanna Dreby

FIVE Children and Power during Separation

Nico was unmistakable in San Ángel for his bleached, spiked hair and for being the youngest hanging around a crowd of older boys. I guessed he was about eleven but learned when I visited his fifth-grade class that he was actually thirteen. On that day, Nico blurted out that his parents lived in the United States, seemingly pleased that I was interested in the experiences of children like himself.

During the week of the town *feria,* Nico was out every night at the rides until late. On the eve of the week's culminating events, Nico was at the rodeo. He and a friend were the youngest groupies hanging around the *jinetes* (cowboys who ride the bulls). I recognized his companion as a local seventh grader. Nico was much quieter than his friend, striking me as a true tagalong. At 1 A.M., I noticed them lying on the unattended trampolines giggling when they called out catcalls to me in English.

Then I saw Nico and his friend at the town dance. In the middle of the crowd they danced wildly to the music, laughing and bumping into each other and an inebriated young man. Shortly thereafter, the boys' older chaperones abandoned them for the company of some ladies. By 3 A.M., Nico was alone, lying on the grass, yawning.

The next afternoon, Nico accompanied a frail old woman to a store downtown. The woman, I learned, was his eighty-three-year-old grandmother, Doña Elizabeth. Later, as we sat in her disarrayed two-room house, Doña Elizabeth told me she recently had had a stroke and had trouble hearing.

> I am the only one to take care of him. He doesn't get along with Flor [a neighbor who helps out]. His oldest brother [an adult] lives down there too, but he doesn't get on with him. . . . You know, he doesn't really love his parents. I noticed this when they first came back to visit. He was like eight years old. When they came, he didn't want to have anything to do with them. Since then, he doesn't want to talk to them on the phone. . . . His parents call, but they talk to me. He says he doesn't want to talk to them. He never does. I will call to him and tell him to come to the phone, but he doesn't show up.

When I asked for permission to interview Nico, Doña Elizabeth consented but explained: "He isn't here now. You can find him downtown. He usually goes to watch the volleyball games in the evening and comes back late. During the day he is always down at the river somewhere." Doña Elizabeth, who had been sitting on the floor despite scattered chicken droppings, grew drowsy as we conversed. Our interview ended when she eventually fell asleep.

Before interviewing Nico, I spoke with a number of members of the family who all confirmed that Doña Elizabeth had absolutely no authority over Nico. Nico had been held back three times in school. His teachers described the fifth-grader as a lost cause.

Given his markedly difficult home life, I was not surprised that Nico was resentful of his parents for having left him when they migrated, especially since his other siblings had all joined their parents in Las Vegas. When I asked him what he spoke to them about on the phone, his answer was curt: "I tell them to send money." This response differed sharply from that of other children, who resisted viewing their relationship with migrant parents as purely an economic one. When I asked Nico for details about his parents, he said, "I don't remember. They left me when I was little," even though his grandmother told me his father was back in February and his mother had come to visit the year before.

Despite being more unruly and outwardly resentful of his parents than others, in many ways Nico's answers to my questions were much like those of other children. Nico told me he did not know why his parents did not come back to Mexico, that he did not want to join them in the United States, and that he wanted them to return to Mexico. Although unsure whether his mother and father love him or whether he loves them, Nico said he felt more affection for his father. Given his general air of ambivalence during the interview, I was surprised at Nico's decisive answer that he would never leave his children to go work in the United States in the future. I asked, "Do you think it is worse for the mom or the dad to go to the United States?" Nico said, "The mom." "Why?" I asked. He answered, "Because . . . the mom [is different] from the dad. . . . The dad doesn't do what a mom should do with her child." Like other children, Nico criticized his mother more harshly for her absence than he did his father.

Nico's case was extreme, as he was one of the few children I interviewed who seemed to lack proper care. Yet it illustrates how central children's expectations of parents are to shaping their experiences while parents are away. Above all else, children expect parents to be better able to provide for them by working in the United States. This is what the sociologist Robert C. Smith calls the "immigrant bargain."[1] Although children's assessments of parents' failures or successes as migrants are complicated by gender, children like Nico are disappointed when parents do not live up to this fairly straightforward expectation that children's lives will be better while parents are away. Some, like Nico, lash out their disappointment by acting uncontrollably, especially when it takes longer than parents expect to fulfill their promises. As the journalist Sonia Nazario writes, such disappointment may lead some desperate children to seek out their parents on harrowing journeys of their own to the United States.[2] The emotional costs of migrant parents' failures to live up to their end of the "immigrant bargain" may be greatest for their nonmigrant children.[3]

EXPECTATIONS OF CHILDREN

The "immigrant bargain," however, is not one-sided. Nico's parents surely did not anticipate him being so wild while they were away. On the surface, expectations of children seem simple. When asked about his expectations of his children in Mexico, a migrant father explained: "Expectations? Well, that sounds a little weird to me. *De allá pa' acá* [from there to here], yes. I feel like there are quite a lot of expectations of those of us working here. But what do I expect of them? What can I say? That they take care of themselves. That they are good. That they study. That is it." There appears to be an imbalance in expectations, with the burden on migrant parents, who must make something of themselves in the United States to prove that the sacrifice of leaving children in Mexico is worthwhile. At least, this is migrant parents' view.

Yet from the perspective of children of migrants in Mexico, the seemingly minor hopes that children study, take care of themselves, and behave are considerable. Underlying these hopes are parents' expectations that children will understand their reasons for leaving, continue to love and respect parents who are not a part of their lives, and—as they get older—show parents' sacrifices to be worthwhile by making something of themselves. All of this must be accomplished without the daily support of parents and often while living in relatives' homes. Aspirations for academic achievement are particularly powerful: children's education is a key feature of "intergenerational contracts" between migrant parents and children.[4] Many parents told me that paying for children's schooling justified their absences. Some even planned to retire to Mexico once their children were professionals and could support them through old age.[5] When intergenerational mobility lies at the heart of migrant parents' sacrifices, the expectations of nonmigrant children in Mexican transnational families are exceedingly high.

Drawing on the theoretical stance most fully developed by the sociologists William Corsaro and Barrie Thorne, I discuss in this chapter how children fare in meeting these expectations during periods of separation by considering children's worlds as partially created by and understood by children themselves.[6] As it is somewhat difficult to glean information about young children's lives from their verbal accounts, my analysis draws on children's accounts as well as those of the adults with whom they interact, especially their parents, caregivers, and other family members, but also in some cases their teachers and me. Taking into account how children understand parental migration shows that because of children's negative experiences while parents are away, most have difficulties meeting parents' expectations.[7] Like Nico, the children of migrants often act out; authority conflicts are common, and in the most severe cases caregivers who feel they cannot control children may even neglect them. Like Nico, many children perform poorly in school despite parents' commitments to fund children's education with their remittances.[8] Children experience great resentment and feelings of loss arising from parents' absences.[9] While parents struggle to meet their goals in the United States, children struggle to live up to their end of the "immigrant bargain."

Children suffer without their parents, but they are far from powerless in their families. Children's negative experiences give them leverage in negotiating their relationships with the adults in their lives. When parents migrate without their children, the needs of children loom large, symbolically and practically.[10] Children who exhibit disappointment at parental absences increase parents' feelings of insecurity about being away. When children have difficulties in meeting parents' goals of upward mobility through academic achievement, parents may allocate more of the family resources to this end. Children who remain in Mexico have little say in their parents' decisions to migrate, yet they negotiate emotional responses to family separation and its economic ramifications. They have an important role in shaping families' migration patterns.

Unlike parents, whose experiences differ by their gender, children's experiences vary most by their age. Aside from some individual variation, young children, teenagers, and young adults respond to parental absence differently. It is not until children become young adults that their own gender begins to shape their experiences. Because children's life stages affect their reactions, family relationships are dynamic and fluctuate according to children's changing needs.

YOUNG CHILDREN

Research suggests that the younger children are at the age of separation from parents, the more deeply they are affected.[11] I find, however, that young children do not describe feeling as distressed by parents' migration as teenagers do.[12] Yet young children have ways of showing that parental absences matter, mostly via different kinds of emotional withholding.

Naming Caregivers and Parents

Five-year-old Marco was not an expert on U.S. migration. When his grandmother mentioned that he was afraid of *gringos,* I called Marco over and asked, "What are *gringos*?" "Police," he answered and ran back to play. Marco also did not know that *el norte* was *Los Estados Unidos* [the United States]. But the young boy demonstrated a clear understanding of his family structure. When I asked whom he lived with, he responded: "mama Carmela" (his grandmother), his "papa Paulo" (his grandfather), and his "tío José" (an uncle). He also said that his mother and father live in *el norte,* and added that he missed them and wanted them to come home.

Doña Carmela, Marco's grandmother, told me that the boy is quite attached to her, since she raised him from infancy. When his parents came to visit two years earlier, he refused to go live with them at their house. "Does he cry for his parents?" I asked.

> No, he doesn't cry for them. Sometimes he cries because he says that I am not his mother. His uncle is always telling him that I am not his mother, that I am his grandmother, and he cries. . . . Sometimes he comes home upset and says he is mad because they [his uncles] said

> that I am not his mother. He says I have this many mothers [shows two fingers] and this many fathers [shows two fingers] and this many grandparents [shows three fingers] because he says he has his mother there and me, his father there and his father here. And his grandparents are his fathers' parents and my mother who is still alive.

Among young children, the naming of caregivers—mostly grandmothers—in Mexico as *mamá* or *mami* is common. Yet all of the children I interviewed—even at the young age of five—understood that they have two mothers and, at times, two fathers, even when they call their grandmother mom. None got mixed up in telling me that their "mother" or "father" lived in the United States. They recounted conversations with, and showed me pictures of, their migrant parents, and they often pointed out the gifts migrant parents had sent. Like Marco, most claimed to have multiple mothers and, at times, multiple fathers.

For some children, the naming of caregivers as mothers is due to parents' instruction. Migrant mothers described the sharing of the title of mother as the price of leaving their children. They conceded that children should call caregivers mom, as they are the ones doing the daily care work. At the same time, mothers may feel offended when children do not also recognize them as mothers. One grandmother explained that her daughter told the children to call her *mamá* instead of *abuelita* [grandmother]. But when her daughter called home and spoke to her son, she would say, "Who am I?" and the little boy would answer, "My sister Rosa," after which she would correct him quickly. "No, no, no, I am your *mother.*"

Calling grandmothers *mamá* may simply be a way of expressing the emotional connection children share with caregivers in Mexico, but when children subsequently refuse to call migrant parents *mamá* or *papá*, they signal their lack of attachment to them. Children seem conscious that their use of names can make their mothers feel bad about being away. A migrant mother, Sandra, told me: "When I call, I ask to speak with my daughter, and although they are not talking to me, I overhear a conversation that goes something like this: They say, 'Come, Raquel, your mom is calling.' And she answers, 'Who? Who wants to talk to me?' 'Your mom.' 'Oh, Saaaaaandra,' she says before coming to talk to me on the phone."

According to one grandmother, her granddaughter "has always called her mother by her first name. I can tell that she doesn't really love her. . . . My daughter gets upset and cries to me over the phone. She says that she doesn't love her." Indeed, with migrant mothers I often sensed underlying anxiety around naming. Migrant Nydia, for example, said that four-year-old Kevin calls her mother mom but was quick to explain, "He doesn't deny [that I am] his mother. He knows that I have my place [in his life]." Although biological mothers are willing to share the name of mother with children's primary caregiver, when children pointedly avoid acknowledging their biological parents, migrant mothers feel offended. Naming demarcates the emotional costs of mothers' absences.

Interestingly, naming does not seem to affect migrant fathers in the same way it affects mothers. Although children often said they have two fathers, no migrant fathers reported taking offense at their children's naming practices. The use of names as a sign of affection challenges migrant mothers' investment in a maternal identity as family caregivers.

Acting Indifferent

Young children also express their distress about separation from parents by pretending to be indifferent toward them. Children speak frequently to their migrant parents on the phone, but they often communicate an "out-of-sight out-of-mind mentality" to them. Nydia said, "The only thing that makes me feel badly about my son is when he doesn't want to talk to me." A woman who looked after her nine-year-old nephew after his mother migrated said the boy often refused to talk to his mother on the phone. "I didn't want my sister to think that I was telling him not to talk to her. So sometimes I would trick him to get him to talk to her on the phone. . . . My sister would cry when he didn't want to talk to her."

Children act most indifferent when parents come home to visit.[13] Even when children anxiously await parents' return, once they arrive, children's behavior indicates to parents that migration is not without a price. One mother I met in San Ángel said she was only away from her three children for a year, but when she came back, her five-year-old twins hid from her. "They said, 'since you left, we don't know you anymore.'" Another said that her son spread the rumor that he wasn't going to accept her and her husband when they returned to San Ángel from the United States. "He would tell his uncles that he wasn't going to love us when we came home." Whereas naming is most distressing for mothers, fathers also feel the sting of children's indifference. Two years after Daniel's children went to live with his mother-in-law in Mexico, he explained: "They don't remember me. You don't know what that is. It is hard. They get [me] confused with a brother of mine; they think he is their dad."

It is, of course, understandable that children feel uncomfortable when their parents come home. Children who have grown up without their parents may want their parents to return but may not know how to feel or deal with conflicting emotions once reunited. A mother and grandmother in San Ángel explained how one eleven-year-old girl reacted to her mother's return.

MOTHER: Well she knew [I was coming], and she was really anxious. She would ask how many days was it until we would arrive.

GRANDMOTHER: Then the car came, and it was outside. So I said to her, "Go, go see your mother." And she said, "No, I don't want to."

MOTHER: But then she came to me, but it was forced, like all of a sudden she was embarrassed and didn't want to come.

Later, the mother explained: "She called me mom ever since I arrived, but she wouldn't get close to me. It is only now [two months later] that she is starting to warm up."

Family members usually described children's feelings of discomfort as temporary. Some researchers have suggested that for young children, distress upon a reunion with parents is typically short-lived.[14] But at age thirty, Paulo still recalled the uneasiness he felt when his father, Enrique, returned to visit. "When he returned after a lot of time, well, I felt really uncomfortable, as if he was a stranger, for the very reason that we didn't really have a relationship, because I was little when he left." Paulo's father left when he was fourteen, and after three years, when

Paulo was seventeen, his father started to visit the family in Mexico annually. Paulo said that although he now gets along with his father, he is still uncomfortable around him. When Paulo visited with his parents, I watched him be outwardly affectionate with his mother yet shy away from his father's company. Children's indifference may have long-term consequences for parent-child relationships.[15]

All of the children I interviewed, even children whose parents left them while they were very young, indicated that their parents were important to them. They commented that they missed their parents, loved them, or wanted them to come home. When young children display indifference to parents, either over the phone or when parents visit, it does not mean that parents are unimportant. Rather by pretending to be indifferent, they express resentment at their powerlessness to affect the migration decisions of their parents, whom they care about deeply.

Parental Authority Disregarded

Young children almost always defer to the authority of their caregivers in Mexico but tend to reject this authority when they become teenagers. Even when parents return, either for temporary visits or more permanently, young children continue to defer to their caregiver's authority during an adjustment period. One grandmother said that when her daughter first came home, her grandchildren were very happy, but it took them a while to adjust to their mother's presence. "At first it was still grandma this and grandma that. Not until now are they leaving me a little and going to their mother." When I asked an eleven-year-old whose parents just returned from the United States, "Who do you ask permission to do things with?" she responded, "I ask my parents for permission only because that is what my grandmother told me I should do."

When parents or single mothers are away, children turn to their grandparents. When fathers are away, children defer to their mother, even when their father visits. As fathers tend to consider themselves the authority figures in Mexican families, children's deference to their mother is often hurtful.[16] Gabriela said that when her husband, Angelo, visits, "the kids always come to me for permission and with their problems. My husband has even commented to them, 'Am I not worth anything here?' Once he told them, 'I am going to leave because you don't respect me.'"

Gabriela's ten-year-old son, Gilberto, demonstrated the way children disregard migrant parents' authority. One day I asked Gilberto for an interview about having his father home for a visit. He agreed. I explained that first we had to ask his parents for permission. We walked down the street together, and seeing that his parents were not at home, Gilberto went across the street to his grandmother's place to look for them. I lagged behind outside but was close enough to see Gilberto ask his father, sitting just inside the door, where his mother was. Learning that she was at a meeting, Gilberto came back out and said his mother was not around, so we would have to do it later. That evening, Angelo laughed about the incident and explained that this was a common occurrence with all of his four children, especially his eight-year-old son. "He is always playing marbles with his friends on the street. He comes into the house and walks by me looking for his mother to ask if he can go play. I stop him and say, 'What's this, *¿y yo qué?*' What about me?"

Whether intentional or subconscious, overlooking migrant parents signals the importance of the primary caregiver in children's lives. Migrant parents may laugh it off but later shake their heads and wonder, as Angelo did, what about me? In effect, ignoring parents' authority underscores the emotional costs of parental absences.

Refusing to Migrate

Many young children resist parents' efforts to reunite the family in the United States, and their parents do not send for children against their will. It is somewhat surprising that more parents do not exert parental authority and send for children regardless of the children's preference, but their unwillingness to do so is consistent with descriptions of minimal-intervention parenting strategies in Mixtec communities of Oaxaca.[17] Such a regional tendency, however, does not necessarily mean that children in the Mixteca wield greater influence in their families than do children in other parts of Mexico. After all, children felt they had little say over their parents' initial decision to migrate. Instead, I believe parents' reluctance shows that their preoccupation with their children's reactions to separation affords children greater power in shaping family migration decisions than they might have had while living with their parents.

Facing children's resistance to migration, parents typically make elaborate plans to return to Mexico to try to win over their children. One mother, for example, wanted to send for her ten-year-old daughter, which would have cost approximately three thousand dollars. Her daughter said no. "I didn't insist, because she has to make the decision herself." Instead, the mother returned to San Ángel for a three-month visit to convince her daughter to migrate. The visit was much costlier than paying for her daughter's migration, as the mother had no income during this period, had to finance her return to the United States, and—if all went as planned—would pay for the undocumented crossing for both herself and her daughter. Similarly, Zelia went back to San Ángel for her son, Juan Luis. On the last day of her three-week visit, the six-year-old decided that he preferred to stay in Mexico. Zelia returned to the United States without him, having spent nearly three thousand dollars during the short visit.

When young children's emotional withholding makes parents feel bad for being away, parents may make significant efforts to be reunited with their children. This involves substantial costs, given their status as low-wage workers in the United States. In this way, young children's reactions to parents' absences may have significant economic repercussions.

TEENAGERS

During adolescence, the consequences of migration are most pronounced, even when children stay home.[18] While younger children's responses to their parents' absences subtly remind migrants about what they are missing, as children grow older, they become more outwardly resentful. Even though many young children I interviewed did not want to join their parents in the United States, the surveys I conducted in the Mixteca show that children ages nine through thirteen more often report wanting to migrate than do children without migrant parents.[19] This pattern reverses for children ages fourteen through seventeen, with 77 percent of children with migrant parents wanting to go to the United States, compared to 82 percent of those without migrant parents.[20] At this stage, children of migrants appear to resist U.S. migration more outwardly. This may be due to increasing distress about parental absences. One fifteen-year-old boy, who had lived with his grandparents his entire life, said his parents' migration was harder to deal with than when he was younger, "Because before I didn't feel anything, and now I understand a lot of things." A grandmother who had raised a total of ten grandchildren said the change occurs at about age ten. "That is when they start to figure things out. I always tried to tell my grandchildren the good things about their parents, and not talk badly about them. But it doesn't matter, because at this age they start questioning things."

It is commonly believed that parent-child conflict increases dramatically during adolescence.[21] Yet, although in certain areas, such as the use of finances, conflicts may increase, in other areas, such as chores or appearance, conflicts may actually decrease.[22] Three areas of conflict among teenagers are different from those I observed among younger children: maneuvering around ambiguous lines of authority, acting out, and experiencing difficulties at school. Such conflicts may not differ greatly from those of children living with their parents, but children of migrants described these tensions as being uniquely shaped by their parents' migrations.

Ambiguous Line of Authority

Most teenagers enjoy relatively high levels of freedom in their daily activities while living with their caregivers in Mexico. A common pattern is for caregivers to be more lenient with young children than parents would be. One grandmother explained: "I have them really spoiled. Anything they ask for, if I have the money, they get it." Once children become teenagers, however, caregivers find it difficult to retain authority over them. A family friend of Nicandra's two teenage children said,

"When their grandmother was here, the boys would trick her. Once she was asleep they would sneak out. They basically have been doing their own thing for years." According to a teacher, one ninth-grade girl "is very bad to her grandmother at home. She yells at her, she disobeys her. Once she tried to assault her, and the grandmother cannot control her. . . . I have seen that girl in the street at ten or eleven at night with her boyfriend." Caregivers concurred. One complained that her nine-year-old nephew "started going out a lot and would get into trouble. He wouldn't listen to me." A grandfather explained that raising his grandchildren was not like raising his own children. "With my grandchildren, it is different. They do what they want." His wife agreed. "I talk to them, and they just don't listen to me."

When teenagers perceive caregivers to be too strict, they turn to their migrant parents, who are thought to be more lenient. "Young people, they are so clever," explained a teacher in describing the discipline problems among children of migrants. "They know what they want and they know how to get it." For example, Tina and Brian's aunt said that authority conflicts occurred in their family because the teen's grandmother, Doña Silvia, does not let them go out. When Tina protested to her father over the phone, he would tell her not to worry, that he would talk to her grandmother. According to the aunt, "Their father is far away and really doesn't know what is going on here. So he can say, be nice to the kids, let them go out, just so they all get along. But he is not here dealing with them. And if the kids get in trouble, like Brian getting some girl pregnant, he will surely blame my mother for not watching over him enough." Along the same lines, a grandmother complained: "Their mother and father have the last word, not us. These girls ask for permission from them over there and then they leave." In effect, unclear lines of authority between parents and caregivers give teenagers greater freedom.

Moreover, migrant parents often attempt to build rapport with teenagers from afar via friendship rather than parental authority. A migrant mother said, "My mother is the strict voice, and I try to be a little bit more compassionate and understanding." Tony, thirteen when first left alone, told me his mother, Nicandra, "has always spoken to us like a friend." A migrant father said that during one recent phone call his son told him that he was hanging out with a group of friends who marked their eyebrows with razor cuts (implying gang membership). "I told my son that I never hung out with a group of friends like that because it is better to be your own person, rather than follow others. But if he wants to be with them . . . I am not going to tell him no." He went on to explain: "I try to be my son's friend."

If teenagers exercise more autonomy because of the ambiguity of authority and migrant parents' eagerness to please from a distance, they are not particularly happy about it. Rather, they described experiences of increased autonomy as something undesirable that would not have been possible if parents were present. Paula's daughter Cindy, who had been in trouble for going out late with her boyfriend, said, "For me it is very exceptional—it is something really painful for me that my mother isn't here with me." Cindy described her mother's discipline in a positive light, as something she missed. "Before, she would scold us and hit us, and now there is no one around to scold or hit us when we come home from school. . . . Now I am alone."

Cindy is not alone in her experience. When I asked Tony what he missed about his mother, he answered, "Everything. The food . . . I even miss that she scolds me." At age thirteen, Tina admitted that over the past year she had started hanging out with the wrong crowd at school. "It's just that, you know, I started hanging out with some friends who have lots of problems, like me." She started cutting class, her mid-year grades plummeted, and she was nearly suspended. Months earlier, Tina was quick to answer my question about what made her miss her migrant parents: "I miss my mother's affection, and as for my father, I miss that he corrects me."

Acting Out

Nico, the boy described in the opening vignette, is an extreme example of the behavioral difficulties that crop up among children of migrant parents. Yet many children I met who lived with loving substitute caregivers and had extensive contact with their parents acted out in similar ways.[23] A teenager complained that her twelve-year-old brother had become a troublemaker since their mother left just a year earlier and had recently been called to the office for breaking a window at school. Another teenager raised by her grandmother said her older brother had already joined their parents in the United States after misbehaving. She explained: "He left because he was very bad. He would go out a lot, and he got in trouble at school." Doña Beatriz, a mother of twelve, seven of whom lived with her while her husband went to work in the United States for two years, lamented: "Everything was destroyed [after he left]. Everyone was sad and didn't eat well anymore. Some of them were insolent and rude to me. I think that they lacked a paternal figure." Another woman said that when she went to the United States for three years, she left two sons in San Ángel. The younger boy studied and even finished high school, but her fourteen-year-old son dropped out of middle school. "He would go and drink, and they would tell me that they found him drunk hanging out on the hill all the time. . . . Then he went to live with his girlfriend's family. He got her pregnant." Complaints about teenage girls were as common as those about teenage boys.[24]

Nicandra's sixteen-year-old son, Miguel, articulated the feelings of abandonment that help explain why children misbehave while parents work abroad. Although Nicandra did not describe Miguel as having problems when she migrated, as did his older brother, Tony, twice Miguel was kept back a grade, and he dropped out at age fourteen. Miguel attributed most of his personal failures to his mother's migration. For example, he told me he started to smoke at the age of twelve, when his mother left, although he has more recently stopped. "I felt desperate because I lived alone with my grandmother and my brother. And I started the habit because, many times, you know, it chills you out, it calms your nerves, and all that." Miguel joined a neighborhood gang and was involved in simple assaults, though he was never caught. "To me it didn't matter. Not having my mother, I felt strange. I felt like what did it matter. If I saw a person staring at me, it was like, what do you want? I would look for a fight." Miguel said he was different when his mother returned to visit. "I dropped all of this when she came back. She came back and I stopped. Having her, I don't feel like smoking or doing things that I am not supposed to do."

Another common misbehavior is older siblings abusing younger siblings. According to one social worker I interviewed, the parents' migration "always affects the older children more . . . because the older ones have a duty, even though they are with their grandparents or their uncles. They have this responsibility to take care of and protect their younger siblings." The grandparents of one seventeen-year-old who had assumed much of the housework after her parents migrated said she often hit her younger siblings inappropriately. Eleven-year-old Eric, eight-year-old Edwin, and seven-year-old Osvaldo had a difficult time after their mother migrated. Their cousin described an incident between the three siblings:

> You know, the oldest one feels very responsible for the other two. It is as if he takes on the role of the father. He hits his brothers. . . . The other day—oh, how it made me want to cry. . . . I heard some shouts from their room, and I went to see what they were doing. The little one [Osvaldo] was on the floor, doubled over and holding his stomach. The middle one [Edwin] was crying that his older brother [Eric] was beating up the little one. But Osvaldo was crying because he said his older brother said, "I've had enough of you." The older one [Eric] came and said that "it is just that I've had enough of everything, me and me all of the time. I love my brother a lot, but I get tired."

Children of migrant parents may "act out" for several reasons. In most cases, while parents are away, children feel that no one cares about what they are doing. Although most have concerned caregivers and parents, during adolescence children of migrants want to feel accountable to their parents. Physical separation prevents this. Also, because of parents' absences, teenagers feel increased responsibility—for themselves and their younger siblings. Some teenagers take out the pressure of this increased responsibility by acting aggressively.

School Performance

Aside from trouble such as gang activity, drinking, and drug abuse, a more widespread problem for teenagers is school performance. Of the sixty children I interviewed, 41 percent over the age of fourteen dropped out of school in the middle of their studies, and 27 percent of those over age seven had been held back a grade at least once, with some having been held back multiple times. Although local dropout rates are not available for comparison, other research shows Mexican children with migrant parents to have a greater propensity to drop out of school than children of nonmigrants.[25] A regional social worker explained: "There are students with good grades that I am about to put on the honor role . . . but of those children, there are not any who are alone because their parents are in the United States. Those children do not figure in." More profoundly, this pattern of poor school performance belies the expectations of most parents. As Angelo told me, "My idea is not to live here [in the United States]. It has always been to have a better life there [in Mexico]. It doesn't matter to me that I sacrifice the present—I want my children to have a career in Mexico." Given parents' expectations and their investments in children's schooling in Mexico, why do teenagers have such trouble in school?

Four reasons for difficulties in school emerge. First, many children experience low levels of depression after their parents' departures.[26] For example, Brian, in the tenth grade, told me that when his mother left while he was in seventh grade, he did not feel like studying much because he missed her. "It lasted about three, no, I think two months." Another fifteen-year-old girl explained that the day her father left she had trouble focusing at school. She recalled not being able to do a standardized test. "I had nothing in my head."

Although a few children bounce back from these episodes, for many a drop in school performance after a parent's departure has long-term ramifications. Doña Beatriz's seventeen-year-old son, Roberto, who described himself as a very sensitive person, told me he felt sad when he was twelve and his father left for the United States. A year later he dropped out of middle school. "What happened? Did you want to go to live with your father?" I asked. "No," he answered. "I missed him. I didn't want to go to the United States, but I simply didn't feel like studying anymore." After two years, his father came home. Roberto went back to school, graduated, and when I met him was in his first year of high school. A few months later, however, Roberto dropped out of school again. Yolanda and Esteban's sixteen-year-old daughter, Cynthia—described by her younger sister as being the most "sensitive" of her siblings and the one most affected by their father's absence—also dropped out of middle school the year before. "Why did you leave?" I asked her.

CYNTHIA: I didn't like it.

J. D.: Did you like school when you were in primary school?

CYNTHIA: Yeah.

J. D.: And did you do well in primary school? What grades did you get?

CYNTHIA: I did okay. Not great, but not bad. I got like eights.[27]

J. D.: So what happened in middle school?

CYNTHIA: I don't know. I just didn't like it anymore.

J. D.: Was it too hard for you?

CYNTHIA: No, it wasn't hard. I did okay. I just didn't like it anymore.

Whereas among young children sadness after a parent's departure may be temporary, during adolescence, sadness is manifested in children's descriptions of apathy about their schooling.

Second, teenagers' misbehavior often affects their school performance. Regional schoolteachers complained of behavioral problems among children of U.S. migrants. When asked how migration affected their schools, the most frequent response was discipline problems. A dean at a middle school said of children of migrants, "They are rebels; they are the ones with out discipline. They are the ones that have the lowest grades." Another described a typical student with a migrant father as "behaving aggressively, [being] violent, [having] low grades." Only when pressed did school employees cite examples of students who did not fit this profile. Moreover, most of the small schools I visited did not have social workers. Even larger schools that are mandated to have social service support for students lacked trained staff in these positions. One dean explained: "The only support we have for young people is to talk to them and provide orientation." Schools in rural Oaxaca are faced with changing demographics owing to high levels of emigration without the funding, training, and other resources to deal with the emotional aftermath. Teenagers take resentment of migrant parents to school; teachers' only recourse for disruptive behavior is to send them back home.

Third, some students described feeling uncomfortable at school because of peer pressure.[28] In San Ángel, when one mother's husband left, her eldest son had trouble with classmates at school. "The oldest boy said his classmates would tell him that he had no dad and that was why he never went to the school meetings. When he would come home from school, he would be sad, and I would tell him no and say that he did have his father, and we would spend the afternoon and evening looking at the pictures of him." Another mother in San Ángel said that it was hard for her twins their first year of middle school, before they dropped out: "They didn't want to study anymore and I felt bad. They would say that they felt bad because they didn't have their father, and I would say that they shouldn't worry because I was going to support them always and they shouldn't worry about it. . . . After I would talk to them, they would put more effort into it, but only for a bit." Her son confirmed this account: "In school the other kids teased me because my dad was gone."

Fourth, the most common sentiment expressed by children of migrant parents was that they lacked academic support from caregivers in Mexico. This is largely because the majority of caregivers are grandparents with very low levels of education. Many grandparents do not read and write well and are unable to monitor children's work. Of the thirty-seven caregivers I interviewed, sixteen—all grandparents—could not read or write well enough to help their grandchildren with homework. The illiteracy rate for elderly Mexicans in rural areas is high at 44 percent for rural men age sixty-five and older and 63 percent for rural women age sixty-five and older.[29] "The gap between the generations," explained a high school social worker, "in terms of knowledge, morals, and technology, is very thick."

Children of migrant parents rarely feel that caregivers in Mexico are invested in their academic progress. Teachers told me students often signed their grandparents' names on homework that was incomplete or incorrect. One explained: "Students live with their grandparents, but many do not know how to read or write—they are illiterate. With grandparents, it is very difficult that, because of their age, they give the same attention to the children. The children tell them, 'I already did my homework,' even though they did not do it."

Brian said he lacked academic support since his mother left. "You see, at school parents are supposed to sign off on our forms. And, well, my grandmother is often too tired to go. My uncle, the one who is supposed to do it, he is never available. So, what I do is sign the papers myself." Brian was one of the few I met who was doing reasonably well in school, so I asked who he goes to when he does not understand his work. "Nobody," he said. "I understand it on my own. Or I study the books. For example, I now take algebra, and it is hard to understand. So today I had a test and tomorrow I have to study again. So what do I do here? My grandmother doesn't know, and my aunts and uncles don't either. I try to explain to the teacher, but he doesn't want to hear it. And, well, no one else has studied a career that can help me with this. So, I explain it to myself from the book, I write it all out and I understand it little by little."

Brian's strategy might have been the same were his parents with him, since neither went to college, although both finished high school. Yet Brian attributed the loneliness he felt facing his schoolwork to his parents' migration. If his mother were around, Brian believed, he would at least get her attention, if not help with his homework.

Furthermore, schools in Oaxaca expect high levels of involvement from parents or substitute caregivers.[30] Most rural schools I visited organized mandatory parent-teacher meetings, implemented compulsory parental review of homework, and required parents' financial and volunteer support of schools events. Any lack of interest or involvement of caregivers in children's education is quite noticeable to children. One fourteen-year-old girl in San Ángel told me that she missed her mother—whom she claimed not to love—most at school, especially on May 10, Mother's Day, when they have a special program and a formal dinner. I asked, "Do you go with your grandmother?" "No," she responded. "She doesn't like to go to those kinds of things at school." A social worker in a nearby community explained: "When the tenth of May comes, there are some children who get really sad and others who do not even recognize the day. I have talked to them, and they tell me, 'May tenth doesn't mean anything to me. I don't have a mother.'" Because the schools that the children attend are organized around, and expect, parental involvement, parents' absences are especially hard.

Teenagers' Troubles and the Distribution of Family Resources

As is true among younger children, teenagers' reactions to parental absence affect parents' decisions about the distribution of family resources. When teenagers have behavioral problems, parents may make the costly decision to return home, even if temporarily. Nicandra, for example, returned twice in response to her son Tony's problems, at a total cost of more than seven thousand dollars. At the time she earned approximately three hundred dollars per week.

In addition, migrant parents often heavily invest in their children's educational expenses, especially for high school and college, when the costs of schooling increase considerably. Laura and Enrique went into debt to send their oldest son to study architecture at the university; he dropped out to migrate to the United States when he learned of the debts the family had incurred on his behalf. In New Jersey, he worked in landscaping. Paula also sent money to enable both Cindy and Mateo to attend private school and to finance Mateo's first year of college. Both eventually dropped out in the midst of their studies.

Migrant parents do not disregard the intense difficulties that their children experience during adolescence. Over time, they deliberate over how to respond to their children's needs during a tumultuous life stage. In this sense, their responses to their teenagers may be similar to those of parents who live with their children.[31] Yet in the transnational context, parents have limited resources to deal with conflicts with teenagers. A response involves a large economic investment for families with already scarce economic resources. Migrant parents want to respond to their teenagers' problems but often are unsure of how to do so. They may funnel family resources into schooling, which does not necessarily enhance children's educational experiences or opportunities during periods of separation.[32]

YOUNG ADULTS

As teenagers grow into adulthood and begin to make decisions about their future, they describe resentment as fading into ambivalence.[33] One nineteen-year-old whose mother left her when she was an infant explained: "I was like thirteen when I started to feel bad about not living with my mother. I saw all my friends talking about their dad or their mom and what they did together, and since I didn't have them, I felt really bad . . . [but later] I changed—I stopped feeling so bad. It didn't affect me anymore." Older children identify a distinct stage of turmoil, roughly between the ages of twelve and sixteen, although individual variations exist. While many do not entirely forgive their parents, and separation has a lasting impact on their relationships, the negative behavior and resentment that children experience wane with time.

Three factors seem to influence the decrease in hostility toward migrant parents among young adults: a greater sense of duty as key players in the family migration strategy, increased empathy toward parents after having their own romantic relationships, and an emerging sense of economic responsibility related to entering the labor force. At this stage, children's own gender identity becomes increasingly salient in shaping their experiences.

Key Players in Family Migration Strategy

Young adults said their ability to understand parents' reasons for leaving them was extremely important. One seventeen-year-old explained that her mother's migration affected her less than it did her younger siblings: "It really affected my younger bother and sister. But for us, the two of us older ones, not nearly as much. We can get used to anything." Trinidad contrasted her feelings of helplessness about her father's departure when she was twelve, and not having been told that he had gone to the United States, to that of her older siblings. "They understood what was going on . . . [but in my case they lied because] my mother did not want me to think he had abandoned us." Trinidad's father came back and migrated again when she was seventeen. The second time was different.

"Well, yes, I felt sad, but I was able to accept it. I understood that he had to go work."

Beyond the capacity to understand the family's migration strategy, young adults described their roles as expanding after their parents left and asserted that their willingness to assume these roles was key to parents' decisions to migrate. When her mother decided to join her father in the United States, an eighteen-year-old told me, "She asked me for advice. She asked me if I could help and take care of my brother and sisters and if she could count on it so she could leave." Tony also supported his mother's decision to migrate. Assuming full responsibilities for paying the family's bills was stressful, but he added, "Someday in the future, it will all be worth it."

Young women's contributions to the housework are particularly important. Cassandra found herself helping out more at home after her father left. "There was a time that it got so difficult that my mother decided to migrate also. I left high school so that I could take care of my siblings. I didn't finish school because I had to take care of them." Cassandra's mother, Laura, never went to the United States and instead took a job in San Ángel. Still, Cassandra assumed much of the housework, since her mother was away most of the day, and she spent entire weekends washing the family's clothes until her hands burned from contact with detergent. "Since I am the oldest daughter, I felt responsible, because I didn't want my siblings to suffer. There were times that I had to act strong . . . because I felt like their mother. There were many things that I had to put up with because who could I talk to about it? I couldn't talk to [my oldest brother], though I think now that he knew about it all as well." Cassandra admitted feeling bad at first for having left school to care for her siblings. "Later it didn't matter to me that I made the sacrifice, as long as my siblings and my mother were okay."

As Cassandra's case illustrates, many older teenagers feel pressured to leave school to help out at home after parents depart. Regional teachers and school administrators often attribute their schools' retention difficulties to the lure of migration, although many students do not appear to drop out in order to migrate directly. A social worker told me, "Those in the ninth grade, when I talk to them about improving their grades . . .

they say, 'What for? I am not interested in school. When I finish I am going north.' . . . It is the mentality of our students that when they finish [ninth grade] they are going to go." A middle-school teacher complained that the dropout problem was concentrated among the boys. He said male dropouts do not necessarily migrate, and there are no employment opportunities for them in town. They leave school because they feel they have to take over their father's responsibilities at home. Such patterns are consistent with findings that dropout rates among Mexican adolescents are 10 percent higher among children in migrant households than in nonmigrant ones and that many adolescents are neither enrolled in school nor working.[34] For young adults, their work and sacrifice at home in Mexico, like that of their parents working in *el norte,* make it all possible.

Intimate Relationships

A sense of investment in the family migration strategy, although often at the cost of leaving school, may help those left as young adults to better adjust to separation. For younger siblings left as small children, romantic relationships as young adults help reduce resentment at parents particularly when it encourages greater personal responsibility. Cassandra explained: "Now that we are all married, we are all more conscious of things and take everything with a greater sense of responsibility." Nicandra said her son Tony stopped being difficult as a teenager once he had a steady girlfriend. "Maybe it was because I sent him to therapy that he was completely reformed, but I feel that what settled him down more was his girlfriend. . . . Now I see him really centered. He says, 'Mom, how is it possible that you can be so unconscious of the harm you did before?' and I tell him, 'It is just part of adolescence.' "

Tony also described his relationship as helping clarify his goals for the future. "Depending on what happens with my girlfriend . . . I hope that I can get a good job and save some money to buy a small business. . . . [My mother] is thinking of coming up with the money for the initial investment, but I want to do it all by myself. I know she would be so proud of me."

Romantic relationships may also help young adults better understand the pressures their parents faced. As a teen, thirty-year-old Paulo was often angry at his father for leaving the family. "I don't remember how old I was. . . . I know I was in a stage, well, it was a difficult time to be far from my father. . . . Like I lacked the paternal figure." As an adult, Paulo sees his father every year during the holidays. He said, "Well, we have had our differences. And we still do. But, now that I got married, I see things in a different way. I now analyze it all and see how we can all make mistakes." Managing their own relationships may help young adults better understand the complexities of their parents' lives that may have precipitated migration.

Work

Experiences in the workforce also reduce young adults' resentment at parents' absences. At work, young adults are surrounded by a more supportive peer culture than they had in school. One sixteen-year-old male explained: "My friends now are different than before. When I was in school it was, like, the other kids would tease me because my dad was gone. Now if my friends ask me about it and I tell them I don't talk to my dad at all, they are like, 'Oh, sorry for asking.'" He explained his change in attitude toward his migrant father over the past few years: "It is one thing to feel nothing, but it is another thing to feel anger. I don't feel anger [anymore]. . . . Now, it is like how we say here, what is done is done."

Employment—or even the idea of entering the workforce—may help young adults come to terms with potential economic hardship and thus better appreciate the difficulties their parents faced in providing for them. A young woman described the pressure she felt to leave school: "I was going to drop out. . . . I kept thinking that the money is just not enough to cover [the family expenditures] and that I should go to work and help out." Trinidad said that when she began to work, she better understood the economic pressures underlying her father's migration. "So when I started to work, I realized how difficult it was to earn this money that everyone was always talking about and what my dad had labored so hard for."

When children of migrant parents begin to think about work, they not only understand economic pressures but are also better able to understand the lure of migration. An eighteen-year-old who described great hardship at being separated from her migrant mother said she would consider leaving her children to work in the United States. "Who knows? It might be necessary, even if I loved my children a lot, just like my parents thought it over very carefully before leaving." Sixteen-year-old twin brothers each said they would be willing to leave their children to work in the United States, despite having felt extremely angry with their father for abandoning them. One explained: "Well, it might be necessary because here there is nothing to do. There is no other way to get ahead. There is no work." The other added: "I would leave them to go there to make something more. I would go and save up my money and then come back and stay here."

Entering the workforce is a key step to young adults making decisions about their own futures. Young adults recognize they can best become economically independent, or at least contribute economically, via migration. Families described a pattern in which children remain in Mexico until they reach a certain age in mid- to late adolescence, at which point they join parents abroad.[35] My surveys in the Mixteca show that of children ages fourteen through seventeen, fewer of those with migrant parents reported wanting to migrate than did those with nonmigrant parents. However, children over the age of eighteen with migrant parents more often reported wanting to migrate than did those with nonmigrant parents.[36] At this stage, young adults may begin to pressure parents to take them north.

Accessing Parents' Social Capital

Migrant father Gonzalo and his son, David, illustrate how parents' social networks become a key resource for young adults who reach this critical age when they are eager to migrate. At the time of our interview, Gonzalo had just arrived from Mexico, yet it was not his first time in New Jersey. Three years before, he had returned from New Jersey to live permanently with his family in Oaxaca. "I put up this little plastics stand. . . .

I sold very little, maybe two hundred pesos [twenty dollars] per day—it wasn't really enough to eat on. I was feeling down because the business wasn't doing well, but I had not thought of coming back north." Gonzalo's fourteen-year-old son, David, changed his mind. David had recently dropped out of school and was helping his father at the plastics stand. "My son told me he wanted to go north, and if I didn't go with him, he would leave with his cousins. I didn't really want to come back, but I didn't want him [David] to come alone either. So I decided I had better come with him while I was still able to." David confirmed his father's story: "He said that I am going to give you the opportunity [to migrate] while I still can."

David told me migrating had been the most significant experience in his life thus far. "I feel much more mature. . . . Everything I do now is with a purpose." He described a whole new world opening up to him in New Jersey. "There [in Mexico], there is nothing to do to have fun, not like here where there are basketball courts and green soccer fields to play at." When we met, David had already started working, joining his father's landscaping crew. He lived with his father in an unfinished basement in the house rented by a cousin. Newly arrived, David had yet to be discouraged. "Everywhere I go, I keep meeting family," he explained, eyes glittering. For David, and others like him, migration was a coming-of-age experience.

Children vary in when they reach a point when they are eager to migrate, affected by their own individual circumstances as well as their families' migration histories. Consider Nicandra's children, Tony and Miguel. In the fall of 2004, nineteen-year-old Tony was finishing high school and, inspired by his steady girlfriend of more than a year, was convinced that his future lay in a stable job in Mexico. Sixteen-year-old Miguel, however, had dropped out of school and had been working full time at a grocery store for more than a year. The younger sibling reasoned that he would make a lot more money if he joined his mother in New York City, and he asked her to take him there. A year later, Nicandra told me she had saved up the money to send for her boys. "What made me decide was the day Miguel told me that he felt lonely without me. I didn't want to bring him [here], but when he said this, I said, 'Yes, I am going to send for him.'" Once Miguel's migration was set, Tony—now having broken up with his girlfriend—did not want to stay in Mexico by himself. "This was not my plan," explained Nicandra. "I always thought I would work until I could go back there. But now I guess that all of us will end up here." A month later, they were reunited.

The process of reaching a critical age of readiness for migration is different for young men and women.[37] Young men often contemplate migration earlier, a decision that has much to do with their lack of success in school and the expectation that they become economically active. Facing few economic possibilities in Mexico, and having low levels of education, young men feel that future employment prospects are much better in the United States. One common pattern is for men to migrate after proposing to their sweethearts in Mexico in order to pay for the wedding. For example, before marrying Silvia, Daniel migrated to save money to wed his girlfriend. "Once I had this girlfriend, I went to the U.S. to make money to marry her. I had an uncle in New York City who had done the same thing, and I viewed him as an example."

Young women's migration, also affected by the need for economic activity, is more often tied to the formation of new family relationships.[38] For some young women, marriage is a direct ticket north. Yolanda's oldest daughter migrated just two months after marrying a man who had previously lived in California. A seventeen-year-old daughter of migrant parents in San Ángel told me: "I would like to get married and then go north with my husband to make our life together [there]." For other young women, the route north via marriage is more circuitous, coming after a failed marriage. One grandmother in San Ángel had three daughters who all migrated to the United States after their failed unions, leaving their children in her care. They did not consider going anywhere else to work, such as Mexico City, "since their father was already working over there [in the United States]." Another young woman grew up in San Ángel with her grandmother while her parents worked in New York City. She ended up migrating after her marriage to a drug user broke up and she was left with the full responsibility for her daughter. Her parents had since returned to San Ángel, and they cared for her infant daughter after her migration. In fact, one in three mothers I interviewed in New Jersey had grown up as a member of a transnational family (with a father, a mother, or both parents working away at some point in their lives).

Despite migrant parents' hopes that remittances will help children become professionals in Mexico, children often follow in their parents' footsteps. Once children reach a critical age of readiness for migration, and the emotional difficulties of separation become less salient, the economic benefits of migration loom large. Young children influence parents by affecting their emotions, and teenagers affect the distribution of family resources by experiencing problems that parents spend money on to solve. Young adults, in contrast, most often take advantage of parents' social capital and—when possible—monetary support in financing a trip north.[39] Young men are more likely to do so at earlier ages than are young women.

CHILDREN AND POWER

The often difficult experiences children of all ages have with separation from their parents are meaningful on a number of levels. They show the costs of separation for the youngest members of transnational families. The difficulties parents encounter as migrants mean they cannot meet their hopes for providing and caring for their children from a distance. Similarly, the emotional wake of parents' absences makes it hard for children to meet parents' expectations for unconditional love and respect, good behavior, and especially academic achievement. Children resent their parents and communicate this resentment openly. Behavioral problems are common. Most children left by their parents do not do well in school, and the schools they attend do not have the resources to help them. Many end up migrating and becoming low-wage workers in the United States as their parents did before them. These are the most disturbing consequences of parental migration.

Yet children's reactions to separation show that they do not lack power in transnational families. Over the past twenty years, an emerging area of research on childhood has focused on children as autonomous actors who create their own social worlds as distinct from and in dynamic relationship to those of the adults in their lives.[40] According to Jens Qvortrup, the new sociology of childhood has been relatively divorced from traditional, structural approaches to understanding children's lives, which emphasize the economic and political inequalities children experience.[41] Ethnographic studies of children's social worlds have not, for the most part, been successful in describing how children's power, or lack of power, in family relationships relates to their families' relative position in the society in which they live.[42]

This analysis reveals that in the transnational context, children may exert leverage, both as intended recipients of the benefits families gain through international migration and as independent agents whose divergent needs are intensified by separation from parents, while simultaneously being the least powerful actors within their families. Like children of divorce caught in custody battles between their parents, children in Mexican transnational families experience a disjuncture between their symbolic role as the primary beneficiaries of migration and their actual experiences of power vis-à-vis the other members of their family.[43]

The adverse consequences of separation—although difficult for all family members—are concentrated among children, who are, after all, dependents in their families. Parents make the initial decision to leave. The young children I interviewed are like other Mexican youth, who "report that they have little influence on their family decision-making processes, with parents tending to make most of the decisions."[44] As minors, children in Mexico cannot directly receive migrant parents' remittances at banks or money transfer agencies. The youngest children do not know how much money their parents send and do not decide how to spend family resources. For older children, the emotional price of separation becomes evident over time, particularly in terms of their educational prospects in Mexico.[45]

Yet children are also symbolically central to migrant families.[46] At the aggregate level, children with migrant parents may have advantages over their nonmigrant peers, presumably owing to the overall economic returns of migration.[47] Also, although the regularity of remittances may vary, the social networks developed during migration prove to be a uniformly important source of social capital for Mexican families.[48] My finding that parents' migrant networks are an important resource for older children has been verified quantitatively, with the intergenerational transmission of migration experience greatest among families headed by migrant parents.[49] This practice, however, does not appear to be a process by which parents pass on pro-migration values or attitudes, what scholars call a "culture of migration" to their children.[50] Instead, it arises out of a combination of life course changes, children's experiences of power in their families during separation, and the lack of educational and professional opportunities available to children in Mexico.[51]

Children wield influence over migrant parents as the beneficiaries of their sacrifices. Young children often express disappointment at parental absence through displays of emotional withholding. These displays affect the emotions of the adults around them in what scholars describe as a process of "emotional transmission."[52] For the most part, young children gain access to their parents' resources indirectly. Although also affecting adults' emotions, teenagers' difficulties at home and at school can produce more direct demands on parental resources than do the problems of younger children. As teenagers mature into young adults and begin to consider employment, they invariably find that employment prospects are better in the United States than in Mexico. For children in many Mexican communities, a key component in the transition to adulthood is reaching a critical age of readiness for migration.[53] At this point, which often comes earlier for young men than it does for young women, parents' ability to translate migration into human capital gains for their children has generally failed. Regional schools do not provide enough structural support for the children of migrants regardless of parents' remittances. When they perform poorly in school, young adults feel the lure of migration.[54] They have an advantage over other youth in their communities in being able to access their parents' social capital in the form of migration networks. And parents' social capital inevitably leads north.

Children's experiences over time suggest that children are not completely powerless within their families. Like research showing that women's relative power in their family enables them to bargain for family resources, children's relative power—as shaped by their negative reactions to parental absences—affords them some ability to bargain in their families.[55] Their symbolic centrality during migration allows children to exert their interests within their families, even if they do so by expressing unhappiness and feelings of powerlessness.

Children's experiences are meaningful in yet another way; they illuminate the dynamic nature of intergenerational relationships over time. Parents and children must adapt to each other's changing needs, and relationships may show significant variability over the passage of even just a few years. This is perhaps true in all families, yet members of transnational families face distinct strains and difficulties. Because parents and children are living apart and contact is infrequent and occurs most often over the phone, parents have many fewer cues to help guide them in reacting to their children's changing needs. One migrant father explained: "I know that my son is big, but when I came here [to the United States], he had just started walking. He was two. I know he is now big, but this is how I remember him. When I see him again, he is going to be so big. He is now seven . . . but I cannot imagine him big, only little, the way I left him."

These time dislocations are particularly difficult for transnational families. With time, parents may easily lose touch with their children's development, which can occur remarkably quickly in contrast to the slow pace in which parents meet their goals as migrant workers. For children, in contrast, each passing year without a parent constitutes an even greater share of their lived experiences. Periods of separation drag on, particularly as children grow and their needs, and interpretations of their parents' absences, change. The emotional consequences of separation eventually overtake the potential benefits of parents' remittances, particularly in financing children's schooling. The unmet expectations of parents and children are a source of great difficulties for families during periods of separation.

A grandmother and her granddaughter at home in Mexico; the girl's parents live and work in *el norte*. Photograph by Joanna Dreby

SIX Middlewomen

> [My daughter] wants to take [my granddaughter] now, but [my granddaughter] doesn't want to go. My heart and soul split in two when I think of the day that she will leave. But I know I will have to let her go at some point, and I will let her go because it is right for her to be with her mother. But I will only let my daughter take her when [my granddaughter] decides to go. . . . I am not going to let [my daughter] take her against her will.
>
> A grandmother in San Ángel

This grandmother's statement illustrates the vastly important role caregivers in Mexico have in mediating relationships between migrant parents and their children. Children often feel attached to their caregivers. Caregivers, in turn, are emotionally attached to the children in their care. When children resist migration, they may find support from their caregivers, who will feel deeply saddened if the children leave. Caregivers may advocate on behalf of the children in their care who do not wish to migrate, further prolonging periods of family separation.

At the same time, caregivers, like the grandmother quoted above, do not question migrants' rights to the children in their care. In the transnational context, caregivers rarely usurp parents' roles in children's lives. They most often act as intermediaries, what I call "middlewomen," in relationships between parents and children. This is because caregivers have their own stake in the child care arrangement; many depend economically on remittances from migrant parents. They may not want children to leave, but in order to stake claim to parents' remittances, they cannot undermine parent-child bonds. Instead, in the context of often lengthy periods of parent-child separation, caregivers' actions almost paradoxically reinforce intergenerational obligations.

This chapter considers the "tangle of reciprocity" involved in these caregiving arrangements, or networks of care, to explore the role of caregivers in shaping how parent-child relationships unfold during periods of separation.[1] Here I focus on families in which the mother has migrated and the children remain with a nonparental caregiver. Migrant parents rely on a very limited set of choices for caregivers during migration. Mothers almost always leave their children with grandparents, usually maternal grandmothers. In a very few cases they choose other relatives, such as an aunt. Reciprocity during periods of separation is more easily accomplished when the caregivers are the children's grandparents, making these arrangements much more long-standing than those with other related caregivers.

Indeed, children's experiences differ depending on the type of caregiver. In what follows I first contrast the two networks of care mothers rely on when migrating—grandparents and other relatives—and then describe the tensions that characterize each care network. The systematic comparison of the two primary caregiving arrangements shows that despite vast differences between the types of care, neither grandparents nor other relatives undermine parents' rights over their children. In essence, when divided by borders, caregivers help in what sociologists call "doing family" in a way that reinforces parent-child obligation.[2] By supporting parent-child relationships, caregivers help make family reunifications more likely.

FAMILIES' NETWORKS OF CHILD CARE

When it comes to caring for their children, American families are not as independent as one would expect given the predominant ideology of the nuclear family.[3] Regardless of class background, contemporary Americans rely on multiple individuals to develop a network of care for their children. Such networks, according to sociologist Karen Hansen, are social creations (as opposed to purely biological or economic exchanges) that involve a process of "staging networks," which includes identifying potential caregivers, linking members through reciprocal relationships, and mobilizing obligation.[4]

Families of different racial and ethnic backgrounds, and in different countries around the world, may stage child care networks in ways that vary from those of white families in the United States. Cultural expectations as well as relative poverty may shape the mutual obligations involved in the care of children. Carol Stack, for example, has shown that reciprocity among African American families in the low-income neighborhood she studied was quite extensive and a coping strategy to deal with economic deprivation.[5] Child care arrangements are often fluid and vary according to the financial needs of not only parents but also extended kin. They may fluctuate over time as children grow and their needs change.[6]

"Child fostering"—what the anthropologist Esther Goody defines as the sharing of one or more parenting tasks between more than one set of parents—is not necessarily mutually beneficial.[7] Research in different parts of Africa, where child fostering is a well-documented practice, shows that power dynamics between the two sets of parents vary depending on the age of the children being fostered (with younger children being more burdensome than older ones) or the circumstances under which a child is fostered (whether rural-to-urban or urban-to-rural, during famine time, after the death of a parent, etc.).[8] In fact, one researcher found that fewer than half of the fostering arrangements were "joint ventures" between caregivers and parents. Most of the time, fostering arrangements were either openly contested or "ambivalent" takeovers in which caregivers completely supplanted parents.[9]

When parents migrate internationally, familial networks of care appear to be more cooperative than conflicting.[10] Families from the West Indies, for example, have used fostering during migration since the early 1900s, and the cultural predisposition toward fostering has been described as "a necessary prerequisite for migration."[11] Scholars suggest that it is fairly normal for West Indian women to have their first children out of wedlock or to have children with different fathers and to rely on their own mothers and family members to care for them.[12] As such, "children are regarded by West Indians as women's wealth, and socially it is the distribution of this wealth that links different generations of women."[13] Men barely figure in to these relationships, and bonds between women are what make international migration possible. In Central America, where community "other-mothers" look after the children of migrants, women are also key to migration strategies, as they are in the Philippines, where mothers often migrate without their husbands and female relatives are primarily responsible for children.[14]

I too find that while men do have a role in Mexican transnational care networks, women are the primary caregivers when mothers migrate. For this reason, I refer to caregivers as middlewomen. Child fostering, however, has rarely been documented as a common practice in Mexico. When they migrate domestically, Mexican women generally take their children with them.[15] This is somewhat surprising given reports that strong extended family ties are a cultural tendency in Mexican families, with *compadres*—or godparents—having important roles in family networks.[16] While Mexican women may rely on each other for short-term child care needs, the sharing of child care tasks as a long-term solution to economic difficulties or as a way of fomenting economic exchange between extended family members and neighbors is not particularly common. In the transnational context, Mexican families' child care networks are primarily intergenerational in orientation.

GRANDPARENTS

Grandparents are the most common caregivers when mothers migrate from the Mixteca.[17] Of the school children I surveyed who had mothers working in the United States, 78 percent lived with grandparents.[18] Only 31 percent of children without migrant mothers reported living with grandparents.[19] There is a strong preference for children to remain with maternal grandparents: surveys show 62 percent of children of migrants in the Mixteca to reside with maternal grandparents and 24 percent to reside with paternal grandparents.[20]

Maternal Grandparents

Migrants believe maternal grandmothers to be the most logical caregivers for their children during their absences. Illustrating the preference for maternal grandmothers as caregivers, one migrant mother explained: "We left them with my husband's mother just because my mother has already passed away." Another migrant mother said, "I felt okay leaving them because I knew they would be with my own mother." One single mother in San Ángel told me that she had often thought of migrating to the United States. "I thought of going in '93, but I didn't. What happened is that my mother got sick at the time I thought of going, so I couldn't go. Later she died. . . . My sisters were here, but I felt I trusted my mother more." Most migrant mothers implied that maternal grandmothers are, due to lineage, an extension of themselves and the best substitute for a mother's love. The child care choices of migrating mothers suggest that in Mexico the most acceptable replacement for unpaid family labor is maternal kin.

The prevalence of the practice of leaving children with maternal grandparents is curious given that anthropologists have documented the predominance of patrilocal residential patterns in the region of Mesoamerica from which the majority of the Mexican parents I met migrate. Typically when a couple marries in southern Mexico, they will live with the husband's parents for a number of years until the couple can move out on their own.[21] We might expect that when mothers leave, children will stay with their paternal grandparents since they have lived with them before. Conflicts between mothers-in-law and daughters-in-law, however, are common. When husbands migrate, wives may prefer to return to their own parents' home.[22] Are mothers leaving children with maternal grandparents simply because they are already living together? Or is a mother's migration what prompts the decision to leave children with maternal grandparents? In the Mixteca, the latter appears to be the case. Among the children I surveyed living with their mother whose father was in the United States, 23 percent lived with maternal grandparents and 25 percent with paternal grandparents.[23] The pattern reverses drastically among children of migrant mothers. It appears that when a mother decides to migrate, she places her children with her own kin.

Mothers may feel they are better able to maintain good relationships with their children from a distance if their own family members are caring for the children. I found that in three-fourths of the families I interviewed in both the United States and Mexico, children lived with maternal kin. Among those who reported weak relationships between mother and child, two-thirds of the children lived with their father's family. For example, in explaining how she came to care for her grandchildren, a paternal grandmother in San Ángel said that her daughter-in-law left her son for another man in the United States. Before her son sent the children back to live in Mexico, their mother would watch them during the day and go back to her new partner's home in the evening. "My son would say to her, 'doesn't it make you sad to see your children [cry] like that [when you leave]?' and she would answer, 'for those children, I cannot lose my happiness.'" Given this account, it is not surprising that when the children's mother returned to San Ángel to visit them, they did not want to talk to her. When mothers leave children with maternal kin, they avoid the risk of having their in-laws speak badly about them. In effect, a migrant mother secures more optimal conditions for maintaining an emotional bond with children from a distance when her own family members care for the children and thus support the migration decision.

Unless there had been a marital breakup, migrant parents usually reported amicable relationships with their in-laws who watched their children. Mothers generally do not express serious concerns about their children's care when grandparents are the caregivers, assuming that grandparental love for grandchildren dictates treatment of them. Ofelia summarized the prevalent attitude of migrant women: "I know my son is missing the love of a mother, but I also know my son doesn't suffer terribly without me. He has food, material things, and love from my own mother. It is more that I am the one who suffers without him."

Caring for Grandchildren

As opposed to grandparents in the United States, who are often reluctant to take over full-time care of their grandchildren, Mexican grandmothers are instrumental in becoming the primary caregivers for their grandchildren when parents migrate.[24] Migrant mothers often said that their own mothers were the ones to give them the confidence to take the final step of leaving. According to one migrant mother, "I wouldn't have done it [if it weren't for my mother]. With my mother, I know that they are okay. She is a little strict, but it is better that way." A grandmother in San Ángel reported that the act of leaving children signified the trust between mother and daughter. She said her daughter told her upon leaving, "I am giving you my daughter because I know that you will take care of her."

Grandmothers may actively encourage daughters to leave grandchildren in Mexico. Nancy said that when she left Mexico to join her husband in California, she wanted to bring her daughter along. Her mother convinced her that after bouts of depression after her husband left, it would be physically impossible to take her two-year-old daughter with her across the border: "How are you—at a mere ninety pounds—going to carry your thirty-pound daughter across the desert?" A grandmother in San Ángel explained that she convinced one of her daughters, a single mother in the United States, to send her granddaughter back to Mexico. "I told her it would be better for her to send me the girl. I convinced her that it was better for her to send her back." When I asked her why she had done so, the older woman explained: "Because I was worried that they were going to take her to someone there, and you don't know how well they will take care of her. They aren't family." Similarly, another grandmother proclaimed: "As I tell my daughter, if it is hard for me to care for them and they are my own blood, how are you going to pay someone else over there to watch them when you don't even have a stable job?"

Many times women described children as their most prized possession. This suggests that leaving them with kin is a way of cementing bonds between women.[25] This dynamic, however, is not limited to mother-daughter relationships. Fathers also expressed trust in children's grandmothers as caregivers. Recall that Armando told me he felt confident when he decided to send for his wife because his children would stay with his own mother: "I know my mother is a very responsible person. I trust her a lot." Even when children stayed with maternal grandparents, migrant fathers spoke of their confidence in the child care arrangement. One father said he never had conflicts with his mother-in-law: "We get along well."

Moreover, some grandmothers I interviewed said their husband, although not the children's primary caregiver, had made the arrangements for their grandchildren to stay in Mexico. One grandmother in San Ángel explained that it was her husband who instructed their daughter to leave their four-year-old granddaughter because "who was going to watch her over there?" Another said that her migrant husband in the United States told her to take care of her grandchildren when he decided to send for his daughters after they had marital problems. And one of the few grandfathers who sat with his wife to be interviewed, told me, "It is more important, and safer, that they be raised here, because over there everyone works and it is important for children to have someone looking after them."

While maternal grandmothers are the preferred caregivers, paternal family members may support the child care arrangement. When Elsa joined José in the United States, for example, their children, Brian and Tina, stayed with Elsa's own mother, but a paternal uncle was designated as the family academic "tutor," responsible for all affairs related to the children's schooling. In another case in San Ángel, one grandmother explained that her adult son had been to the United States once before. The first time his wife joined him, the couple's two sons stayed with her. Then the couple returned to town and had another baby. When her son left again for Nebraska and his wife followed within a few months, the grandmother explained: "I told her [the daughter-in-law] it was better for her to leave [the baby] with her mother because he was so small, and that I would keep the older boys." In the relationship between mothers-in-law and daughters-in-law, a shadow of a man (a son or husband) is often present.[26]

If children in the West Indies are considered "women's wealth" and child fostering a way of cementing ties between female kin, then children in Mexican families are the wealth that unites men and women of different generations to each other.[27] For older couples, grandchildren are the tie that binds them in old age. One couple I interviewed defended each other in describing the difficulties they had raising their teenage granddaughters. Doña Ana struggled at times with her husband's drinking habits but praised his great attention to and interest in raising their grandson, Kevin. "We raise chickens to sell. He [Doña Ana's husband] cares for the animals, but every day I take them to sell. So when Kevin was a baby and I was out selling the chickens, he would stay with the baby. The two 'men' are very close." Although caring for grandchildren can be a source of tension in marriages, it also can improve marital relationships when husbands and wives have the time to share child care tasks.[28] Care for children cements ties between husbands and wives and parents and children.

Economic Benefits of Separation

Remittances from adult children working abroad are a significant source of income for older people in Mexico, particularly elderly women living in rural areas like San Ángel.[29] Indeed, a study in 1990 found that 69 percent of Mexican men between the ages of sixty and sixty-four, but only 9 percent of women in the same age group, were economically active. The gender disparity in economic activity was even greater in rural areas, where 75 percent of men between sixty and sixty-four were active compared to only 6 percent of women.[30] Many elderly women do not have the support of economically active husbands as they are not living with a partner. While 87 percent of men aged sixty to sixty-four were married, only two-thirds of women were.[31] Moreover, the social security system in Mexico is not universal but is administered by a number of different organizations covering different classes of workers, usually in urban areas. Estimates suggest that in 1990, as many as 82 percent of elderly individuals in Mexico lacked pension benefits.[32]

Faced with economic hardship in old age, grandmothers may actively encourage their daughters and sons to leave children in their care for economic reasons. By keeping children, grandparents are able to stake a claim to migrant parents' remittances. A number of grandmothers I interviewed had numerous children living in the United States and had cared for multiple grandchildren over the years. All reported that those responsible for sending money home were invariably those who had children in their care. In one case, a grandmother had raised a total of ten grandchildren, and nine of her ten children lived in the United States. At the time of the interview, only one fourteen-year-old granddaughter remained in her care. The only person who regularly sent her money was the fourteen-year-old's mother. However, since she had cared for so many different grandchildren, the responsibility of providing for her had been distributed among a number of her migrant children over the years.

While money is a motivation for grandparents to care for grandchildren, only a few I interviewed felt economically stable. Most grandparents described ongoing financial difficulties despite the support of remittances. Regardless of the amount sent home, grandparents did not feel they had enough to adequately cover the costs of living. One grandmother said she received two hundred dollars per month and explained: "That is not enough to raise four children." Another's husband worked as a taxi driver and also had a small corner store to help support one daughter and two grandchildren in her care. She received between one hundred and two hundred dollars per month from her migrant daughter, but she said it was just enough for her to pay for the medicine for her chronically ill grandson. Yet another grandmother and her husband in San Ángel had owned a corner grocery store for more than twenty years. But, she said, they never made a profit; instead, sales only covered food expenses for the family. Her daughter, a single mother, sent just fifty dollars home per month. "It isn't enough, but we do what we can."

Yet grandparents may be reluctant to ask migrant parents for money. When they do not have enough money, they cope on their own. When I asked a grandmother if she called her daughter to ask for money when she needed it, she answered, "No, I don't ask anyone [for money]. I don't ask anything of my children. I wait for their kindness." According to another grandmother, "They [my daughters] send me money twice a month. It isn't enough. . . . But, no, no I don't call them [when money is tight]. I get the money here on loan." At least in San Ángel, money lending within the community is the preferred way of dealing with economic shortage. For example, when I finally caught up with Doña Dalia, who cared for two children and four grandchildren, to arrange an interview, it was just after I noticed two other women at the house. I returned the next day at 9 A.M. at Doña Dalia's request, but as I turned the corner of her street, I saw the same two women receive no answer at the door. I immediately feared I would have trouble finding Doña Dalia again, but after I waited patiently at the door for a time, it eventually opened and she let me in. Now entertaining a guest, Doña Dalia left the door to the street ajar. About a half hour later, the women returned, but Doña Dalia dismissed the women—who I now understood were debt collectors—quickly at the door. She told them: "They haven't sent me any money yet." Later Doña Dalia told me that since her daughter left nine months earlier, she had sent three packages of clothing and between 100 and 150 dollars per week. Doña Dalia lauded her daughter's commitment, apparently sending more than Doña Dalia's own husband, who also worked abroad. "She sends clothes and shoes, and since she learned that her sister left [leaving another grandson with Doña Dalia], she sends things for him also." Nonetheless, "It is not enough, but what can I do?"

Instead of reporting economic hardships to migrant parents, grandparents prefer to highlight how well children are thriving under their care. According to one grandmother,

> [My son] sends between 150 and 200 dollars every two or three weeks. Depending on what he sends, I take good care of his children [three boys]. They are all well fed. For example, I give them each a whole fried fish to themselves two or three times a year. I give them their sausages, and I buy them the milk that comes in the box [as opposed to powdered milk]. When he sends money, I buy a whole carton of milk boxes so that every morning they have a cup of milk before school. And I give them a sandwich before school. They also get five pesos [fifty cents] each so that during break they can buy whatever they want so they aren't hungry the rest of the day.

The sociologist Leah Schmalzbauer suggests that a communication gap exists between migrant parents and their children in Honduras, with children knowing little about the daily lives of their parents. Parents "relativize their communication with family back 'home,' choosing what and who to tell about the reality of their lives in the USA."[33] A similar communication gap may exist regarding children's care in Mexico, with grandparents playing a crucial role in mediating the information parents receive about their children. One reason grandparents put a positive spin on their grandchildren's care despite feeling they lack economic resources may be their fear of losing access to remittances if parents decide to send for their children. It also may be that grandparents understand that it is difficult for migrant parents to send money home as they work in low-wage jobs and may have multiple obligations in the United States.[34] They may not want to worry migrant parents, who are, after all, their own children. Finally, grandparents may fear that if they complain of economic hardship, migrant parents will take away their grandchildren, with whom they have developed significant emotional bonds.

Emotional Ties

Migrant parents often told me that one of the reasons they had not sent for their children was that they did not want to leave their own parents alone, without the company of grandchildren. Grandparents may not only encourage migrants to leave children in their care, but they may also actively discourage migrant parents' efforts at reunification. According to one migrant mother, her mother-in-law "says they are fine there. She doesn't want us to bring them here because they have always been there with them." Migrant mother Silvia said, "My parents dissuaded me from the idea [of bringing them over]. And the idea of pulling them out of there from one moment to the next seemed a difficult one." One grandmother who cared for three grandchildren and whose husband lived in the United States near the children's mother said, "He [her husband] says that there [in the United States], the children don't have any freedom to play and only stay cooped up in the house. He doesn't want her [the mother] to take them. He tells his daughter that he doesn't want her to end up in jail because that is what they do there if you leave children home alone." Ironically, I had gone looking for this grandmother twice before finding her at home; both times she was out and the six children in her care were home alone in the two-bedroom house.

Grandparents are proud of the loyalty their grandchildren show them. Doña María laughed when recounting how concerned grandson Germán gets when she is ill, nervously tending to her by asking, "What can I do?" "Do you want soup?" and "Why don't I take you to the doctor?" One grandmother reported that she does not read or write well enough to help her grandchildren with homework, but she beamed in explaining that her six-year-old grandson says, "Don't worry, mama, I am going to study hard and learn well so that I can help you do the books for the store." Another grandmother laughed with pleasure in telling a story about her grandson: "Then sometimes he would come home from school and he would caress my breasts and he would ask me what it was like when he would drink from my breasts. I told him that he didn't drink from my breasts, that his uncles yes, but not him. And he cried and cried saying why didn't he drink from my breasts. So I thought better of it and told him, yes, that he did, so that he wouldn't cry anymore."

Despite the strong emotional ties grandparents have with their grandchildren, grandparents rarely question biological parents' attachments to their children. They believe it is best for children to live with their own parents and that they themselves are merely substitutes for parents. Grandparents like living with their grandchildren but recognize that parents have ultimate rights over their children. According to one grandmother, "Well, how are we going to want her [our granddaughter] to go? But, if her mother decides to take her, what can we do?" Another said that she would not let her grandchildren go to New York City unless their parents came back for them. "But if they come for them, I know that they have a right over their own children."

Grandparents' worries about parents' plans for children's migration often reflect, at least in part, a genuine concern over how the children will react to reunification. They want to ensure that their grandchildren are emotionally and developmentally prepared to migrate. In essence, they are closer to understanding the needs of their grandchildren than migrant parents are, as they have been living with the children and feel confident in advocating for those needs to the parents.

Grandparents Are Not the Same as Parents

The emotional ties grandparents have with the children in their care do not challenge parent-child relationships. Instead, grandparents seem to prefer to relate to children as grandparents and not as parents. Research in the United States suggests that the absence of parental responsibility is one of the most positive aspects of grandparenting.[35] Likewise, all family members I interviewed said grandparents are more indulgent than parents in caring for children. One migrant mother whose two daughters live with her mother-in-law explained: "It isn't the same [when they are] with grandparents. The grandparents may feed them, but they don't insist. If the children don't want to eat, they don't eat. But a mother insists that [her child] eat and then knows that he eats well." A grandmother said, "I have them very spoiled." A seven-year-old boy told me that living with his grandmother was different from living with his parents, "because when I lived in the other house, they wouldn't give me money and here they do. . . . Here they spoil me more." An eleven-year-old said life with her grandmother was different than with her mother. "My grandmom sometimes tells me to hurry up and do my work because if I don't, she won't give me money. And my mom [when she was here], if I didn't hurry up, she would hit me."

Many grandparents said they do not use physical punishment with their grandchildren. This was one of the major differences between raising one's own children and raising grandchildren. Doña Beatriz, for example, was in her early fifties when I met her; for three years she raised her oldest daughter Silvia's three young children alongside three of her own children, with all six under the age of ten. She said that she treats all of the children equally. However, "I might hit my own children to discipline them, but I don't hit my grandchildren." Another grandmother told me, "Since they aren't my children, I'd feel bad to really hit them."

Members of Mexican families see the roles of grandparents as different from those of parents. Grandparents spoil their grandchildren and treat them more gently than they do their own children. They are ever mindful that biological parents have the ultimate rights over making decisions about children's lives. If anything, grandparents intervene in parent-child relationships only to ensure that parents respect the wishes of grandchildren, such as Doña María, who had suggested that Germán stay in Mexico not to keep her company, but rather until he graduated from the sixth grade. Grandparents rarely express their own self-interest in parents' migration. They benefit financially from caring for grandchildren but do not pressure migrants for money for children's care.

OTHER RELATIVES

When grandparents are caregivers, the costs and benefits of child care arrangements for caregivers are subtle and subsumed under the expectation of a loving bond based on grandparents' "natural" tendency to indulge their grandchildren. In contrast, child care arrangements with other relatives are more explicit. I met only six families in which children lived with relatives other than the grandparents. Ties to extended kin and *compadres* are important in Mexico, and the social networks they provide are key for facilitating migration.[36] However, these ties do not appear to be strong enough to be suitable for the care of children when parents migrate internationally. When parents leave children with other relatives, it is usually due to a lack of other options. The terms of child care are generally agreed upon in advance and often are much more carefully monitored by migrant parents than when children remain with grandparents.

Only if You Must Go

Unlike grandparents, other relatives generally do not encourage migrants to leave children in their care. Some agree to help because they recognize that single mothers are in a bind. For example, one migrant mother moved in with her sister, also a single mother of two, after her husband left her for another woman. After working for a few months cleaning hotel rooms and barely earning enough to survive, this mother's siblings living in New Jersey helped her to migrate. She left her children with the sister in Mexico and sent money home to support her sister and all four children. For the most part, however, other relatives are reluctant to take on the responsibility of caring for other children. One migrant mother, for example, joined her husband in the United States after he had been away for a time, leaving two daughters, ages six and nine, with her sister-in-law. When I asked, "How did you decide that the girls would stay with your sister-in-law?" she explained: "My husband decided. My sister-in-law didn't want to take them. She said that the children are going to suffer. But then she said yes, but only accepted it for a year."

"Who made the arrangements with her?" I asked.

"I told her to talk to my husband about it. . . . The girls didn't want to live with their aunt either. They wanted to stay with their grandmother, my mother-in-law, because my mother passed away. Then they asked to live with their godmother, but I had to tell them no, because their father had already decided that they would live with their aunt and that was the way it would be."

When other relatives decide to take care of children, they do so out of obligation to migrant parents. In contrast, grandparents feel equally obligated to parents (their children) and their grandchildren.

Financial Arrangements

The economic terms of the child care arrangement are explicit when children stay with other relatives. One aunt broke down in tears when she told me that her own now-adult children who migrated to the United States rarely send her money and she is forced to sell fruit to make ends meet. Because children's obligation to their parents is an ambiguous expectation, she was hurt when they did not provide for her. In contrast, she said her migrant sister sent a thousand pesos (one hundred dollars) per month while she cared for her nephew. "She knows she has to send money for his expenses." In another case, the migrant mother described in the previous paragraph did not know what financial arrangements her husband made with her sister-in-law but said that every time she calls to talk to her daughters, her husband spends much of the twenty-minute phone call discussing these arrangements. An aunt who was watching her nieces temporarily said of her sisters in New York: "Oh, they know they have to send money for their expenses. Last week one of my sisters sent money, and now we are waiting for the other one to."

Remittances to grandparents are part and parcel of intergenerational responsibilities, and migrant parents implicitly trust that grandparents will spend the money wisely, keeping the best interests of their grandchildren in mind. But when children live with other relatives, there is a high level of distrust over whether remittances are used to support the children. Migrant Paula, for example, emphasized on numerous occasions how closely she monitored the use of the money she sent back to her children, Cindy and Mateo, in Mexico. Once Mateo complained that when he asked his caregivers (Paula's cousins) for money, they claimed they did not have any. In response, Paula started sending 250 to 300 dollars a month to her cousins for food and sent money separately to Mateo, who at the age of eighteen could receive money directly, to pay for Cindy and Mateo's school and clothing expenses. "He is very responsible and conscientious with the money I send," Paula said. Later, when Cindy left Paula's uncle's home and moved to a different city temporarily with another family, Paula explained the specific terms of the arrangement carefully.

> I send the money to him [the father in the family she's staying with]. And he is a good person because at home, since they knew my daughter, I could send money to the telegraph office in her name. But in the city, I can't, because she is a minor. So he said I can send the money to him, and I just tell him how much is for him and how much to give to her, and he will give her every last penny. And my daughter has told me that he gives it all to her . . . he gives her all that I send for her.

Not only do migrant parents like Paula make careful arrangements to ensure that their children are provided for, but they also do their best to scrutinize these arrangements. As children grow older, parents may rely on their reports about how caregivers manage the money they send.

Emotional Ties

Other kin generally do not view emotional bonds with migrant parents' children as a potential benefit of the transnational child care arrangement. This does not mean that they do not become attached to the children in their care. One aunt said that she would be sad to see her nieces leave. "Well, I think I will feel bad, and that is why I am trying not to get used to them too much." Another aunt explained: "I thought of [my nephew] as my son. I cried a lot when he left." Cindy and Mateo told me that they have two mothers and love both women. Blanca—their second mother—recalled fondly that after Paula's first trip to the United States, Cindy did not recognize her biological mother and instead asked Blanca, "Who is that woman who is going to live downstairs in our house?"

During one interview, an aunt who had previously cared for her nine-year-old nephew when her sister migrated began to cry. Not only had she grown close to her nephew and felt bad when he left, but she was offended that her sister did not consult her about the decision to send the boy to Mexico City to live with another sister. One day, she simply got a call and was told that the boy would be moving out. She admitted that the boy was a handful and got in trouble in part because she worked and could not supervise him as she would have wanted. She also said that she believed he was doing better in Mexico City. What hurt her was that she was not consulted in the decision-making process.[37]

Powerlessness

This aunt was not the only one to say her advice was ignored. As I describe further in the next chapter, Blanca claimed that when Paula decided to return to the United States and take her son, Mateo, with her, she warned Paula that it would not be a good idea. She implied that Mateo's difficulty in adapting to life in New Jersey and his subsequent return to her home in Mexico was evidence that she had been correct. The mother of Eric, Osvaldo, and Edwin also apparently ignored the advice of her children's caregivers in Mexico. She had recently decided to send for eleven-year-old Eric, thus causing emotional turmoil for the brothers, particularly seven-year-old Osvaldo, who broke down crying talking about the prospect of his older brother's imminent departure. According to the boys' cousin, "My father doesn't want the older boy to go. He says that since my aunt is over there alone and working that the boy will end up being alone. He says that there will be no one to take care of him and that the boys are going to come back [to Mexico] all gangster-like."

Relatives' feelings of powerlessness in advocating on behalf of the children in their care contrast with those of grandparents, who feel that speaking on the children's behalf is their only means of influencing migrant parents' decisions. It is possible that this disparity arises from migrant parents' general distrust of other relatives' motivations. While migrant parents believe that grandparents will put the interests of their grandchildren above self-interest, they may consider either self-interest or pity to be the core of the child care arrangement with other relatives. As such, migrant parents consider advice from grandparents carefully but may ignore advice from other relatives because they believe financial motivations, rather than emotional ties, may underlie the advice.

Migrant parents are inherently distrustful of other relatives' motivations. They may be justified in their misgivings, as conflicts with other relatives are common and these arrangements are often fragile and short-lived.

RISKS TO RELATIONSHIPS OVER TIME

The sources of tension in child care arrangements over time reveal the norms of reciprocity that underlie these arrangements. When children live with other relatives, conflicts arise from distrust over the equity of the exchange of care for money. In contrast, financial considerations do not cause strains when caregivers are grandparents. Instead, it is grandparents' physical ability to care for children as they grow older or the mother's jealous feelings over children's increased attachment to grandparents that cause tension in these relationships. In all cases, relationship tensions increase the longer children remain with caregivers in Mexico and as children grow older.

Paying for Care

Conflicts with other relatives stem from concerns that the terms of the child care arrangement are not being fulfilled, either by the migrant parent or by the relative caregivers in Mexico. Parents often doubt that their children are receiving sufficient care given the remittances being sent for this purpose. Relatives, for their part, feel that parents are not sending money regularly enough and in sufficient amounts to cover their expectations of care for their children. An aunt's account about her experiences in Guatemala caring for her niece illustrates the monetary concerns also typical among Mexican families: "When we spoke on the telephone, my brother-in-law would even insult me. He would say that I didn't want to send their child because I was taking the money, the U.S. dollars they sent. But I never took any of the money for myself. I did, however, lump it together with mine to use for the household expenses, but even that wasn't enough."[38] As is clear in this example, child care arrangements with other relatives typically incorporate a wider range of family members than when children live with grandparents, in this case a brother-in-law, who may have strong opinions about the equity of the arrangement.

While I heard rumors that the misuse of money was a problem for migrant parents, all those whose children lived with grandparents denied this. For example, when I asked one migrant father of two children living with his mother-in-law in Mexico if he ever had problems with money, he shook his head. "No, I have never had a problem with my mother-in-law. I have heard from other friends that they sometimes have problems like that, like her buying a gold chain with the money instead of spending it on food. But me, no, I have never had that kind of problem." The only families to admit to any disagreements over money were those whose children lived with other relatives.

No case better exemplifies how money can become a source of conflict for families than that of Eric, age eleven, Edwin, age eight, and Osvaldo, age seven, who had lived with their parents and an older sister in Mexico City until their parents' marriage ended in a bitter divorce. The boys' father moved in with a girlfriend, and their mother, distraught over the divorce and suddenly having to support the children, migrated to the United States. The three boys stayed with their sister, fifteen at the time, in a house occupied by four of their maternal aunts and their ailing grandmother. The boys were immediately subject to abuse from their older sister, "who once put one of the boys head first in the washing machine," and from their aunts, one of whom "used to force feed Osvaldo *menudo* [cow intestines] even though she knew it made him throw up." Another aunt living nearby felt sorry for the boys and took them to live at her house. The money problems began at that point. According to cousin Faviola, who related the story, the boys' mother had arranged to send three hundred dollars every two weeks to support the children. Faviola explained: "Sometimes she wasn't able to send the money. Then her brother-in-law would complain. Their mother began to wonder what they were doing with the money she sent, because you don't need all that much just to feed the boys." The three boys continued to behave badly, and—to make matters worse—"I think they humiliated my aunt because they would say to her that you eat because of my mom."

After a few months, the boys' mother arranged to send remittances to another sister as she began to think that the money she sent was not being used to support her children. The sister who lived nearby would buy food for the boys and take it to them every week. The brother-in-law who had complained about the money got upset. He threatened to call the DIF, the Mexican equivalent of Child Protective Services, to report the boys as abandoned by their mother.

At this point, cousin Faviola's family intervened. Faviola often traveled to Mexico City from the small town in Oaxaca, where she lived with her parents and witnessed the escalation of the family's problems. When Faviola's father also traveled on business, the elderly grandmother came crying to him, saying that she was too old to stop her daughters from abusing the boys. After a desperate call from the boys' mother in the United States, Faviola brought the three boys and their sister back with her to Oaxaca. Shortly thereafter, the sister ran away, back to Mexico City, to live with a boyfriend. At the time I visited the family, the boys had not seen either their mother or their father, who lived in Mexico City, in more than a year.

The boys' mother continued to send money for their support, now to the family in Oaxaca. Faviola explained: "We didn't make an agreement like they did in Mexico [City]. We did it to help her out. We told her to send what she can and that she shouldn't worry because here her children are going to eat; they won't go hungry." Faviola's family was motivated in part by their religious commitment as Jehovah's Witnesses. However, supporting three additional boys put financial strains on the family budget. When I interviewed the family at the end of February, Faviola told me that the boys' mother had last sent about 550 dollars before the holidays. The money had since run out. Faviola's father drove a truck that transported local residents to the nearest big city, but much of the time his salary went to repairs on the vehicle. Faviola and her sister earned modest incomes as part-time community educators, but Faviola also had a number of medical expenses related to her chronic illness. Moreover, Faviola has two younger siblings, so the combined family income had to support five young children and four adults. When I asked Faviola if caring for the boys is ever a burden, she explained:

> No, it is not a burden. But it does affect us as a family. My other little sister got really jealous when they first arrived. And the littlest one felt bad because I couldn't bring him things like I used to. Before, when I got paid, I would always bring him something small. But now I would have to bring five and that is too many. For example, the other day I was in a good mood and I invited the kids to an ice cream. But they all picked the ones on the cones, which are like seven pesos [seventy cents] each. Then we had some too. In the end, I spent about fifty pesos [five dollars] only on ice cream.

Within a year, the three boys were no longer living in Oaxaca. The crisis support Faviola's family provided could only be temporary owing to the precarious nature of her family's economic situation. In this case, like others, the migrant mother resolved the financial conflicts by sending for her children as quickly as she could. However, the instability of the care arrangement, albeit short-lived, came with a price; as I have previously described, the boys were quite emotionally distraught over the upheaval they experienced after their mother's departure.

Jealousy

When children stay with grandparents, money does not cause such conflicts. Unlike reports from the Caribbean, where financial support is key to children's experiences in their grandparents' homes, none of the grandparents I interviewed complained that migrant parents did not send enough money.[39] They did acknowledge that remittances were insufficient, but they did not blame migrant parents for the lack of funds. Although some grandparents questioned single mothers' romantic involvements in the United States, they were entirely sympathetic to the financial difficulties faced by their migrant children. One grandmother, for example, said that she did not receive enough money to cover the costs of raising four grandchildren. However, her main complaint was, "My poor daughter is over there suffering for her children, and they don't know how to take advantage of her sacrifice."

Instead, tension between migrant parents and grandparents arises most often over children's loyalties. Grandparents recognize biological parents' rights to their children and tend not to flaunt children's attachment to them as compared to their lack of warmth toward their parents. Yet migrant parents feel upset over their children's affections for their grandparents and feel that they cannot complain about it. Migrants have to balance allegiance to their own parents and also to their children, which at times is very difficult to do.

Nydia's problems managing her relationships with her parents, children, and husband illustrate this difficulty in finding balance. Nydia had decided to migrate to New Jersey to reunite with her husband, who had been away for a little over a year. She had worked as a teacher prior to migration, traveling to a town nearly three hours from her home every week and leaving her son, Kevin, with her parents. So when Nydia migrated, Kevin stayed with his maternal grandparents.

When I met Nydia, she was pregnant and had recently left her job as a waitress. Nydia and her husband, Carlos, who worked in landscaping, had decided that after the birth of their second child, they would return to Mexico to reunite the family. In our first conversation, Nydia said, "Sometimes there is a little distance between us, and he doesn't want to talk [over the phone]. When I was there, he was a little closer to me."

Nydia's mother, Doña Ana, emphasized how important four-year-old Kevin was to her and her husband when I visited the family in the coastal town where they lived. Kevin's parents were going to send for him, and Kevin didn't want to go. Doña Ana said she and her husband, too, felt that he shouldn't go, because if the boy left, her husband would grow ill. She said her husband is very close to the child because Kevin has always lived with them, and her husband has helped take care of him. On one visit, when Nydia took Kevin to see his other grandparents for a week, Nydia's father was sick with worry the whole time. Nydia sometimes questioned her father about this, wondering why he wasn't as loving with her when she herself was little. Doña Ana has tried to explain to Nydia that he was simply busy working.

I had visited Doña Ana in mid-October. Nydia, Carlos, and their new baby, true to plan, returned home in December. I spoke with Nydia a few times over the phone, learning she had difficulties with Carlos after coming home. That March, I visited Nydia again. She explained her separation from Carlos, saying that she refused to leave Kevin again, but she also felt she could not take the boy away from her parents. Carlos, however, would not stay with her parents and went back to live with his own family. She explained: "The first time, I left my son for my husband. This time I will stay with my son." Nydia did not consider taking Kevin from her parents. Doing so would have permanently damaged her ties with them.

Nydia's experience shows how children's attachment to their grandparents can create lasting tensions within a family and even contribute to the dissolution of a marriage (although their separation had multiple causes, as Nydia and Carlos had experienced earlier conflicts). In this case and others, tensions arising from jealousy do not erupt in overt conflicts, as when parents and other relatives dispute the financial terms of the child care arrangement. Rather, jealousy is an undercurrent to the relationship that increases the longer a child remains with a grandparent. In fact, neither Nydia nor Doña Ana explained their problem as one of jealousy, although I believe their actions exhibit conflicting claims over four-year-old Kevin's loyalties.

Of Health and Old Age

Grandparents are aware that their declining health poses a risk to their ability to look after their grandchildren. One grandmother, who described enjoying her grandson's attachment to her, explained: "I am conscious that he is not my son. I recognize this. It would make me happy that he would live with his mother. Because I am old. Maybe right now I am strong, but I will not always be like this. And as the boy grows up, and I grow old, he is going to need his mother." Like tensions over children's affection, the declining health of grandparents typically does not lead to outright conflicts in families.

During interviews, many grandparents spoke of their health as limiting their capacity to care for their grandchildren. One sixty-nine-year-old grandmother who lived with her seventy-three-year-old husband told me, "Since we already finished raising our children, yes, sometimes it is tiring to be doing this again, caring for and educating them." Another grandmother, in her fifties, who cares for four grandchildren and two of her own teenage children, also complained: "Sometimes I feel desperate because there are so many, and I already went through mine. But really it is because there are so many of them. Sometimes I don't even have anything to give them to eat." A sixty-eight-year-old woman caring for grandsons ages seven and eleven offered: "Oh yeah, I get tired, how wouldn't I? But what else can I do? I wash their clothes, I grind—yes, I grind my tortillas by hand still. . . . Sometimes I think I'll be watching grandkids until I am ten feet under." Most grandparents want to care for their grandchildren, even though it becomes increasingly difficult to do so over time. One grandmother told me, "Sometimes it is hard with all these kids here, but I love them and I want them to stay. I wouldn't change anything, because this way there is more love in the house."

Curiously, migrant parents in the United States did not describe the health or exhaustion of grandparents in Mexico as a cause for concern. However, grandparents' health does cause conflict between migrant parents and other family members.[40] Ofelia, for example, complained that her mother was too old to look after the three young children of her cousin who had recently migrated. Nicandra recounted that her siblings were upset when she migrated and her mother moved in with her children. "They [her siblings] did not agree, because they said it was my responsibility. They said that my mother could not be in charge of them because she was too old. The criticism of my siblings was very difficult. But at the same time, in my house my mother did not work. And, in her house, she did. She was always working. So they said she was too old for it, but nobody did anything to keep her from working before."

I encountered surprisingly few cases in which grandparents actually fell ill while caring for grandchildren. Mostly, it appears that migrant parents assess health issues prior to their departure. For example, one migrant mother said she left her children with their paternal grandparents because they were younger and more physically fit than her own parents, whom she otherwise would have preferred as caregivers. Grandparents' health mostly becomes problematic when aging grandmothers are unable to look after teenage grandsons.[41] Nico's grandmother could no longer effectively monitor the teenager's activities after her stroke. In Nicandra's case, her mother—also a single mother—had trouble controlling ten-year-old Miguel and thirteen-year-old Tony when she moved in after Nicandra migrated. Both boys described periods of gang involvement after their mother left, although in a city where this is common, they might have done the same had their mother been present. Eventually the grandmother passed away, and Nicandra's children remained in the family apartment on their own.

Despite evidence of these grandmothers' failing health, their ability to care for their grandchildren did not create overt tensions with migrant parents, although the migrants' siblings did complain, as did some neighbors. Nonetheless, the risk of being unable to live up to their responsibilities because of ill health constantly preoccupied the grandmothers I interviewed.

The Potential Costs of Conflict

The sources of tension in caregiving arrangements affect relationships between migrants and the people watching their children in Mexico. They also have real consequences for the children. Most children, I found, lived with caregivers who loved them, but this did not mean that children's home environments were free from conflict. As the examples in this chapter show, when care arrangements are full of tension, children in extreme cases may face the risk of abuse or neglect. This was true in the case of Nico (see chapter 5), whose grandmother's health had deteriorated significantly. It was also the case for the three brothers—Eric, Edwin, and Osvaldo—whose family fought over money matters. Indeed, child maltreatment is a threat to child well-being globally, and especially in Mexico and in the United States, where one study shows nearly identical rates of child death from maltreatment, rates that are much higher than in nearly all other industrialized nations.[42] Although I did not specifically seek out stories of child abuse (nor would I have received accurate reports using my methods), I do not believe that child abuse and neglect are as big of a problem as we might expect given news stories about unaccompanied migrant children fleeing violence to join parents in the United States.[43] Most children live with grandparents, and perpetrators of child maltreatment tend to concentrate among younger age groups.[44] More research is needed to shed light on the prevalence of child maltreatment among transnational families. Nonetheless, this study suggests a pattern in which children are at greater risk of maltreatment when tensions in child care arrangements are high. Stress in child care arrangements can have a negative impact on children.

Stress in child care arrangements also can have negative consequences for aging caregivers. Research findings on health outcomes among custodial grandparents in the United States have been mixed, with some showing poorer health outcomes among grandparent caregivers and others finding little to no difference in overall health.[45] "Caring for a grandchild will affect a grandparent's health," proposes one study of grandparent caregivers, "to the extent that it affects the balance of resources and demands in grandparents' lives."[46] For grandparents caring for the children of migrants in Mexico, there appears to be a considerable shift over time in the balance between resources and demands. When children are young, they require a lot of physical care, but parents ensure that grandparents are fit enough at the time of migration to meet these physical demands. Grandparents caring for young children describe great emotional rewards from the arrangement and also benefit from their access to remittances. Care for older children does not have as many physical demands, but it requires a great deal of emotional energy, as caregivers who look after teenagers are likely to experience higher levels of conflict related to authority disputes and children's conflicting loyalties. And with time, grandparents' health is more likely to decline, as they themselves grow older. Although my data are limited, I suspect that negative health outcomes for caregivers are likely to be highest among grandparents who are older and those who look after adolescents. Moreover, tensions in child care relationships at this stage are likely to have a spiraling effect, with caregivers' health problems making them feel ineffective in being able to properly care for teenage children, who, in turn, find they lack oversight and engage in more problem behaviors, furthering the stress they and their caregivers experience.

Remarkably, given how prominent the behavioral problems among children of migrants are and their potential consequences, neither caregivers nor migrant parents described children's behavior as a source of conflict in the child care arrangement. Clearly, children's behavioral difficulties affect the adults in their lives, and ambiguous lines of authority can be a problem for both parents and caregivers. Although caregivers—like other family members—may be critical of migrant mothers for not living up to gender expectations of caregiving from a distance, they did not typically complain that the children in their care acted badly because migrant parents had abandoned them. Nor did migrant parents fault caregivers—whether relatives or grandparents—for the behavioral problems their children experience. This is interesting because many neighbors, teachers, and administrators blame both parents and caregivers for children's behavior.[47] Although tensions with caregivers may have negative consequences for both children and caregivers, they do not undermine the basic logic of parents' migration as a sacrifice for the sake of children to the degree that might occur if family members openly complained about the adequacy of the care children received.

RECIPROCITY IN CHILD CARE

Child care networks are fundamentally based on reciprocity. "Network members," writes Karen Hansen, "evaluate situations and assess each other's commitments, 'needs,' intentions, reliability, and capacities in light of their own. Through this process of perception, valuation, and interpretation, they negotiate reciprocity."[48] Once migrant parents identify caregivers, the resulting reciprocal relationships—or norms of exchange—differ depending on whether grandparents or other relatives remain with children in Mexico.

As I summarize in the accompanying table, other relatives feel motivated to care for children out of obligation to migrant parents. Similar to families in West Africa, the arrangement is not so much about children as it is an agreement between parents and "pro-parents," in this case, other relatives.[49] Since they offer (reluctantly) to take care of children in exchange for the migrant parents covering the costs of children's care, the remittances migrant parents send are the key aspect of the arrangement. Given the emphasis on exchange between parents and other relatives, both parties scrutinize this explicitly defined exchange according to norms of equity. Disagreements over the equity of the arrangement are common, particularly as children grow older and can report on expenditures to migrant parents. Significantly, a wider range of relatives, including aunts and uncles, cousins and in-laws, may intervene in attempting to regulate and monitor the financial arrangements. Monetary exchange forms the basis of the reciprocity among those with limited financial resources. Child care arrangements with other relatives are overtly exchange-based. They are also often conflictive.

In contrast, when grandparents are the caregivers, the lines of obligation that motivate the arrangement are more complex. Grandparents feel obligated both to migrant parents and to their grandchildren. Migrant parents feel they are able to fulfill economic obligations to their parents and to their children simultaneously.[50] Grandchildren also may be able to fulfill certain obligations to their grandparents by providing them with companionship during old age. The expectations of exchange

Reciprocity in Relationships with Caregivers in Mexico

	Grandparents	*Other Relatives*
On leaving	Grandparents encourage migrant parents to leave grandchildren in their care.	Relatives are reluctant to take on the responsibility for the children.
Main actors	Arrangements involve intergenerational obligations in multiple directions between grandparents, parents, and children.	Arrangements are primarily between adults: namely, migrant parents and other relatives. Other family members are often involved.
Economics	Grandparents depend on migrants' remittances but don't feel they can stake claim to the remittances unless in the name of the children in their care.	Economic exchange of remittances for child care expenses is at the heart of the relationship.
Emotions	Grandparents are emotionally tied to grandchildren but do not believe their bonds to children negate parental rights.	Relatives try to avoid emotional bonds to children (usually unsuccessfully).
Influence	Grandparents can wield influence on migrant parents' decisions.	Relatives feel powerless to influence migrant parents.
Conflict	Conflicts are covert and related to grandparents' declining health and children's bonds to grandparents.	Conflicts are overt and related to the use of remittances.

embedded in these kin obligations are also more complicated.[51] Unlike the overt economic exchange with relatives, money matters are more implicit, since family members expect emotional bonds to trump financial ones. Emotional bonds may substitute for economic exchange, especially during periods of financial instability common during periods of separation, particularly for single mothers. A frequent interchange between the economic and emotional logic of reciprocity means these arrangements are often more durable in the transnational context, and they are highly cooperative.

DOING FAMILY

"Families," write Deborah Bryceson and Ulla Vuorela, "are imagined communities."[52] What part do caregivers play in the ways Mexican families imagine themselves in the transnational context? Mexican caregivers, either other relatives or grandparents, have two options in the roles they assume with the children in their care. They can become "substitute" parents of sorts, adopting parenting duties of nurturance, training, and sponsorship.[53] Or they can act as middlewomen by temporarily taking over only the "tasks of nurturance" while parents are away.[54] Given the differences in reciprocity and obligation when grandparents care for children as compared to relatives, we might not expect that both grandparents and other relatives adopt roles as middlewomen. Yet neither attempt to displace biological parents' rights to their children. Both kinds of caregivers are intermediaries in these relationships. As such, extended family ties in Mexican families ultimately support and reinforce parent-child obligations during migration.

Care arrangements with other relatives are generally short-lived. Other relatives may decide to care for children out of pity toward the parents or in order to gain some access to remittances. While they do feel attached to the children, they feel powerless in shaping migrant parents' decisions regarding the care of the children. Given the economic expectations underlying the arrangement, it is not in relatives' interests to alienate migrant parents on emotional grounds. Doing so would jeopardize access to the remittances. Because a general air of mistrust between relatives and migrant parents predominates, parents often strive for reunification as quickly as possible. So, for example, by the summer of 2005, Eric, Osvaldo, and Edwin were all reunited with their mother in the United States, ending a rather difficult year and a half of hardship after she migrated. Similarly, neither of Paula's children continues to live with her uncle; both chose to be independent once they came of age. When relatives care for migrant parents' children, child care arrangements tend to be highly fragile, spurring migrant parents to keep periods of separation from children as short in duration as possible.

Grandparents are more willing caregivers for children and may assume the caregiver role for a longer period. Even so, grandparents remain as intermediary caregivers and prefer to relate to the children in their care as grandparents, rather than as parents. Grandparents are reluctant to physically discipline their grandchildren and are indulgent toward them, which may cause disciplinary conflicts during adolescence, when children of migrant parents seek more personal freedom in their lives. Particularly given the constraints of aging, grandparents prefer to enjoy the affection of their grandchildren without carrying the full weight of responsibility for their development. Grandparents also feel obligated to their own children, the migrant parents. Grandparents do not pressure migrant parents for funds, even though they often feel they lack sufficient economic resources, and research indicates that the elderly in Mexico are badly in need of financial support from their children. To their grandchildren they often praise the parents' sacrifice. They constantly highlight their grandchildren's need for biological parents and acknowledge biological parents' rights to their children. Grandparents do not want to undermine migrant parents' efforts; they are, after all, their own children, and grandparents hope to support their endeavors to care for their family, albeit from a distance. Despite young children's practices of calling grandmothers "mama," rarely do these women consider themselves their grandchildren's mothers. Instead, they too position themselves as middlewomen in the transnational caregiving relationship.

As middlewomen, both grandparents and other relative caregivers bolster an ideological model of the Mexican family in which the parent-child bond is paramount even when international borders separate parents and children. They enable parents to leave their children and do not try to replace the parents in the children's lives. As intermediaries, caregivers suggest that the ultimate reunification of parents and children is not only a possibility but also a probability.

According to Margaret Nelson, not only do women and men, boys and girls, "do gender" in their ongoing interactions; they also "do family" in the ways they construct meaningful family relationships.[55] When parent-child obligation is the primary definition of the family even when parents and children live apart, family members reinforce a specific definition of the family as composed primarily of mothers' and fathers' commitments to their children. This nuclear family ideal is striking, because scholars typically describe Mexicans as placing high value on extended family ties and Mixtecans, specifically, as including friendships in their definitions of their families.[56] It is also striking because parents and children are not actually living together; they do not interact on a daily basis as the ideal nuclear family does. In some families whose living arrangements differ from dominant cultural norms, such as those of lesbian and gay parents in the United States, family members may create new meanings of kinship.[57] I find, however, that like the single mothers whom Margaret Nelson interviewed, "although circumstances might require doing family in complex and even atypical ways," parents and children divided by borders "sustain quite traditional ideological notions of what a family is and should be."[58] Like the expectations that mothers be caregivers and fathers be providers, a rather singular notion of the family as composed primarily of parents and children exists when parents and children live apart.

An emphasis on parent-child ties in Mexican migrant families is not a reflection of the persistence of cultural values of the family during migration. Cultural values of familism do influence the choices families make about child care when parents migrate, as does the "tangle of reciprocity" involved in these relationships.[59] However the "doing of family" in a way that reinforces parent-children ties during periods of separation has less to do with the strength of cultural values and more to do with the way families set up child care networks across borders, the reciprocity of such arrangements, and the expectations of parents and children that continue during periods of separation. Mothers continue to be caregivers from a distance and fathers continue to be providers because of the way family members interpret parental absences or "do gender" in their interactions. Likewise, family ties are strong in Mexican transnational families because family members, including middlewomen who have their own stakes in the relationship, "do family" in a way that highlights parents' sacrifices for children.

Lola's room (top) and Cindy's room. Photographs by Joanna Dreby

SEVEN Cindy Rodríguez between Two Worlds

January 2005. It was my second visit to the Mexican home of migrant Paula Rodríguez's cousin, Pedro, his wife, Blanca, and their daughters, Lola and Jessy. Paula's fifteen-year-old daughter, Cindy, lived with the family, as Cindy's older brother, Mateo, had done previously. The family lived just four blocks up the hill from the center of the city (a sign of status in small cities in Mexico) in a house perched on the side of the hill. The street-level entrance was through the storefront—a turquoise painted and tiled room filled with vegetables and fruit. Through the store was the living room. Out the back, stairs wound down to a spacious backyard patio and the kitchen; a balcony walkway led to a large covered garage and the stairs to the second floor.

After a late night of food and festivities, the next day I woke up to fully take in the surroundings of the second-floor bedroom where I had slept.

There was no door to the room, just an archway of bricks opening onto another bedroom with bunk beds, where eight-year-old Jessy had slept with her cousins the night before. The rooms were quite beautiful; the walls were painted peach, and new tile shone from the floor. Downstairs I found seventeen-year-old Lola watching TV, and I asked about the house. She told me the second-floor addition had been built two years earlier. There were four bedrooms upstairs, as well as a bathroom, and they also had added the covered driveway where the party had been the evening before. I asked about who slept where. "Well, my parents sleep in the master bedroom, and I have the front room. My sister, Jessy, sleeps where the bunk beds are, and when Mateo was here, he used to sleep in the bed where you stayed last night."

"What about Cindy?" I asked.

"Oh, her room is downstairs, by the kitchen. She didn't want to move upstairs with us."

As we talked, I looked at the family photographs decorating the living room walls. There were a handful of portraits of Lola from her *quinceañera.* In New Jersey, Paula had told me about the party, complaining that she had yet to be repaid for helping to finance the extravagant event. I saw pictures of Jessy as a baby and a number of shots of Blanca and her family dressed in the traditional garb of the Isthmo region of Oaxaca. There were also some photos of Pedro and Blanca's wedding. Notably, there were no portraits of Paula, nor pictures of Paula's son, Mateo, who had been raised in the home. And there were no images of Cindy displayed on the walls.

Later I returned upstairs to look again at the new rooms. Each had the same fancy tile and brightly painted peach walls. In Lola's bedroom was a set of new white furniture, adding to the cheery decor. After breakfast, I asked for Cindy and learned that she was in her bedroom. I went to look for her and found that the only entrance to the ample room was a curtained doorway off the kitchen. Tarnished blue and white tiles and turquoise blue walls matched the decor of the living room and the store above. However, the blue paint was faded and had peeled off in a number of places. Cindy had attempted to cover the spots with posters of school projects. Despite being a comfortable space as compared to many I had seen in other Mexican homes, Cindy's room was markedly dreary compared to the rest of the family's living quarters. I was struck by what seemed to be a Cinderella phenomenon, albeit of Cindy's own choosing. While her mother was away, Cindy preferred to live apart from the others, in the dark, windowless first-floor room by the kitchen: the servant's quarters. She appeared to feel that she was different from the others in her family.

OUT OF PLACE

When caregivers act as middlewomen and parents are thousands of miles away, where do children of migrants fit? To which family do they belong? Where do their allegiances lie? Cindy's experiences suggest that some children feel that they do not truly fit anywhere. As middlewomen, caregivers constantly remind children of the important roles migrant parents play in their lives. Children expect fathers to provide for them and mothers to care for and love them even when these expectations go unmet. They expect that parents' migration will make their lives better in Mexico, even when they have difficulties living up to their parents' educational expectations. Meanwhile, children living with grandparents love their caregivers dearly, but as they grow older, they become aware that their aging grandparents cannot offer them the same support that their parents could, such as helping with schoolwork. Children living with other relatives are often in these homes temporarily and may feel like outsiders. Even Cindy, who was born and raised in Pedro and Blanca's home and loved them like a second set of parents, was at some level uncomfortable in their home. She felt different, in limbo between two families: the one she imagined with her mother and the one of her day-to-day interactions.

The sacrifices of migrant parents like Paula reinforce parents' symbolic role in their children's life even when they are not present on a daily basis. The terms of this sacrifice create a "cultural construct" of kinship in which parent-child ties are symbolically central.[1] During periods of separation, parents come to matter more than ever, making children feel even more distraught about their parents' absences. Meanwhile, the lack of temporal coordination between migrant parents' lives in the United States, where meeting goals is extremely time-consuming, and the lives of their children in Mexico, who change dramatically during periods of separation, intensifies children's disappointment in their parents over time and their feelings that their lives are somehow inadequate without them.

Paradoxically, Cindy's experiences also suggest that what resolves the feeling of a life in limbo is the passage of time. Over time, children like Cindy come of age and start their own families. Indeed, the lives of the daughters and sons of migrants unfold in different ways while a parent is away. Although gender does not significantly shape children's experiences at young ages, gender matters when children grow older. As Cindy's experiences illustrate, young men—like her brother, Mateo—are often better able to take advantage of a parent's social capital and migrate north, reuniting with their parents more quickly than young women are able to. Daughters, in contrast, are likely to remain in a state of limbo for much longer or until they find an outlet by forming a new family, often while they are still young. Just as migrant mothers experience the greatest burdens of transnational parenting, so too over time daughters struggle disproportionately to manage a life in limbo between two families.

SURMOUNTING POVERTY

March 2004. Paula grew teary when I first asked if I could interview her about her two children in Mexico. Still, she agreed to the interview, which we scheduled for a Tuesday morning. Since Paula worked two full-time jobs at two different fast-food restaurants, that was her only day off from her seventy-hour per week work schedule. Walking by a dark blue sheet that had converted the living room into an extra bedroom, we sat in the meticulously clean kitchen in the first-floor two-bedroom apartment of a house by the train tracks in an upscale New Jersey town. At the kitchen table, Paula recounted her story.

A heavy-set woman with kind eyes, Paula had come to New Jersey about five years earlier with the help of her sister; she had two children, a boy, eighteen, and a girl, fifteen, whom she supported in Mexico. She was one of six siblings, all of whom were in the United States. She lived with her boyfriend in New Jersey; one sister lived nearby, a brother lived in Queens, and three brothers lived in Texas. The family was originally from outside of a small city in the state of Puebla. Paula studied the six years of *primaria*, or grammar school, and after that she did not work—but rather helped her mother out at home.

Suddenly, Paula started to cry, not profusely, but by closing her eyes and squinting. She said she felt ashamed about her past. After taking a moment, Paula explained that she had met the father of her children when she was about eighteen. When her daughter was only eight months old, he left her. She felt embarrassed because he left for no reason. One day he went away and did not tell her why. As far as she knows, to this day he has not remarried and lives with his parents. He is not in contact with her, and her children do not know their father.

More than a year later, I learned more details of these early years from Paula's relatives in Mexico. Paula had been living with her mother in a small town when she got pregnant by a neighborhood boyfriend. Paula's mother was furious about the pregnancy. A cousin, Pedro, offered Paula refuge at his house in the nearby city. Since Pedro and his wife, Blanca, worked as schoolteachers, Paula stayed at their home throughout her pregnancy in exchange for housekeeping duties. When the couple had a daughter a year later, Paula helped with child care as well. Then she got pregnant again and continued to live with her cousin's family. Paula told me that by this time she could not go back home to her mother, who was struggling alone since Paula's own father had died while she was just a child.

About a year after Paula's daughter was born, she met four women through her cousin who were planning to migrate. She decided to try her luck, like her brothers had before her, in *el norte*. "Why didn't you go to your brothers already living in Texas for help?" I asked Paula. "Well, you see, my pride has never folded. Ever."

Paula went to the state of Washington in 1989, leaving her four-year-old son, Mateo, and her one-year-old daughter, Cindy, with her cousin Pedro and his wife, Blanca. There she lived with the relatives of one of her travel companions and got a job at a McDonald's restaurant. As she worked both the opening and closing shifts, Paula was home during the middle of the day and cooked for the family she lived with in exchange for her share of the grocery bill. By cutting daily living costs to a minimum, Paula was able to send 150 to 200 dollars a week home for the care of her kids. This was necessary because Blanca had to hire help to care for the children in her absence.

When I interviewed Blanca in Mexico, she described the turmoil surrounding Paula's first departure. Although Paula had discussed the possibility of migrating with Blanca and Pedro, she, like most migrants from Mexico who cross the border without proper documentation, did not know the specific departure date. When the time for departure came, Blanca and her husband were away on vacation with their daughter and Paula's oldest son Mateo. "When we came back, she was gone. She left the baby [Cindy] with a neighbor until we got back. . . . Paula was only away for a year, but this was a difficult time for me because we were left with three small children," explained Blanca. "The older boy was in kindergarten, and we took the younger two kids to a day care center before we went to work. Fortunately, by that time the kids were not using diapers, but it was still very hard since they were all young."

After just eighteen months in the United States, Paula went home. "I couldn't stand it," she said. "I missed my children way too much. During the time I was away, my daughter forgot about me. But when my son would get on the phone, he would ask, 'Mama when are you coming?' and 'Mama why did you leave me?'" The adjustment upon Paula's return was not smooth: both Paula and Blanca recalled that when Paula first came home, Cindy did not recognize her mother. Blanca said little Cindy eventually learned to follow her older brother's lead and began recognizing Paula as her mother again after seven or eight months.

Back with the family in Puebla, Paula moved into a bedroom adjoining the kitchen and, as before, took care of the cooking, cleaning, and child care while Blanca and Pedro were at work. Her responsibilities expanded over the next ten years that she stayed in Mexico. Blanca and

Pedro had another daughter, whom Paula helped to raise. They also set up a store selling fruits and vegetables in the front of their house, which Paula tended during the day. Paula explained with a note of pride in her voice that when she left the second time, "they closed the store [for a time] because there was no one around to tend to it."

For more than two years, Paula planned her second undocumented trip north before eventually migrating again in 1999. Paula patiently waited until her son, Mateo, graduated from the ninth grade; this time she had decided to take him with her. Blanca said Paula was insistent on taking Mateo with her, even against her advice. "I said it was going to be more difficult there with him and that what was he going to do while she worked. But she insisted on taking him. 'He, I am taking with me,' Paula said. And she did." Paula admitted that Mateo was not crazy about leaving their home in Mexico. Moreover, "My daughter often asked why [I was going to leave], but I explained to her that there was no future for me in Mexico. There I wasn't able to save any money." Paula did not want to take the younger Cindy along for two reasons. First, the expense of crossing for three people, rather than two, was too much. Second, Paula worried about the danger a young girl faced in crossing the border. "Cindy eventually accepted that I leave, but only with the condition that I go back for her after a few months."

According to Blanca, the second departure was much easier for the family in Mexico. "I was prepared. I put my younger daughter into a day care center a whole year before she left. Paula, since she had always cared for her, said, 'Oh, Blanca, don't take her there. Why, since I am here?' But this time I wanted to be prepared since I knew she would be leaving." The housework was also easier for Blanca to assume once the children were older. "I am the kind of person that always did everything with her [Paula], together. We washed the clothes together, we cooked together, we washed dishes together, so that when she left, it was not so hard for me to keep doing everything."

This time, Paula moved to New Jersey with the help of her sister. Within just a day, she started working at a local fast-food restaurant. Mateo was left alone. Paula planned that he would attend high school during the day and even spoke to her manager about a part-time position in the evenings.

But they arrived in New Jersey in July, giving Mateo almost two months with little to do. Quickly he decided he did not like the United States or where he lived with his mother in New Jersey. According to Mateo, it was really hard to be away from his family home. "It really isn't the same to be with your mother than it is to be living with everyone in the family. . . . It was really hard for me to get used to the way of life" in the United States. That fall, Mateo never signed up for high school. Instead, he turned to an uncle in Texas, who offered to take him in and cover all the costs associated with a high school education. "The opportunity arose for me to study in Houston, and that was how I saw it, as a great opportunity that I should take." Mateo left for Texas that January.

Mateo completed two years of high school in eighteen months by going to summer school. However, he still disliked living in the United States, "so much that he would call me crying," explained Paula. Mateo decided it would be best to return to Mexico to study. Before leaving for Mexico, Mateo moved back in with his mother in New Jersey. He worked as a cashier at a fast-food restaurant for four months at six dollars per hour. Paula said she felt bad when her son left for Texas, "mostly because of his rejection after I brought him here. But when he left for Mexico, it hurt more, because I knew the separation would be more permanent."

Paula said her daughter, Cindy, felt jealous about having been left in Mexico. "I didn't really realize this until once when we were talking on the phone. Cindy blurted out, 'Mom, you don't love me because you took Mateo and not me.'" Paula explained that it is much more dangerous for a girl on the border and that life in the United States was really no good. "Eventually she understood that it wasn't that I don't love her, but that I had her best interests in mind."

At the time of my initial interview with Paula, Mateo had been back in Mexico for nearly two years and it had been five years since Paula had seen Cindy. Mateo, now fluent in English, wanted to get a college degree in tourism. According to Paula, he still needed two more years of high school in Mexico and four years of college to this end. Paula calculated six more years of schooling for Cindy, who wanted to be a schoolteacher and had just started studying at a private high school, financed by her mother's remittances. Working two full-time jobs at two fast-food restaurants in New Jersey, Paula believed she could finance both of her children's education. She expected to continue with her grueling schedule for the six years necessary to provide her children with professional degrees that could give them the independence that she never had at their age. If all went according to plan, Paula hoped eventually to return to Mexico for an early retirement.

"LEFT BEHIND"

November 2004. I met Cindy and Mateo more than six months after first interviewing Paula in New Jersey. By a stroke of luck, the day I visited, Mateo, who was living and attending school in the capital, was home for a weekend visit. During this first visit I quickly picked up on the language of the family relationships: Mateo, Cindy, Lola, and Jessy were all siblings; Blanca and Paula were the two mothers, and Pedro the father. The following excerpts from my interview with Cindy that first day reveal her emotions regarding her mother having migrated without her.

On Paula's migration: "She told us that she had to leave because, above all else, she had to support us and, also, so that when she comes back she can return to her own house and not to the house of another. . . . At first I agreed that she go because we were all going to go together. She asked me if I wanted to go, and at first I told her no because I was afraid. Later I told her yes, but then, well, it was too late."

On conversations with her mother: "She asks if we are okay and, well, about money. We don't do that so much because at school we sell tickets to get money for school supplies. And she asks if we've been to see my grandmother. She asks me how we are here and if we eat well. I tell her yes, that we are eating well. And then when we have vacations, she asks if they take us with them and how they treat us. I say that yes, because they always take me along . . . and they treat me well. . . . Well, yes I feel bad when she doesn't call, because I don't know where she lives or who she lives with, and I worry that she is going to get sick there, and we aren't going to know about it."

On the differences of living without her mother: "Before, when we would come back from school, well, she was here and then after she left, there was no one here. . . . Before, I slept with her in the same room; now I am alone. . . . You see with them [Blanca and Pedro], I cannot talk about personal things, and I don't know. I just don't like to talk to them. I don't trust them really. . . . It is hard to trust my mother over the phone; you can do it, but it isn't the same. If she was here, it would feel different.

"My mother told me that she wanted to do a big party for my fifteenth birthday, but I told her that I didn't want a party, because I didn't want to celebrate that big day without her here. . . . It feels really bad, because I see my classmates and some of my friends with their mothers and, I don't know, they go out, they talk, and I feel bad, I guess, because I cannot talk to my mother. That is why I don't like to go out much. When I see my friends, I feel jealous.

"When I have children, I wouldn't want to leave them, because it feels really bad, and I wouldn't want them to suffer. . . . For me, the money is not really important." Cindy was clear during our interview: she wanted her mother to come home. Cindy explained how she is different from her brother: "I don't think it really matters to him that she is over there—I think it is all the same to him. And, well, not for me. For me it is very exceptional—it is something really painful for me that my mother isn't here with me. He takes it much more lightly."

According to Mateo, his mother's stint in the United States is more like an investment. Mateo said he did not regret his time in the United States and that he was eager to take advantage of his mother's work so that he could study. "The truth is, it is something impossible for me to have her [my mother] here. Because then I would have to work—I would have to leave school . . . At least I want to finish my career, and then I can say, you know what, come back here. Now it is my turn. . . . If I have children someday and I have to leave them, I would do it. I think any father would do that for their children. It is not so much a sacrifice, but I see it as an investment. I know that today it is for them, and maybe one day when I am old, they will do the same for me."

OF DAUGHTERS AND SONS

January 2005. On my second visit to Paula's family in Mexico, I was in for a surprise. I walked into the house to find lying on the sofa an older woman decked in the traditional clothing of the Isthmo region, where Blanca's family is from. Across from her, and virtually everywhere in the room, were stacks and stacks of plastic baskets and buckets filled with fruit and candy. That evening, Blanca and her husband would be hosting an *acostadita,* a religiously based party. After being invited to the midday meal of goat meat with hot green salsa and corn tortillas, I whiled away the afternoon feeling slightly out of place in the festive atmosphere. Marginal to the flurry of activity around the house, mostly I sat with Blanca's mother watching TV. Hours later, after taking invitations for the party to some neighbors, Cindy joined me on the sofa. Now relaxed in a lull from the excitement, she asked if I was going to Mass. I had not known we were to go to church and was not sure how to answer until she announced that she was not going. I stayed with Cindy.

Once the rest of the family left, Cindy shared the latest news on Mateo. Just a week before, Paula had called to say she could not send money and instructed Cindy to withdraw money from their savings account. When she did, Cindy found the account balance to be only about a third of what it had been just months before. Apparently Mateo had borrowed the money and had not repaid it. Cindy suspected the unauthorized loans started in October, because she heard through the grapevine that Mateo liked to drink with his friends. "I think he used up the money buying liquor and was spending it on stupid stuff with his friends."

"Your mom must be mad," I said.

"Yeah, but I tell her it is her fault," answered Cindy. "All the time she is always giving him everything that he wants, and look how he repays her."

"And your dad and mom here?" I asked.

"My dad is furious. He is going to change all the locks."

Cindy seemed to get satisfaction from describing every last lock in the house that her father was going to change so that Mateo would not be able to figure out how to get in. "He also says he is going to go to the apartment and take away Mateo's computer and stereo to sell them to get the money back."

I never heard anything more about Mateo's alleged misuse of his mother's savings, so I do not know whether Cindy's accusations were true. True or not, they reflect Cindy's feelings that her mother had always favored her older brother. "I feel upset sometimes at my mother for not calling more often. When she doesn't call anymore, I feel like she has abandoned me. When she does call, the first thing she always asks about is my brother. She doesn't even ask about what I am doing, just, 'How is your brother?' So after this [alleged stealing of money], I told her. I said, 'Mom, you don't even call or care about me, just your son, and look what he does to you.'"

Cindy acknowledged that her mother had been responsive and was calling more often. In fact, later that evening, Paula called. She spoke briefly with Blanca, and I talked to her for about ten minutes. Then Cindy took over the phone and talked to her mother for nearly an hour before heading off to bed.

THROUGH THE EYES OF OTHERS

Despite her many reasons to feel bitter, I found Cindy to be a very pleasant young woman. She was playful with my son, Temo, and seemed quite close with her cousins who visited from Oaxaca for the party. When the rest of the family did not return from Mass by the time the first guests arrived, Cindy welcomed them into the home and offered them food and drink. She introduced me to two other women to interview who had family members abroad. To me, her difficulties seemed more related to her mother's migration than a personality trait. Her family members seemed to agree. On my next visit to Blanca and Pedro's house, accounts from both Blanca and Lola further confirmed the costs of Paula's migration for Cindy.

March 2005. After spending the day at a *quinceañera* party and visiting family together, I had the opportunity to speak with Blanca. Like Paula,

Cindy, and Mateo, she articulated the overall family narrative as one of a united front. "We have never treated them [Cindy and Mateo] differently. As you saw today, if we go to a party, we all go like one family. And it has always been this way. We all go together." But Blanca also admitted that she notes some differences between the girls. She described Cindy as the most aggressive of the three sisters. "Sometimes Cindy hits little Jessy a lot, and my other daughter, the older one [Lola], gets upset and defends her little sister. She tells [Cindy] not to hit her. I think it is because they aren't from the same blood, and that is why she hits her. In contrast, since the other two are sisters, they defend each other."

I had noticed throughout the day that Cindy seemed more affectionate with Pedro than with Blanca, and I asked Blanca if this was so. Blanca smiled. "I think so. It is because since she was little, he was the only father figure that she had. He is the only father that she knows." Blanca implied that since Cindy has a mother, her role is not as important. In line with Blanca's biological logic, I asked if she thinks it matters that he is a blood relative. Blanca nodded in agreement. "Well, yes, it is also because of the blood."

Blanca initially claimed that Cindy's aggressive behavior was a personality trait, but later she added that she thinks Paula's departure has affected Cindy more than it has Mateo, "because she is so aggressive and sometimes she seems really sad." Blanca also explained that Cindy has seemed to be affected in school. "Well last year she failed [was held back a year], and I said, 'Cindy, you have to study and make an effort at school, because your mom isn't there suffering and working so that you do nothing here. She is sacrificing herself there so that you have a better life here. You have to take advantage of her sacrifice.'"

"Do you think Cindy wants to go live with her mom in the United States?" I asked.

Blanca paused. "I would say no. One time I had problems with her because she was going out a lot. She isn't like Lola, who always comes back when she says she will. [Cindy] would go out and she wouldn't come back. So then I said, 'What are we going to do?' I told her if she keeps it up, I would call her mother and tell her to take her over there."

I asked, "And she stopped?"

"Yes, she stopped. That is why I say I don't think she wants to go there."

I got a similar version of a rebellious Cindy from seventeen-year-old Lola. Lola told me that during the upcoming holiday (Holy Week), neither she nor Cindy was going to go on vacation with Pedro and Blanca to Oaxaca. On the last visit, Cindy had spent so much time out late with her boyfriend that Pedro and Blanca got angry and prohibited the next holiday trip for both girls. "It isn't the first time that I got burned for putting my hands in the fire for her."

Lola complained that the summer before, Cindy wanted to go to the pool to be with her boyfriend. It was complicated because neither knew how to swim. But Lola went to bat for Cindy and convinced Blanca to let Cindy go. Then Cindy did not come home until after seven that evening. Now Lola was upset because Cindy was arranging for her boyfriend to come visit over the holidays while Pedro and Blanca were away. "And the worst is that she is insisting that he come and stay at the house. If she wants to do this, she could at least be proper. He can stay at a hotel, and they can visit during the day."

Lola explained that this is how she did it once. She smiled deviously, adding that Cindy was not the only one with a boyfriend in Oaxaca. Lola was also seeing a young man studying at the university. Once, she said, he came to visit her in a nearby city where her cousins lived. He stayed at the hotel, she stayed at her cousins' house, and they visited during the day. "But Cindy is so stubborn; she wants to do everything her own way."

I asked Lola, "Has Cindy always been this way, or has she changed since her mother left?"

"She has always been aggressive. When we were little, she would hit me a lot. And now in school, she also fights with the other kids."

"You mean physically?" I asked.

"Once, yes. I remember they told me that my sister was fighting, and I went to see, but I don't like to get involved in those kinds of things. I saw her all in a ball with another girl. The other girl was crying. But Cindy, she just got up and [acts out Cindy combing bangs behind her ears and with a defiant smile], like it was nothing."

"Was there a change after her mother left?" I asked again.

"When her mother left, well, we all cried. Me too, because she [Paula] was the one to watch us since we were little. We missed her a lot. And I think that, yes, although [Cindy] has always been aggressive, it has been more so since her mother left."

CHANGE OF PLANS

July 2005. After returning to New Jersey, I learned from Paula that drastic changes in the family's relationships had occurred over a period of just a few months. First, Paula told me that Mateo had dropped out of school. Apparently Paula had continued to send money to Mateo for school until she learned that he had not been studying for more than two months. She was furious: "I cut him off." It was not long after she stopped sending money that Mateo called and asked to come to the United States to join Paula. He did not want to study anymore. He wanted to work. Paula agreed to send for him and was waiting for her boyfriend to return from his trip to Mexico to help make the arrangements for the crossing. Mateo arrived later that summer and began working as a cashier at the local supermarket.

Cindy's life had also changed drastically since I had seen her in Mexico. In a rather remarkable show of independence, Cindy decided that she wanted to move away from home and go to the capital city to finish her studies, as Mateo had done. She found a family she knew from vacations in Oaxaca to offer her a room to rent with them in the city.

"I didn't want to let her go," explained Paula. "I told her it would be better for me to send for her to come here if she isn't going to put effort into her studies. But then the man [the father of the family with whom Cindy was living] told me that he went to get her and picked up her grades at the end of the school year, and she had done very well last year. He told me she is very motivated to keep studying, and so I guess we will see what happens this year."

"Do you think Cindy misses her family at home?" I asked Paula.

"What is she going to miss?" Paula retorted. "Now she doesn't have to sweep and clean and everything. She is much happier now."

October 2005. I attended a small party for Mateo's twentieth birthday. I arrived while food preparations were still in progress and had the opportunity to visit with Paula before her attentions were diverted to the other guests. When I briefly asked about Cindy, Paula looked distressed. "Is she still studying in the city?" I asked. Paula shrugged her shoulders and answered in a hushed voice: "She went off with her boyfriend."

Not long after, when the others went out for soda, Paula told me that sometime in September Cindy—again acting as an independent decision maker—had left the city to move in with her boyfriend and his family in Oaxaca. "I was really, really angry for a while. I wanted her to have a career so much! And now she just left with her boyfriend. But, since it was about a month ago, I have since calmed down."

"Do you talk to her?" I asked.

"Oh yes," she answered. "I would never abandon my daughter. I talk to her every day I have off. I don't want her to feel like she is alone. She is just so young to have gone off with her boyfriend. You know, she isn't even seventeen for another few months! I don't want her to feel like if something goes wrong, she has to stay there. She just has to say the word, and I will bring her here with me."

Paula said she spoke often with Cindy's boyfriend's mother, since she wanted to make sure that Cindy was being treated well. "I don't want her to treat my daughter badly. I tell her that Cindy isn't used to doing housework. I tell her she doesn't know how to cook, nor wash the clothes. I have asked her to be patient with my daughter. Cindy's boyfriend's mother tells me not to worry, that she is teaching her how to cook and all. But . . . you see? That is why I wanted her to have a profession . . . so she wouldn't have to cook and clean for the rest of her life."

For the time being, it appeared that Cindy might continue her studies. At eighteen, her boyfriend was not yet out of school. He had one more year before getting a degree in teaching. "He says that his uncle has a teacher's contract there in town and is planning on retiring next year, so he [the boyfriend] will take over the contract there in town.[2] But who knows? That is what he says. I don't know the family. . . . I tell Cindy that I want her to have a career, to finish school. Her boyfriend tells me not to worry and that they will try to get her a place to study there in town at the school for teachers." In the meantime, aside from learning domestic duties, sixteen-year-old Cindy planned to open a beauty salon in a house her boyfriend inherited from his grandparents that sits in the center of town.

Paula said she had misgivings about her daughter's emotional state. "You know? She told me all these things about her brother, Mateo, that he was a drunk, that he was doing drugs. And you know how terrible that feels? When Mateo came, I had a doubt in my heart whether or not my son could really have done all these terrible things that she said. But you see him here? There he is, playing at his computer."

She pointed toward Mateo, who was in sight but in another room sitting at the computer with my son, Temo, watching a movie. "That is all he does. He works here at the supermarket, and he also has a part-time job with me at the McDonald's. Then, in the afternoons, he comes back and is at home, like this, playing with his computer. My sister and others say, 'Listen, Paula, if Mateo was into drugs and other things like that, do you really think he could be so calm for all these four months that he has been here? Don't you think,' they say, 'that if he was into those things he would be bored, nervous, and anxious all the time?'"

As for Cindy, Paula said she felt that all she could do now was to support her daughter. "For me, right now, the most important thing is to be in communication with her. I don't want her to feel that she is alone in this. I am her mother, and no matter what happens, I have to support her. But you know, I wanted her to have a professional career so much."

Paula had been stirring the chicken she was boiling on the stove. Now she came to sit at the table next to me. "And you know what hurts the most?" she added. "I feel like I have been a bad mother. I feel guilty—I think to myself, maybe if I had been there when she needed me, watching her, all of this would not have happened."

UNINTENDED CONSEQUENCES

In many ways, Paula beat the odds stacked against her as a single teenage mother in rural Mexico. Paula went from being a house servant for her cousin to being able to pay for a private education for her two children. Had she stayed in Mexico, she never would have been able to provide her children with the opportunities they received. Nor would she have achieved the level of independence and self-worth that I believe migration provided her as an individual. Moreover, after her first trip to Oregon, Paula took painstaking efforts to plan her migration in order to lessen the impact of her absence on her children. She waited through what she deemed to be important years before migrating a second time. She believed the best course of action would be to take her older son with her so she could provide him with opportunities in the United States. Afraid of the border crossing for her daughter, Paula left Cindy with the same people with whom she had lived all her adult life.

Despite Paula's careful planning and the opportunities her migration gave her children, her absence had unintended consequences. Cindy had difficulties in school while her mother was away, being held back one year. Cindy—according to her family members—was aggressive and had some behavioral problems. She did not live up to her mother's expectations of academic achievement (at least not on the time line her mother had proposed) and instead dropped out of school and went to live with her boyfriend at the age of sixteen. For Cindy, Paula's migration was not a success story.

I believe that one of the reasons Cindy had difficulties while her mother was away was that she experienced feelings of dislocation from living in someone else's home without a mother to give her a sense of having her own family. Cindy did not feel the same as her cousins Lola and Jessy, despite her caregivers' efforts to treat all the children equally. Cindy's pictures were not on the living room wall. She chose to live in the basement room by the kitchen. Cindy might have felt different had she lived with a grandparent, as many other children did. Yet when children live with grandparents, there are other issues, like the generation gap, that may make children feel disconnected from them in a similar way. Grandparents are family, but they are nonetheless family once removed. Children are clearly aware that their grandparents relate to them differently than their parents would. Unlike children living apart from parents for other reasons, such as those in long-term foster care homes, children do not look to their caregivers in Mexico to replace their parents.[3]

Cindy also felt left out of her mother's life to a greater extent than her brother did. Unlike Mateo, she had not migrated and glimpsed the world in which her mother operated. She was constantly aware of her mother's absence and felt jealous of friends who had mothers to take them shopping. Cindy felt caught between her attachment to her life in Mexico (she did not want to migrate to the United States) and her attachment to her mother. Despite all of Paula's efforts, in the end, Cindy did not feel fully a part of either her family in Mexico or the family her mother represented. It is perhaps no wonder that she decided to form her own family instead.

Kinship ties are highly symbolic.[4] The anthropologist David M. Schneider writes that "one essential problem is to chart the relationship between the actual states of affairs and the cultural constructs so that we can discover how the cultural constructs are generated."[5] Cindy's experiences illustrate the way migration engenders strong parent-child ties in Mexican families divided by borders, even when children feel disappointed and distraught by their parents' absences. Cindy felt in limbo between two families because her migrant mother, Paula, loomed symbolically large in her life. Cindy did not fully fold into Pedro and Blanca's family, because her ties to her mother, who worked in the United States to provide for her, remained strong.

The symbolic importance of migrant parents to children in Mexico is interesting, given that definitions of family ties in the region appear to be more inclusive than among U.S. families.[6] We might expect that extended families provide sufficient social support for children in Mexico. After all, when Paula was a young unmarried mother in Mexico, it was her extended family who took her in and helped her survive. Yet when mothers like Paula migrate, relationships with extended families do not suffice. Parents undertake migration for the sake of their children. The sacrifice inherent in parents' migration heightens children's awareness of parents' absences. Children may have caring adults in their lives in Mexico and live in relatively secure home environments, but this does not mean that they have stable lives while parents are away. Children of migrants experience instability over time because of the troubles they have in school, the generation gap they experience with caregivers, the emotional difficulties they have with separation and—most important—because they have a keen sense that their needs go unmet because their parents are away.

THE SHORT END OF THE STICK

April 2007. I visited Paula in the same two-bedroom apartment where we had first met more than three years before. On the surface, her life seemed similar. She worked at the same two jobs she had had since arriving in New Jersey eight years earlier. After a brief time renting a room to her sister, once again Paula was living with male boarders. She shared a room with the same boyfriend. Physically she looked the same.

Yet Paula's relationship with her children had changed. When we first met, she labored away to pay for Cindy and Mateo's education in Mexico. Now, Cindy was married. "Cindy hasn't had a baby yet, has she?" I asked Paula.

"No, it has been two years since she went to live with her husband, but not yet."

"Well, it is good that she wait; she is still young," I offered.

"Not that young," Paula answered, sounding slightly critical. "She is already nineteen." Paula's expectations of Cindy seemed to have taken a drastic turn from what they had been just a few years before.

Cindy may not have been pregnant, but Paula was a grandmother. Mateo had moved out more than a year earlier, not long after I had last seen him, to Maryland. We spoke on the phone, and I learned from him that he was not working; the twenty-one-year-old had left his job so he could spend time at home taking care of his three-month-old baby.

Cindy's and Mateo's lives had taken markedly different paths, with Cindy staying in Mexico and Mateo forging his life in the United States. This is in part because when Paula migrated she made a calculated effort to be sensitive to what she perceived to be her two children's different needs. She offered Mateo a pathway to the United States, where she believed he would safely be able to work and study and help her meet their family goals in the United States. In contrast, in part because of her fears regarding the dangers of the border crossing for young girls, Paula urged Cindy to remain in Mexico and gain a professional career there. Although neither child accomplished what Paula had hoped for them, there was a major difference between Cindy and Mateo. Mateo felt that his mother's migration was ultimately worthwhile. Cindy did not.

The newly built wall on the U.S.-Mexican border is not the only thing that divides migrant parents from their children living in Mexico. Photograph by Wesley Huber

EIGHT Divided by Borders

La consecuencia más grande de este dicho—el sueño americano—es la desintegración familiar.

The greatest consequence of the so-called American Dream is the disintegration of the family.

Thirty-year-old Paulo, whose father, Enrique, migrated while he was a teenager

Paulo's comment expresses a common sentiment about the impact of migration on Mexican families. I came across this sentiment repeatedly in interviews with teachers, in my casual conversations with Mexican immigrants and residents of San Ángel, and even in local newspapers in both New Jersey and Mexico. According to one school social worker I interviewed, "The fathers just leave, the mothers leave, and it is very worrisome that we have students who live with their grandparents. It is a severe problem." Another told me, "In some ways it is good that we have migration. Economically speaking, it is good. But it has an impact because that family member, that father [or] that brother who left, well now, it is very difficult that we get them back." An interview with an official from the Mexican Child Protective Services agency printed on the front page of the newspaper *El Sol de Tehuacán* reveals how pervasive attitudes about the effect of migration on the family are throughout Mexico. "The moment that there is a migrant father or migrant mother, the family is disintegrated. Do you know how fragile a child who doesn't have a father in the home is? There are cases in which the father leaves and maybe he sends economic resources, but in many cases he leaves and the family doesn't hear from him again, the family is left homeless."[1] In Mexico, migration is increasingly seen as the cause of the problems afflicting Mexican youth.[2] Migration is a necessary evil. The toll it takes is meted out on the family and, above all else, on the children. Families divided by borders, popular sentiment suggests, essentially fall apart.

Indeed, in this book I have documented many of the hardships parents and children endure. The consequences of family separation, I have argued, are best understood by examining how migratory processes internally divide families and affect each member of the family in different ways. And although all family members experience hardships, children and migrant mothers do so to a greater degree than do other family members. Yet I find that, contrary to the predictions of the press, community members, and even some of the family members I interviewed, these hardships do not appear to destroy the bonds between migrant parents and their children. In this concluding chapter, I suggest that paradoxically the very migration processes that strain and can potentially erode family relationships become the means by which family ties are reinforced and even intensified during periods of separation.

Recently, social scientists have begun to describe migrant families as strategically adjusting to economic circumstances, what the sociologists Phyllis Moen and Elaine Wethington call "family adaptive strategies."[3] They suggest that families prevail over the economic forces that cause tensions in their lives because families are able to react in flexible ways to such tensions by, for example, sending different members of the family into the workforce.[4] Similarly, I find that relationships between parents and children are remarkably resilient. But it is not the strength of family values that makes for enduring ties between Mexican family members when they live apart. I have shown that the hardships family members experience arise from a combination of family members' relative participation in migration and their relative position in their families. Likewise, parent-child ties persist despite these hardships because over time, migration alters family members' experiences of power within their families and their stakes in the family migration strategy.

FAMILIES DIVIDED

When parents migrate to the United States, leaving their children in Mexico, their families are internally divided by geography. Yet this decision is generally not one made out of desperation, at the spur of the moment. Rather, in leaving their children, migrant parents are both thoughtful and proactive. They take advantage of their available resources to move to a place where they can earn more for their labor. They weigh the costs and benefits of migration and decide that leaving their children temporarily is sensible, even if heart-wrenching. They consider this difficult decision a sacrifice. They hope to make the most of their sacrifices by working hard in the United States.

In *el norte,* migrant parents have access to opportunities, but in order to make these opportunities bear fruit, they live frugally, sending as much of their earnings as possible back to Mexico. They are primarily low-wage workers; nearly all in my sample were undocumented. Because of these structural constraints, parents find that their economic goals are increasingly difficult to meet the longer they are in the United States. Over time, many parents develop new personal commitments. Some marry or move in with a boyfriend or girlfriend. Many have U.S.-born children. These commitments require parents to spend a greater proportion of their meager incomes in the United States. They may send less money home.[5] Parents find their goals are ever more elusive.

Migrant parents' experiences are further divided by gender. Economic adversity affects men's relationships with their children. When men are not economically productive, they tend not to communicate with family members at home. For mothers, new caregiving commitments to U.S.-born children or a new boyfriend or spouse may erode relationships with children in Mexico. Fathers may be able to reestablish relationships with children, or at the very least feel entitled to reestablish relationships with their children, when they are able to provide for their children economically. Mothers, in contrast, have a difficult time establishing ties with their children the longer they are away from home. They feel guilty for having left their children, even when they provide financially for them via remittances. Children evaluate mothers more harshly for having left them. Migrant mothers bear the moral burdens of transnational parenting.

In contrast to parents who proactively seek opportunities in the United States, children are family dependents who do not make the decision for their parents to migrate. Many live in communities with high levels of emigration, where most productive activity occurs in the United States. They benefit to some degree from parents' remittances, but as children grow, their needs change. Children's developmental needs evolve at a fast pace; parents who have difficulties meeting their goals in the United States often feel they cannot keep up with the changes in their children's lives. Parents may send clothes back in the wrong sizes. Their mental image of their children is as they were years before. The lack of temporal coordination contributes to the problems parents and children face in their relationships from afar.

Children's reactions to parental absence are not static. Although emotionally attached to caregivers in Mexico, with time children feel frustrated when parents do not live up to their promises of what migration will provide the family in a timely manner. Children may refuse to talk to their parents over the phone, disregard parents' authority, and decline parents' offers to send for them. As teenagers, children have trouble meeting the expectation that they make their parents' sacrifices worthwhile. They may become outwardly resentful of parents and exhibit behavioral problems. They flounder in school, many either being kept back a year or dropping out, and do not meet their parents' expectations of educational achievement. These are the most distressing aspects of parents' migrations, the unintended consequences of parents' sacrifices.

Migrant parents loom large in transnational families, increasing the emotional pain children undergo while parents are away. This is in part due to the role of caregivers in Mexico. Grandparents do not replace parents. They have their own stakes in the caregiving arrangement based on intergenerational reciprocity. Grandparents enjoy caring for their grandchildren but do not want to take over parental responsibilities. They are aware that their health and physical stamina may eventually prevent them from being long-term caregivers for their grandchildren. Many struggle to look after older children who become outwardly resentful of parents and misbehave. Neither are parents replaced by caregivers who are relatives other than grandparents, such as aunts. Conflicts between migrant parents and these caregivers over financial arrangements are common, as intergenerational reciprocity does not operate. Children may find themselves at risk in the center of such conflicts. Even in rare cases like that of Cindy Rodríguez, who lived in the same home her entire life, children may not feel fully part of their caregivers' families in Mexico. Mexican caregivers do not supplant parents, because children are ever aware of parents' sacrifices; migrant parents are important to sustaining their daily lives. Children, particularly daughters who do not migrate as quickly as sons, feel in limbo between their idealized family that consists of their migrant parents and the family they interact with on a daily basis.

Mexican migrant families experience hardships because they are internally divided. Migrants live in the United States, where opportunities and lifestyle are vastly different from those of children and caregivers in Mexico. Men's and women's experiences as migrants differ, creating particular challenges for mothers. Children's experiences vary depending on their age and, as they grow up, their gender. Children's troubles are concentrated during early adolescence. Caregivers' relationships to migrant parents—as either a parent or another relative—determine their stakes in the child care arrangement, making arrangements with other relatives especially volatile for children. Each family member has a different position within the family and a different relationship to migration processes. Geography, gender, and generation determine the types of problems family members experience while living apart. Women and children experience difficulties disproportionately.

FAMILIES UNITED

One could view the deep emotional hardships that accompany family separation, including fathers' feelings of inadequacy as providers, mothers' guilt, and children's resentment, as eroding family relationships. Yet this is not the full story. Because separation heightens emotions during periods of separation, obligations between migrant parents and the children they do not live with intensify. In the end, the very same migration processes that are the source of hardship also lead family members to act in ways that promote their continued commitments to each other. This is because during periods of separation, family members' position in their families, as well as their stakes in migrant parents' sacrifices, change.

When migrant parents are away, the mother's role as family caregiver and the father's role as family provider are exaggerated. Family members evaluate parents' sacrifices by "doing gender," not only in a conventional way but also in a way that reinforces parent-child ties. Fathers feel pressured to send money back home and to continue to support their family in Mexico even when they have new commitments in the United States. Mothers feel guilty about being away and pressured to be reunited with their children as quickly as possible. Granted, migrant parents are often not able to fulfill these obligations. Yet I have found that when the difficulties that have prevented fathers and mothers from contacting children in Mexico—including marital conflict and economic insecurity—subside, many migrants attempt to reinsert themselves in their children's lives. Even though it is extremely difficult for mothers to demonstrate care from a distance, they make remarkable efforts to be reunited with their children. In fact, mothers spend less time away from their children on average than do fathers. One study of family reunification found that 77 percent of Mexican children separated from mothers prior to coming to the United States were reunited with their mothers within two years, compared to only 35 percent who were reunited with fathers within two years.[6] Of the forty-five parents I interviewed in New Jersey, mothers averaged 3.5 years away from their children, whereas fathers averaged 8.3 years away.

Although parents have a difficult time keeping up with the changes in their children's lives, feelings of responsibility to their children in Mexico do not wane as children grow older. Both mothers and fathers make significant efforts to adapt to their children's changing needs. This adaptation is not always easy. At times parents suppress their own desires to be reunited with their children, as they deem it better for their children to remain with caregivers in Mexico. The case of Ofelia and her son, Germán, is a prime example. Ofelia wanted to bring Germán to the United States, but given his resistance to the idea, she allowed him to stay with his grandmother in Mexico. Parents also modify their own goals in response to their children. This was true for Paula Rodríguez, who planned to move back to Mexico with her children once she was able to provide them with the educational and career opportunities she herself never had. Paula's plans radically changed when Mateo left college to migrate to work in the United States and Cindy dropped out of school to move in with her boyfriend.

The case of parents who divorce after migrating illustrates how migration may further accentuate parents' obligations to their children in Mexico, even when the other major feature of the family has broken. After a divorce in the United States, fathers like Armando López may actually seek to expand their role in the lives of their children in Mexico, as they are able to continue to provide for children when migrant mothers appear not to live up to the moral expectations of motherhood. Fathers' ability to earn money in the United States makes them feel entitled to their children in Mexico and free to develop more caring roles with their children, which is notable given the lack of involvement in children's lives typical of nonresidential fathers in the United States.[7] Yet even migrant mothers who transgress do not typically abandon their children. Once mothers feel their lives have stabilized, they, like Armando's ex-wife, may return for their children.

Meanwhile, while living apart from their parents, children in Mexico experience greater power in their relationships with the adults in their lives than they did prior to their parents' migration.[8] Young children's acts of emotional withholding make parents feel bad for being away and motivate parents to work as quickly as possible toward reunification. Parents may return to visit children periodically when they sense that children's loyalties are waning. They continue to call home, even if children do not want to talk to them, remaining a presence in children's lives. Teenagers' academic and behavioral difficulties oblige parents to send more of their economic resources to children in Mexico to address these problems. Although often feeling that they had little say in their parents' initial decision to migrate, children of migrant parents are able to influence parents' subsequent migration decisions and the expenditure of family resources. Children's influence on their family's migration trajectory grows even more as they become young adults. When children's resentment toward their migrant parents fades, they often take advantage of parents' social capital and pressure parents to take them north. Young men may request that parents support their migration while single. Young women may rely upon parents' social networks to migrate after having formed new families in Mexico.[9] Insecurity in parent-child relationships during separation affords children the ability to influence the adults in their lives. Children decide to migrate once they see few paths for mobility in Mexico.

Children's caregivers, too, play an important role in "doing family" when parents and children live apart in a way that supports their ultimate reunification. Whether an arrangement based on intergenerational reciprocity with grandparents or a more explicit financial agreement with other relatives, caregivers act as middlewomen, highlighting the symbolic centrality of migrant parents' sacrifice to the children in their care. Their stakes in the caregiving arrangement reinforce parent-child obligation. Physical distance resulting from migration ironically allows a singular concept of the family, defined as stemming first and foremost from the obligations between parents and children, to prevail even if on a day-to-day basis, mothers, fathers, and children do not live together and as a consequence their relationships are strained.

Parents' continued significance for children during periods of migration is highlighted in the drawings of their families I asked 423 Mexican school students in the first through sixth grades to make. When I gave the general instruction "Draw a picture of your family," 92 percent of children with both parents in the United States drew both of their parents in their picture.[10] Of the children with at least one migrant parent,

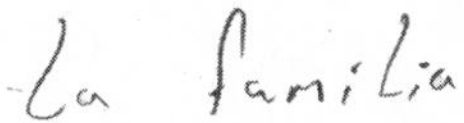

Family drawing by a thirteen-year-old boy who lives with his grandparents in Mexico. Even though his mother and father live and work in the United States, they are prominent in the drawing.

70 percent drew both parents in their picture, although they did not live with both parents and in many cases the parents had divorced or separated after migration. Of the children living without a parent because of a divorce or separation in Mexico, only 38 percent drew both of their parents in their picture.[11] Clearly, divorce or marital separation within Mexico may alter children's perceptions of their family. Likewise, children living in long-term foster care in the United States rarely depict biological parents as the primary figures in their families.[12] When parents and children live apart because of international migration, however, parents appear to be central to the ways children define their families.

Indeed, reunifications among the families I studied were common. Among the twelve families I followed most closely in this study, at the time of this writing, three-fourths had been reunited (at least in part). I am not able to calculate reunification rates across my entire sample, as my ability to follow up with all of the families I interviewed in San

Family drawing by a six-year-old girl who lives in Mexico with her mother and siblings. Her father lives in the United States but is very much a part of how she imagines her family.

Ángel and New Jersey is limited. Yet family reunification, although at times temporary, was a recurring experience. While in San Ángel, for example, eleven of the children I interviewed were either temporarily or permanently reunited with their parents in Mexico. An additional three children I interviewed in San Ángel have since joined their parents in the United States. In New Jersey, nine mothers and three fathers I interviewed have been reunited with some or all of their children during this study.

Reunification does not end the difficulties for migrant families but rather introduces new problems for parents and children, who must come to terms with the resentment and hurt separation has caused. Indeed, research focusing on immigrant adaptation in the United States suggests that parent-child relationships are a source of conflict after reunification.[13] Expectations during reunification may continue to be unmet for children, who imagine life in the United States to be affluent and secure, as well as for parents, who expect children's difficulties to dissolve once separation is over.[14] Moreover, children who have not done well academically in Mexico are likely to continue to struggle when they enter schools in the United States. Better data are needed to shed light on patterns of family reunification, especially on the timing during a child's life course, as I have shown that children's experiences of parental absence vary between preadolescence, early adolescence, and late adolescence. Another key area for future research is children's relationships with their mother and father after migration, as well as how dealings with caregivers back in Mexico evolve after children leave.

Parent-child relationships during periods of separation are not easy. Parents' sacrifices are certainly well intended, but they do not pan out as expected. The balance between work and family that parents seek via migration creates painful experiences for all members of the family and does not appear to result in educational gains for children who do not migrate. Prolonged periods of separation leave few opportunities for family members to work out their difficulties, making family relationships constantly up in the air and under negotiation. Yet during these periods of separation, family members' relative power within their families changes. So do their stakes in the family migration strategy. Over time, changing family dynamics cause family members eventually to seek reunification despite the difficulties that separation causes.

FAMILY RELATIONSHIPS IN CONTEXT

In focusing on the consequences of family separation as a migration strategy, this study describes the trajectories of the lives of migrant parents, their children, and the children's caregivers as evolving from the interplay between hardship and intense feelings of obligation. Yet Mexican parents' migration is ultimately an effort to reconcile the demands of work and family in a global economy. One way social scientists theorize the relationship between individuals' lives and broader social change is through a life course perspective. "Life-course ideas," Glen H. Elder and Monica Kirkpatrick Johnson write, "focus on the changing contexts of lives and their consequences for human development and aging. The individual life course is structured by social influences and the life choices people make in constrained situations."[15] Four key principles stand out in life course theory: individuals exert agency and chart their own life course through the choices they make, given available opportunities and constraints; individuals' lives are linked through shared social networks; the timing of events in an individual's life span matters; and historical time and place shape individuals' lives.[16] The experiences of Mexican families divided by borders illustrate these four principles.

First, during migration, mothers, fathers, children, and caregivers actively adapt to their life circumstances. None act as victims. Facing economic difficulties and drawing on available social networks, parents carefully consider their decisions to migrate without their children. Children express their frustrations at feeling "left behind" in communities that offer them few opportunities for future mobility. Lacking the benefits of a social security system, grandparents in Mexico seek their own economic and emotional benefits from family adaptive strategies. Some of their decisions may seem misguided or naive, yet family members' reactions to living apart illustrate the principle of human agency. They "do gender" and they "do family." Children exert power in their relationships vis-à-vis adults.

Second, Mexican migrant family members' lives unfold in dynamic relationship to those of other family members. Each reacts to changes in each other's lives even when living apart and, at times, when having little information about each other's lives. Children grow frustrated at parents who never seem to accomplish what they propose. Parents attempt to respond to the changes they perceive their children to be experiencing. Caregivers mediate relationships between parents and children. Even when thousands of miles apart, family members' lives are inexorably linked.

Third, the timing of separation in individuals' lives, particularly for children, but also for aging caregivers and parents, is crucial to understanding the lives of Mexican transnational families. As children age, their needs change. Parental absence has different meanings for children at different life stages. So too, as caregivers age, the benefits of the child care arrangement decrease. Even parents find their feelings about having left children in Mexico change as they adjust to life in the United States.

Fourth, historical timing helps explain family dynamics during periods of separation. I have focused much throughout this book on the interpersonal relations in families, yet features of the U.S. economy and immigration policy in the early twenty-first century create the circumstances in which family members decide to live apart and shape their experiences of separation.[17] Mexicans have migrated to the United States for years, but recently labor demands have caused an unprecedented growth of Mexican populations in new destinations throughout the continental United States.[18] Mexican women are migrating at higher rates than ever before, whether to join husbands or alone.[19] Moreover, the increasingly militarized border and the high costs and dangers of the border crossing have led more and more Mexicans to settle in the United States.[20] Circular migration patterns have decreased. Many Mexicans are unable to regularize their immigration status or migrate legally. More than half of new Mexican immigrants are undocumented.[21] I show that parents' lack of legal status contributes substantially to their decision to leave children in Mexico. Parents are not able to migrate legally with their children. Crossing the border with children is expensive and dangerous, and more so for women and daughters than for men and sons. These conditions underlie parents' decisions to leave their children in Mexico when they come to work in the United States.

Parents' status as low-wage, undocumented workers affects how their lives unfold in the United States. Financial difficulties related to low-wage work and lack of health insurance, among other things, make economic goals difficult to meet and prolong separation as parents are reluctant to return to children in Mexico without proving their sacrifices worthwhile. The lack of options to regularize their immigration status once in the United States prevents parents from sponsoring the legal migration of their children or even from having their children come visit them, possibilities for migrants living in other countries.[22] Ongoing legal restraints increase the stakes involved in parents' sacrifices. And the stakes of parents' migration increase the longer a parent stays in the United States. Many families reunite in spite of these difficulties. But the resources it takes to orchestrate such reunifications are exceedingly high. Such difficulties make the ongoing obligations between parents and children over time even more impressive.

The historical prevalence of migration between the United States and Mexico also influences the lives of children in Mexico while their parents are away. What some scholars call a "culture of migration" is pervasive in many Mexican communities where emigration is high, such as San Ángel, where I collected much of the data for this study.[23] We might expect that in such communities, parents' migrations are the norm. Family separation appears to be a particularly common experience for children, especially for those living in areas where a culture of migration predominates. One survey of 7,061 students in grades six to twelve in Zacatecas, a state in Central Mexico with a long history of emigration to the United States, found that 38 percent of students had a father who had been to the United States at least once.[24] My own surveys show that in communities in the Mixteca region of Oaxaca, nearly one in four students had one or both parents working in the United States in 2005.

Surprisingly, even when parental migration is common, not only do children feel distraught about parents' absences, but they also feel different from their peers because of it. Most of the sixty children I interviewed in Mexico said they had friends with parents in the United States. Only five children (four of whom were teenage girls) told me they talked about their parents with their friends and felt supported by their peers. Most children seemed simply to avoid calling attention to differences in their family situation. In a handful of cases, children described being teased by their peers for having a parent away. Although community emigration is a norm, children's individual experiences are not typically supported in their peer groups.

Do these children's feelings translate into different aspirations for their future as compared to their peers? We might expect that living in a place with high levels of U.S. migration would impact children's aspirations so much that their own family's migratory patterns have little to no impact on their lives. Indeed, in analyzing the surveys I collected in the Mixteca, there are no significant differences in migratory aspirations between children of migrants and children of nonmigrant parents.[25] However, differences do exist in children's educational aspirations by family migration pattern. Having a mother abroad significantly *increases* children's educational aspirations, while having both parents abroad significantly *decreases* their aspirations as compared to children with neither parent in the United States.[26] Yet having just a father abroad has no effect on children's educational goals, as compared to having neither parent in the United States. Thus, while the sole migration of fathers, a historically common pattern, is not particularly influential in shaping children's educational goals, the new migration patterns of mothers do affect children differentially. While both the culture of migration and intrafamilial experiences are important in shaping children's lives, Glen Elder has found that family resources and strategies are a better predictor of youth outcomes than are neighborhood influences.[27] In this case, it appears that intrafamilial experiences during periods of separation are more influential than community-wide factors only when mothers migrate, at the very least in terms of children's educational goals. Children of migrant mothers, in particular, may experience dissonance between their individual experiences and those of other young people in their communities, which may aggravate feelings of dislocation.

IMMIGRATION POLICY AND FAMILIES

At the turn of the twenty-first century, U.S. immigration policy has created an unprecedented situation for Mexican families. In the past, Mexican families have endured family separation of a temporary nature while one or more of their family members worked abroad. Today, however, separation has become a long-term feature of Mexican families' experiences of U.S. migration. Mothers, fathers, and children live apart for longer periods than ever before, and the consequences such separations have for families are exacerbated.

Mexicans are not, however, unique in their situation. Scholars describe other immigrant groups around the world as enduring similar experiences of family separation.[28] Yet Mexican migration is distinctive in that Mexican-U.S. migration is long-standing, and the U.S.-Mexican border is the busiest in the world. We might expect prolonged periods of family separation among Mexicans in the United States to be relatively uncommon, particularly compared to immigrants who are separated by continents and oceans. Geographic proximity and the high levels of movement across the U.S.-Mexican border, both historically and today, should give Mexican family members more choices in terms of family migration patterns. Although true to some extent, Mexicans' experiences of family separation reveal the ways that recent changes in U.S. immigration policy can have an immediate impact on family life. Some final thoughts on the policies that have resulted in lengthy family separations under the circumstances in which we would least expect them to occur are instructive on how public policy can better attend to the needs of families. My purpose here is not to provide a comprehensive review of immigration policy, but simply to point out some of the legal problems the Mexican families I interviewed faced.[29]

One of the historically exceptional features of U.S. immigration policy at the start of the twenty-first century is the emphasis on border enforcement and security. Since 2000, federal government funding for border enforcement has increased by 150 percent, and between fiscal years 2008 and 2009 alone by 19 percent.[30] Yet as the political scientist Wayne Cornelius has shown, a more difficult and dangerous border crossing has not deterred initial migration to the United States.[31] Rather, it makes the crossing more expensive and more dangerous. Moreover, Douglas Massey and colleagues demonstrate that when the border is increasingly militarized, return migration rates decrease.[32] This is not because people are desperate to live in the United States permanently but because comings and goings are expensive and difficult to arrange and require greater investment. Parents need more time not only to reach their goals in the United States but also to arrange for family reunifications. As we know from the experiences of Central Americans who must cross the dangerous southern border with Mexico, a high level of risk at the border is correlated with lengthy family separation during migration.[33] As I have shown, it also contributes to the time dislocations families experience while living apart. The militarization of the U.S.-Mexican border has not deterred migration but has increased hardships among Mexican migrant families.

A second historically unique feature of contemporary U.S. immigration policy is the lack of pathways to legal status for the estimated 7 million undocumented Mexicans living in the country as of 2008.[34] One major barrier for Mexican families is strict penalties for immigration status violations implemented in 1996. This legislation (the Illegal Immigration Reform and Immigrant Responsibility Act) instituted three-year, ten-year, and permanent bars on readmission to the United States for those who have been unlawfully present for six to twelve months, more than twelve months, or more than once (repeat offenders), respectively. Moreover, after 2001, the provision that had previously allowed immigrants to pay a fine for unlawful presence and remain in the country to adjust their status was removed. This means that an undocumented immigrant who marries a U.S. citizen, and even has children with this spouse (as was the case for two of the migrant parents I interviewed), cannot regularize his or her status without leaving the United States and being subject to the long-term separation imposed by the bars to readmission. Today thousands of individuals remain in undocumented status because of the fear of long separations, a situation that could easily be solved by reinstituting the opportunity to adjust status from within the United States.

Because laws are complicated, and in some cases waivers are available, many immigrants remain hopeful that a case can be made on their behalf, something unscrupulous lawyers, immigration "consultants" (who often call themselves *notarios*), take advantage of by submitting fraudulent or inappropriate applications.[35] Recently, for example, one migrant father told me that he and his employer split the fifteen-thousand-dollar cost of filing for his legal permanent residence status. Although in this case the application seems to have been granted, for others who receive inadequate and often expensive legal services, the end result has been deportation proceedings. A system that does not provide a coherent pathway for the undocumented to legalize their status places families in a vulnerable position and contributes to the difficult time parents have in amassing the resources necessary to reunite their families.

If U.S. employment is so necessary for Mexican parents, why then do they not come to the United States legally? A third historically unique feature of immigration policy is that there are currently very few options for Mexicans to migrate legally to the United States. There are three principal routes to U.S. immigration: work sponsorship, family sponsorship, or political/refugee status (which rarely applies to Mexicans). Using a system of preference categories, the United States limits the total number of family- and work-based immigration cases. Although the details of such limits are complex, keeping in mind that in 2008 there were an estimated 11.9 million unauthorized immigrants of all nationalities, it is useful to consider the overall limits to immigration.[36] In 2009, employment-based sponsorship for legal permanent residents was capped worldwide at 140,000, and the total number of temporary work visas was capped at approximately 85,000.[37] Although temporary agricultural visas are not capped, many Mexicans today—like all of those I interviewed in New Jersey—are ineligible for these visas, as they work in the meatpacking industry, construction, landscaping, factories, and the service industry.[38] In terms of family-based petitions, caps allot the same number of visas for those from Mexico as those from vastly smaller countries such as Haiti. This creates a backlog and means that families from Mexico can wait years for their applications to be approved, as was the case for one family in this study. For example, in April 2009, the applications being processed for Mexican unmarried sons and daughters (over the age of twenty-one) of U.S. citizens had been filed seventeen years before, in October 1992. Those for the Mexican spouses and minor children of permanent residents had been filed seven years before, in April 2002.[39] Although there are theoretically no wait times on applications for the spouses and minor children of U.S. citizens, in the experience of families in New Jersey, these applications can take anywhere from a few months to more than two years to be approved. Family reunification is one of the ideological principals underlying U.S. immigration policy.[40] However, family members are rarely able to migrate together unless, ironically, they are coming over through a work-based petition.[41]

Lengthy wait periods do not bode well for families who must remain apart for years while their applications are processed. Neither do penalties for unlawful presence, like those implemented in 1996. The sociologist Cecilia Menjívar has shown that a state of "liminal legality," or long-term uncertainty in terms of legal status, has an enormous impact on the family life of Central American immigrants, lengthening periods of separation and creating conflicts among family members.[42] Contemporary immigration policy places Mexican immigrants, who outnumber Central Americans in the United States by five to one, in a similar state of legal limbo.[43] This is particularly difficult for mixed-status families, that is, families in which parents and children do not have the same legal status. Approximately 65 percent of the children of immigrants of all nationalities in the United States are members of mixed-status families.[44]

Today, perhaps more than ever before, lacking a legal immigration status has a vast impact on family members' daily lives. According to the immigration scholar Nancy Foner, "A hundred years ago, the nature of immigration restrictions and immigrant travel meant that very few newcomers lived in New York 'illegally.'"[45] In 2009, workers in New Jersey, as in the rest of the nation, must have proof of authorization to work in the United States to be eligible for employment. After the terrorist attacks of 2001, obtaining a driver's license—a necessity in many parts of the state—has become more complex and requires various types of identification, including proof of legal status in the United States. As a consequence, many migrants find they have no choice but to drive without a license or without car insurance. Although immigrants are less likely to engage in criminal activities than are U.S. citizens, such a restrictive environment means that immigrants end up breaking an increasing number of laws by simply going about their daily lives.[46]

A rising anti-immigrant climate at the local level over the past few years has made matters worse. When I first began interviews, many parents rode to work in vans and described occasional traffic stops in which drivers were asked for proper documentation. Their experiences as passengers were at times scary but rarely led to legal problems. By 2008, however, police in areas of New Jersey were known to ask all vehicle passengers at traffic stops for proper identification.[47] Those who cannot provide identification may be reported to the U.S. Immigration and Customs Enforcement (ICE). Some towns in New Jersey, like Morristown in 2006, have taken an even stronger stance and have sought to deputize local police officers as ad hoc immigration officers.[48] Other municipalities in New Jersey, including Riverside, Middletown, and Bound Brook, have tried to criminalize the renting of homes to those without proper legal status.[49] Efforts to ameliorate barriers for migrants, such as then-governor Elliot Spitzer's 2007 proposal to offer licenses to all New York state drivers regardless of legal status to reduce the risks and costs associated with a high number of unlicensed drivers, have faced wide resistance at the local level.[50] Latino immigrants in both New Jersey and New York have been victims in a rash of hate crimes; most recently at the time of this writing, a thirty-seven-year-old immigrant from Ecuador was stabbed to death on Long Island by a group of teenage boys who had gone out looking for "a Mexican."[51] Regional tensions over immigration at the local level reflect a nationwide trend.[52] The difficulties families face on a day-to-day basis because of their undocumented status have not diminished over the past few years but rather have increased.

Moreover, today immigrants nationwide are at greater risk of a different sort of family separation—one that is enforced by the state. In the past few years, ICE raids have stepped up considerably, with a sevenfold increase in administrative arrests between 2007 and 2006.[53] In New Jersey, twice as many people were detained as a result of ICE raids in 2006 as in 2007, and deportations statewide increased 25 percent between federal fiscal years 2007 and 2008, higher than the national average.[54] When parents are detained and deported, they are often separated from their children who are U.S. citizens. Indeed, a report by the National Council of La Raza and the Urban Institute estimates that two-thirds of the children of those arrested in workplace raids between 2006 and 2007 were U.S. citizens.[55] Large-scale raids, including one in New Bedford, Massachusetts, in which 361 undocumented workers were detained in 2007, and another in Postville, Iowa, detaining 389 people in May 2008, draw attention to the social costs of raids when children are left stranded after school and without their family caregivers. Yet forced separations take a toll on families even on the smallest scale. In one case in November

2007 in Ohio, for example, a nursing mother was detained for eleven days, leaving social workers at a loss as to how to calm the nine-month-old infant, who was a U.S. citizen and had been nourished only by breast-milk until that point.[56] Since I completed this study, forced family separations have become increasingly common. The consequences for families of such direct actions by the state, and particularly on second-generation children, need to be investigated further.[57]

Underlying contemporary immigration policy is the expectation that individuals are ultimately responsible for their unauthorized status in this country. It is their fault, according to popular rhetoric, for deciding to break the law. It is, however, an outdated law that defines individuals as illegal. The logic that individuals, rather than legal structures, are responsible for immigrant status is devastating for families. This is not unlike contemporary workplace policies that do not support parents.[58] Employers in the United States want workers but do not want to support their families with family-friendly work policies. This is also not unlike the existing child care system in the United States. While education for older children is publicly funded, parents are left on their own to figure out child care arrangements for the smallest, most vulnerable children.[59] Likewise, the U.S. economy benefits from and desperately needs low-wage immigrant workers but does not want to play a role in maintaining workers' families.[60] In contrast to child care and employment policies that are piecemeal and vary by employer, industry, and state, immigration is already a federally regulated system. Immigration reform provides a unique opportunity for policy makers to put the needs of those most adversely affected by the system—families—first.

Parent-child ties intensify during periods of separation and eventually, as this study has shown, undocumented migrants manage to find ways to reunite with their children. The question is whether the United States implements laws that allow families to live together legally or perpetuates laws that make family separations and undocumented migration even more difficult and more likely. Sociologists have shown that militarizing the border and criminalizing immigrants does not keep Mexicans from coming to the United States but only changes the processes and strategies by which they do so.[61] This study demonstrates the human toll political and legal decisions have for families, women, and above all others, children. The barriers that Mexican immigrants face in obtaining legal status combined with the necessity of documents to undertake simple daily routines, create a new set of structural inequalities based on legal restrictions. These inequalities, in turn, are replicated within families who live apart. One reason that current immigration policy fails is because criminalizing immigration divides families across borders, exacting what eventually becomes an unbearable toll on families.

SUPPORTING FAMILIES

Immigration reform promises to continue to be a major policy agenda over the next few years.[62] It is my hope that future changes in U.S. immigration policy will make my descriptions of families' experiences of separation obsolete. Perhaps in ten years we will look back on the struggles of Ofelia and Germán Cruz, Armando López, and Paula and Cindy Rodríguez as arising out of a very specific historical moment in which there was a mismatch between national policy and the realities of global migration patterns. Given the recent turn toward even more punitive policies toward immigrants, I fear that the opposite might be the case. It is entirely possible that family separation will take on new forms even more difficult than those I have described in which families exert some autonomy in determining their migration patterns.

Short of broad changes in immigration policy, my findings suggest other arenas in which we can better support families divided by borders. First, there is the need for social support that is attuned to the nuances of Mexican migrant families' experiences. Given that migrant women's wages lag behind those of men and require greater time commitments, labor organizing to improve conditions in female-dominated professions where transnational mothers concentrate, like domestic work, is highly important.[63] Fathers also would benefit from labor-organizing efforts in industries such as landscaping and construction, to provide greater employment security. Outside of the workplace, church groups, social service providers, and other nonprofit agencies can be encouraged to create programs, like support groups and counseling, specifically geared to address the distresses migrants face in trying to care for their children from a distance. Direct-service professionals, like social workers, need to be trained not to further aggravate mothers' guilt at living apart from their children. They ought to encourage fathers to establish relationships with children in their home countries based on more than their ability to provide economically for them. Unions and other agencies that work with immigrants can also open computer facilities and fund technologies to facilitate parents' communication with children in Mexico. Such technologies have proved useful for Mexican transnational community organizations but were not typically used by the family members in this study.[64] Research has found that mothers in the Philippines, for example, often rely on text-messaging and e-mail to communicate with their children.[65] The Mexican parents I interviewed did not, for the most part, have access to these technologies.

Second, I have found that children in Mexico lack supportive environments while their parents are away, aggravating their feelings of loss, undermining parents' efforts to invest in children's schooling, and setting the stage for children to eventually join their parents as low-wage undocumented workers in the United States. Mexican schools are a crucial and underutilized resource for supporting the children of migrants. The children I met felt uncomfortable at school and different because school practices were not responsive to their needs. Textbooks I reviewed addressed migration in a cursory manner that did not reflect the realities of the lives of children who had extensive experiences with the consequences of migration. School curricula, practices, and services can be modified in Mexico to better meet children's needs.[66] Also, there are no structural supports in place to help teachers address students' problems while parents are away. A high school social worker explained: "There are not enough resources, which is one of the factors that limits my job." This social worker was paid on an hourly basis and was capped at only twenty hours per week because of the size of the school. He added that what is needed is "full-time work and the resources to go out in the communities to visit the parents." When I asked another social worker if migration was a topic discussed at the regional supervisors' meetings, she answered: "[Do we talk] about migration? No, we have not talked about it, even though it would be very interesting. In our report that we sent in to the educational services, it says that most of the young people live with sponsors, in this case grandparents or aunts and uncles, because the parents are [in the United States], but we have not dealt with the issues, no." One possibility is regional-specific training in areas with high levels of emigration to educate Mexican teachers and school administrators about both the positive and negative impacts of migration on families. Children need not feel stigmatized for having parents away, and schools are in a prime position to help accomplish this goal.

ON REUNITING

May 2005. I sat dining with José at a local Mexican restaurant in New Jersey. I had brought pictures and a few other items for him from his family in Mexico. My son, Temo, sat in the booth mesmerized by the TV, while José's newborn baby slept quietly in his car seat on the table. José's life had changed since I had met him two years earlier. When we first met, he had recently divorced and rented space for a mattress in the living room of a friend's apartment. During the past year, José had moved into a new apartment in another town with his American girlfriend. They had a baby together. José continued to work as a short-order cook at a restaurant but felt overwhelmed by the changes in his life.

"I look at these pictures," he said, as he slowly examined each photograph in the envelope I brought for him, "and I feel like fleeing back there. But I cannot go yet. I want my children to study. I want them to have careers. So I plan to stay here and be able to send them [money] to support them better."

José flipped to a picture of himself and his son Brian at Brian's sixth-grade graduation. The picture was taken shortly before José had left for the United States. José's eyes welled up with tears, explaining that he remembered staying up all night the day before sewing the pants and the jacket for his son. "But you know," he went on, "with my first son, I never touched him as a baby. I never changed a diaper. I never cared for him. He was the first grandchild. My mother-in-law and sisters-in-law would all take him. Sometimes I would get upset; he was my son, and it made me feel bad sometimes. I never touched him. My daughter was a little different . . . and now with this baby, oh yes, I carry him a lot. I change his diapers. I feed him. I do everything."

José worried about his commitment to his new partner and their U.S.-born child. He asked for advice on how to regularize his immigration status if he married. José wanted papers. The first thing he would do, he explained, is go home and visit his children in Mexico. He would then sponsor his children's migration so that if they wanted, they would be able to study in New Jersey. Unfortunately, I told José, as I understood the law, it was unlikely that he would be able to do so, even if his wife was a U.S. citizen. I gave José phone numbers for local lawyers anyway.

June 2007. This time, José came to my house for lunch. It seemed easier with the boys: my now five-year-old son, Temo, and José's now two-and-a-half-year-old son played in the backyard and José held my one-year-old son, Dylan, on his lap in the kitchen. I made lunch, refusing to let José help any more than with the recipe, since he cooked all day at work.

Although the children had changed a lot, José's life was still in limbo. He described ongoing struggles with his second wife, whom he had married a year earlier and who was pregnant with their second child. Their difficulties were compounded by the fact that he had not been able to fix his legal situation. José remained undocumented, although he had contracted a lawyer hoping to find a loophole that would enable him to apply for legal permanent residency.

"I never imagined myself like this, Joanna," he said, as he instructed me on how to properly cut the zucchinis. "I never thought my life would be like this. I thought that I would be married with my [ex-wife] for the rest of my life. And now look at me." José described his relationship with his wife as amicable. "We get along. I don't interfere in her life, and she doesn't interfere in mine."

But José worried about his son Brian, who had recently turned eighteen. When I met Brian, the then fifteen-year-old was a stellar student. "He is failing me," José explained. Although Brian's younger sister, Tina, was doing better in school than before, Brian had failed tests in two of his subject areas, and he had trouble passing his last year of high school. José was thinking of bringing Brian to the United States. "It would be temporary, so that he could see things here. I feel like he needs to get away a little from everything there." José's main concern about bringing Brian north was the conflicts that might develop with his wife if Brian came. "If he comes, I will have to put my son first. I do not know what she will think of that. . . . I may need to separate from her and go live with my son alone."

Winter 2008. Brian arrived at his father's suburban home in central New Jersey on his nineteenth birthday. Tina continued to study in Mexico. Contrary to his father's concerns, Brian got along well with his stepmother, even babysitting for his two half-siblings, and visited his mother, Elsa, frequently. Despite Brian's earlier feelings of disappointment, with time mother and son appeared to be reconciling. Father and son, however, struggled to get along, and Brian did not plan on staying long. Having suspended his matriculation at the Mexican university, Brian hoped to earn enough money within a year to return home to finish his studies. After a few months, Brian moved in with his mother permanently.

February 2008. The phone startled me. "It's Ofelia," a distant voice on the other end of the line explained. As if sensing my harried effort to place the name with a face, she added, "Germán's mother."

Ofelia went on to explain: "*Es qué ya llegó.* It's that he is here. Germán got here yesterday night, and ever since the morning he has been bugging me to call you. I told him you are not in New Jersey anymore, but he said he had to call to tell you he made it."

Finally, after eleven years and numerous failed attempts, Ofelia was reunited with her son, Germán. Her husband, Ricardo, had returned to Mexico in December for the first time in the twelve years he had lived and worked in the United States. In mid-January, he had brought Germán north. It took them twenty days to cross the border, and it cost more than seven thousand dollars to secure passage for both Germán and Ricardo. Ofelia said Germán suffered a lot, but Germán shrugged off the hardship: "We only walked for about an hour."

The next day, Germán's parents would take him to take the test to enter school. "Your vacation is over," I joked, a feeble attempt to ease the anxious-sounding voice at the other end of the line. Germán had been out of school since the previous June anticipating his migration north.

A few months shy of his fourteenth birthday, Germán would now start a new life in the United States. Unlike his younger sister, a U.S. citizen, it is unlikely that Germán will be able to study past high school, since New Jersey has not passed a law allowing in-state tuition for undocumented students.[67] Although no longer physically separated, inequalities within this immigrant family remain.

The dedication of parents like José and Ofelia toward their children in Mexico and their struggles to decide how best to manage their complicated family relationships during migration are both touching and heart-wrenching. Their experiences are a product of the current legal system that makes it extremely difficult for parents to devise plans for reuniting their family until their children have grown and many years have gone by.

Mexican migrant families' experiences are uniquely shaped by the historical relationship between the United States and Mexico, previous migration patterns, and current U.S. immigration law. Yet families divided by borders are not unheard of in other parts of the world. Transnational families span the globe in the early twenty-first century, and the legal and geographic circumstances they face fluctuate. But the underlying process does not. Labor demands in what Saskia Sassen calls "global cities" combined with a deteriorating standard of living in many countries worldwide provide the impetus for families to make the decision to divide internally.[68] Even though the context of migration varies considerably, I expect that the process by which migration patterns both divide families and ultimately unite them by altering members' relative power in family relationships does not.

The experiences of the men, women, and children depicted in this book may at times sound strikingly familiar. Families in all parts of the world negotiate their relationships. Gender and generational struggles are common. Parents struggle to communicate with their children and to

The son of migrant parents relaxes in Mexico. Photograph by Joanna Dreby

meet their children's changing needs. Many teenagers have trouble relating to parents until they grow older and begin to reevaluate their relationships with parents from the perspective of adulthood. These themes are not extraordinary or unusual, yet transnational migration creates unique dynamics in families. Ultimately, this study focuses on how contemporary global migration patterns both strain and intensify the most intimate relationships of people's lives—the bonds between family members. Although the courses of action taken by many parents, children, and caregivers may at times seem impractical and their expectations unrealistic, I suggest that their choices might not be so different, in the end, from those any of us would make if faced with similar circumstances.

APPENDIX A Research Design

Lives unfold in layers. So has this project. The constant international movement of people and things common at the turn of the twenty-first century has fostered new methods of social research, particularly in the development of ethnographies that "follow the people."[1] In the tradition of other migration scholars, I have learned about the layers of family life by employing multisited methods.[2] In doing so, I found that not only did I need to travel back and forth between Mexico and the United States, but I also had to gather data from many different sources, including parents and children, and also caregivers, community members, teachers, and school students. This study draws on four sources of data: 142 formal interviews: 45 with migrant parents, 60 with children, and 37 with caregivers; detailed field notes taken from a site in Mexico where I lived for seven months and also from central New Jersey, especially with parents whom I met with on more than one occasion; in-depth interviews and observations with a select group of twelve transnational families over a period of approximately four years;

and research in schools including more than three thousand surveys of Mexican school students, interviews with twenty-three teachers and administrators (in the United States and in Mexico), and drawings from 425 Mexican elementary school students. These multiple sources of data shed light on different aspects of family life.

Exploring family relationships required foregrounding four analytical themes in the project's methodology. First, as the migration of Mexican mothers without their children is a relatively new pattern, and since gender has been shown to be key to power relations within families, a comparison between families in which mothers and fathers migrate was paramount. Second, given the lack of attention to children's experiences in migration, the study required the inclusion of young children's perspectives on their family's migration. Third, as family relationships are often in flux and may be more so during periods of migration, it was critical to explore families' experiences over time. Fourth, I needed to frame families' experiences within the context of their respective communities and their families. In what follows, I describe how the research design addressed each of these themes as well as some insights about families' experiences these four methodological concerns yielded.

INTERVIEWING PARENTS: GENDER AND MEXICAN MIGRATION

Initially, I sought interviews with Mexican migrants residing in central New Jersey in and around a city where I was already familiar with the Mexican immigrant community, having worked in the community in social services and as an ESL teacher starting in 1997. When I started the project, I was interested in the little-known experiences of mothers migrating without their children. One Saturday morning English class is salient in my memory. I was reviewing the future tense with fourteen adults at a local church by asking each of them to complete the sentence "I hope that . . . " Ten of the fourteen students, mostly female, said they hoped to live with their children again soon.

My contacts with Mexican mothers primarily came through my friends and co-organizers at this grassroots ESL school. Unlike Latinas in California featured in research on domestic workers, the transnational mothers I met typically worked in fast-food restaurants, in factories, and for cleaning companies.[3] In many ways, their labor experiences were similar to those of men who worked in factories and relied on temporary agencies to find work upon their arrival in the United States. In other ways, however, women's experiences were distinct. I decided rather quickly that I could not understand the experiences of mothers without also talking to fathers. Starting in 2003, I conducted systematic interviews in Spanish with twenty-two mothers and twenty-three fathers who had lived apart from their minor children in Mexico.[4] I did not elicit interviews through any of the organizations with which I had worked; rather I approached individuals I already knew and received referrals from the friends and families of parents with children in Mexico. Nonetheless, many people I interviewed knew that I had worked with different social service organizations, and they often asked my advice on English classes and legal services.

During interviews I asked parents about why they migrated to the United States, the care arrangements they made for their children in Mexico, how often they were in touch with their children and in what ways, how they felt about living apart, and their plans for the future. I met thirteen parents on two or three occasions and another nine parents, some of whom I had known for years, even more frequently. Aware of the importance of technology to the maintenance of transnational ties, I often viewed videotapes or photographs of parents' children and their hometowns and was able to listen in on some phone conversations with children in Mexico. Interviews were open-ended in format; my goal was to address the issues listed on my interview schedule, but not necessarily in any given order. Only four parents allowed me to tape-record them. In most cases I took detailed notes during interviews or, sometimes, afterward.

I interviewed more than half of the parents in their own homes. As all families lived with others, parents often requested I interview them when no one else was home. Mothers in particular asked that I come before their husband returned home from work. When parents did not have enough privacy or a comfortable place to sit and talk in the rooms they rented in area apartments, I invited them to my home for the interview. Some fathers, for example, rented sleeping quarters in unfinished basements, and one lived at a tree farm where he worked. Since members of the ESL school where I volunteered often conducted committee meetings in my living room, it was normal to invite parents to my home. Indeed, some parents seemed most comfortable speaking about what they considered a private topic at my home. One mother, for example, met with me first in her living room, where a number of relatives walked in and out during our conversation. The next week I invited her to coffee, and she disclosed many more details sitting at my kitchen table. In three cases I interviewed fathers in public spaces, such as the local Dunkin' Donuts.

Many mothers and fathers were initially reluctant to discuss their experiences as transnational parents, even some of those whom I had known for years. Parents were also reluctant to refer me to others. Snowball sampling did not work in the traditional sense, and I generally gained access to parents one person at a time through people I knew without children living in Mexico. The one exception was a young mother from the state of Puebla, who had actually been reunited with her six-year-old son a year before. She said she knew a number of women whom I might interview, but she seemed reluctant when I asked if I could call her later to see if she could set something up. Instead, she referred me to her neighbor, pointing toward the house where the neighbor lived. She agreed to walk me over, but when we got there, the bell did not work. It took a while for someone to come to the door, but when the neighbor did come, and my hostess explained who I was, the neighbor frowned. I got the sense that she was uncomfortable. She suggested I come another day and gave me her phone number.

I was not hopeful about this particular interview and was surprised that when I phoned the neighbor agreed to talk to me. I later learned that while the two women were from the same town, they were not friends. The first mother was unwilling to refer me to her friends, so she recommended me to an adversary instead.

Once parents agreed to an interview, they seemed to enjoy disclosing their stories to me. Fathers, for example, were often candid in revealing marital infidelities; I suspected this was in part due to the perception that women in the United States have liberal attitudes about sex.[5] I also suspected that as a community outsider, I offered a sympathetic ear, and telling me about personal matters did not risk the migrant parent's reputation with other Mexican families. Some parents continue to update me about these personal aspects of their lives years after our initial interview.

One of the most useful means for gaining Mexican parents' trust during interviews was my son, Temo. Mexican mothers and I often shared anecdotes about our children. Mothers seemed particularly at ease when I shared snippets about my relationship with my son's father, since I too had lived with a Mexican man. Fathers also felt at ease with my son, who has a Mexican name (Temo is short for Cuauhtémoc, the last emperor of the Aztecs). They often played with him and offered him small toys as gifts, demonstrating an affection for children, which I found to be common among the Mexican men I met.[6] "We enter the field," write Tamara Mose Brown and Erynn Masi de Casanova, "not only as gendered, raced, classed individuals, but also as members of families, as mothers and fathers."[7] I most often related to those I interviewed in this study as a fellow parent.

The sensitivity migrant parents displayed in talking about their children in Mexico suggests that family separation may be touchy for a variety of reasons that differ along gender lines. Both mothers and fathers viewed family matters as private affairs. Many were sad about their separation and simply did not want to talk about it. Yet the mothers I met feared that they would be judged as being "bad" parents for having left their children. Fathers were reluctant to talk about children whom they did not provide for financially on a regular basis. The mothers and fathers I interviewed were thus remarkable for opening up about a very personal aspect of their lives.

EXPLORING CHILDREN'S EXPERIENCES

Between 2004 and 2005, I received a Fulbright grant to study the lives of children living in Mexico whose parents had migrated to the United States, as well as the children's caregivers. While I had been to Mexico before, this was the first time I was able to travel to the many places in Oaxaca and Puebla I heard immigrants in New Jersey reminisce about at parties and informal gatherings. For seven of the nine months I lived in Mexico, I was based in a small town of roughly two thousand residents.[8] The town—which I call San Ángel—is located in the Lower Mixteca region of Oaxaca, about an hour and a half's drive from one of the major cities in the region. Although indigenous Mixtec communities are nearby, residents of San Ángel speak Spanish and do not ethnically identify as Mixtecs.

I went to San Ángel out of convenience; a family I knew from New Jersey offered me a room in their house whose second floor they occupied for only half of the year. Living in the house, just a block from the municipal square, was ideal because of the location and also because the downstairs housed a *caseta,* or public phone booth, where town residents often came to wait for phone calls from the United States. I also chose San Ángel because the lower Mixteca of Oaxaca is a region with high levels of U.S. migration.[9] An anthropological study in the Mixteca during the 1950s found that a number of men in the region had worked in the United States as *braceros.*[10] I too found that a surprising number of old-timers in town had been north as *braceros.* While I was in San Ángel, a local committee was aiding former *braceros* in reclaiming money owed to them. I helped translate documents, viewed pictures of these early migrants on cotton fields in Alabama, and heard stories of harvesting cucumber and cherry crops in Minnesota.

The effects of U.S. migration in San Ángel were visibly evident. Before arriving in the Mixteca, I had traveled in areas of rural Veracruz and was accustomed to seeing houses with aluminum roofs, makeshift walls, and dirt floors. In San Ángel, 500 of 510 houses were made of cement in 2004; only 10 remained that were made entirely of adobe, or mud bricks. Only

13 percent of the dwellings had dirt floors, and no houses in town had aluminum, cardboard, wood, or palm tree roofs.[11] There are no statistics on motor vehicles, but notable were the number of cars, mostly trucks, in town. Quite a few had license plates from destinations as far as Washington, Oregon, and my home state of New Jersey.

In San Ángel, I used a snowball sample to locate children with parents in the United States. Initially, I found it difficult to identify families and children to interview. Although within a week of our arrival, whenever we were out, people recognized us—or really my son, by calling out his name, "Temo"—no one greeted me. Proper decorum in small Mexican towns means saying *buenos días, buenas tardes,* or *buenas noches* to everyone who passes. It took me a while to get the timing right, for the greeting actually should come from the person who passes and not the one who is passed (and yes, it can be hard to tell at times). Rules of decorum are reserved for adult members of the community; children are either greeted affectionately by name, as people often did with Temo, or ignored. Young men defy the rules, not greeting anyone except with the occasional catcall. Actually, when in February we were visited by Temo's father, Raúl, he said I was greeting people in the wrong way, because I often greeted after I had passed residents by a step or two. He explained that this could be taken as an offense, and I should look people in the eye with my *buenos días* before going by. I had learned my style from observation, so it is possible everyone had been slighting me for months.

At that point, however, it did not seem to matter, for in mid-January, after living in town for four months, I finally felt I had been accepted as at least a temporary feature in the town. After I came back from a weeklong trip to the city of Oaxaca over Christmas and New Year's, people suddenly started greeting me: "*¿Ya se hallo Usted aquí?* [You got used to it here already?]" It was a simple line to invite conversation, but to me it was symbolic, as if people realized I had not been scared away and was now worthy of some consideration.

I took this as a cue. After January, I actively sought interviews with children in San Ángel and miraculously wrapped up my research in town at an amazing speed of six weeks' time. At first I felt reluctant to cold-call families, wanting referrals, as was a requisite in New Jersey. But I soon learned this was unnecessary in a small town. No one, in fact, seemed to question my motives. No one refused an interview. It was the easiest string of interviews I had ever done.

I ended up interviewing forty-five children of U.S. migrants in San Ángel. I also interviewed three adult children of U.S. migrants. Eleven children ranged in age from five to seven, eight children from eight to ten, nine children from eleven to thirteen, ten children from fourteen to sixteen, and nine children were over seventeen. When interviewing younger children, I used a structured interview schedule. Younger children generally did not want me to record our interviews, but because they typically did not give lengthy answers, I was able to take almost exact notes of our conversations. With older children, I used a semistructured interview schedule; interviews with young adults resembled those I had done with migrant parents in being relatively open-ended and characterized by free-flowing conversations. I tape-recorded eight interviews with older children and took detailed notes of our interactions. The relatively equal distribution of interviews with children of all ages allowed for insight into the ways children of different ages described parents' migration.

I gained access to children in San Ángel through the adults in their lives. Many children agreed to talk to me because they were instructed to do so by their grandparents or mothers. At first I was uncomfortable using the power imbalance to my advantage, especially since the goal of the study was to give children the opportunity to voice their own opinions on migration. I had no choice, however, because I needed their guardian's permission for an interview. Also, when I first started interviewing children, I was wary of many children's curt and matter-of-fact style of answering my questions until I realized that even those who were eager to be interviewed and tape-recorded spoke to me in that way. In retrospect, I think this reflects a combination of the young ages of those I interviewed and the mix between the local accent and what Rob Smith working in a town in the same region calls the "ranchero culture."[12] Moreover, children in San Ángel were not always taught to speak their mind, unlike children in middle-class America.[13] The result was that children (and even some adults) had a hard time articulating their thoughts and emotions, particularly in the relatively formal setting of an interview with an adult. Sometimes children clammed up and said they did not know the answer, saying *"no sé,"* when a topic was emotional or something they did not understand. Simple answers of yes or no were at times wrought with emotion. I began to pay more attention to, and take field notes on, children's actions and nonverbal cues as well as reports on their behavior from caregivers. Attention to how children acted became an important analytical tool.

Interviews with children's caregivers in San Ángel provided key insights into children's experiences while parents were away, particularly those of the younger children who were not terribly verbal in their interviews. In San Ángel, I was able to interview twenty-seven caregivers; most were grandmothers, although I also spoke to grandfathers, aunts, and mothers whose husband lived in the United States. None of the interviews with caregivers were tape-recorded; all were open-ended informal conversations, which seemed to put the older residents in town most at ease.

CAPTURING CHANGING FAMILY DYNAMICS

Interviews in New Jersey and San Ángel provided me with two sides of the story, so to speak, but not two sides of the same story. Thus I also interviewed a smaller sample of families whose members resided in both Mexico and New Jersey. This type of triangulation in research with families has been found useful in verifying self-reports of family interactions, as well as in accounting for ways that individual family members view similar events differently.[14] I identified constellations of migrant parents (either mother, father, or both when possible), their children in Mexico, and their children's caregiver. Although I often spoke to neighbors, friends, and other family members who were actively involved in these arrangements, my primary focus was the parent-child-caregiver constellation.

Selecting family constellations was complicated by geography. Contrary to expectations informed by prior research on transnational migration, the Mexican community in central New Jersey is not tightly bound to any one place in Mexico, but rather to a number of towns and cities in the Mixteca and on the coast of Oaxaca and Guerrero, as well as Mexico City.[15] In addition, family members in both New Jersey and Mexico had to be willing to participate in the study. In the end, I identified a subsample of twelve family constellations representing the four main variations in migration patterns I had observed: three families of father-only migrants, three families of single-mother migrants, three families with married migrant couples, and three families in which both parents migrated but divorced once they were in the United States. Two of these families had already been reunited with some of their children in the United States (in one case, the children were adults), in order to account for the changing impact of separation on families over time.

In all but one case, I interviewed the parents first in the United States, meeting with parents on multiple occasions, and then visited children and caregivers while I was living in San Ángel. Altogether half of the families lived in the Mixteca region, and all but one of the others in the nearby Costa Chica region of Guerrero and Oaxaca. Four families lived in major cities, two in small cities, two in large towns, and four in the small town of San Ángel. The diversity of the subsample enabled me to gauge the importance of factors specific to San Ángel, such as educational opportunity, to family dynamics during periods of separation. In San Ángel I visited with families frequently, and I resided in the home of one of the families while I stayed in town. I traveled to visit other families on public transportation for shorter trips and hired a taxi driver from San Ángel to take me on two longer trips to visit the families farthest away. I almost always visited families with my son, Temo. On occasion, we traveled with a seventeen-year-old girl who helped me with child care.[16] My Mexican companions, along with Temo, eased my initial interactions with the families.

Given travel and time constraints, I spent different amounts of time with each family depending on the location. In San Ángel, I observed families repeatedly on a daily basis, although I interviewed each family member just once. We interacted frequently and often talked about migration informally, and I had the opportunity to observe how some children reacted to parents' phone calls and return visits. I visited two of the families living outside of San Ángel on four different day trips. Each visit consisted of conversations directly related to my research; we discussed changes in the family or feelings about separation since my last visit, and I interviewed different family members for their versions of the migration story. The other six families I visited during two to four overnight trips of varying durations. In most cases, the first visit was shorter than the second. I was able to observe daily routines in addition to engaging in specific conversations and interviews about family separation. Between visits I often phoned families, especially over the holiday season.

In these twelve families, Mexican hospitality prevailed. Because I was an invited guest and a friend of a relative in the United States, I was generally treated with great respect. In a few cases, I felt undeserving because I did not know the migrant parents that well. However, by the time my stay in Mexico ended, ties with most families were cemented, giving me an even greater connection to migrant parents back in New Jersey.

The methodological approach of interviewing and observing people in a select group of family constellations proved key in a number of ways. For one, it provided me with firsthand insight and greater depth into the multiple social worlds in which migrants operated and how they managed their lives transnationally. In addition, I was able to compare the contemporaneous accounts of different family members and achieve some level of internal validity regarding the salient themes in families. Also, in-depth involvement with the families enabled me to more fully explore issues I found to be important in the larger samples of interviews in Mexico and New Jersey. One of the most useful aspects of tracking transnational families over time—or doing this longitudinal ethnography—was being able to observe how family configurations often changed and to appreciate the fluid movement of people to and from the United States (and even within the continental United States), despite the difficulties of the border crossing and migrants' undocumented status upon arrival.

ASSESSING FAMILY AND COMMUNITY CONTEXTS

Most of the data I draw on focus on family members' accounts of their experiences, but I also sought information on the broader family and community in which they lived their lives. Over the ten years I lived in central New Jersey, I had many opportunities to speak with Mexican immigrants who did not have children in Mexico about their experiences. For the project, I formally met with leaders of the local Mexican American Organization and discussed the topic of family separation in eight formal interviews with local Latino social workers and schoolteachers. The focus of this book is not these outside assessments, and thus I have not emphasized the Latino community's reaction to family separation in the United States. Yet the overall consensus of these leaders and professionals in the community is that leaving children in Mexico is abnormal, reflects bad choices by migrant parents, and causes severe problems for families. For example, one Latina social worker I spoke with described children living in Mexico as migrant parents' "dirty laundry." These views by professionals working in the Mexican immigrant community help explain why migrant parents were initially reluctant to discuss their experiences with me. They also indicate the moral edge family separation inevitably involves.

In Mexico, I undertook a more systematic exploration of the context in which children "left behind" operate. In San Ángel, I spent time attending community events, particularly extracurricular activities organized by the local schools. I taught English to children in the community with the support of an elementary school teacher. I attended parties during the holidays, including *Las Posadas* (Advent-season house-to-house reenactments of Joseph and Mary's search for a place to stay), rodeos, weddings, and municipally organized town dances.

I also sought information about children's lives by doing research in area schools. In total I visited twenty-three elementary, middle, and high schools in order to survey more than three thousand students about their family migration history and views of international migration. In the book I refer only to the surveys I collected in the Mixteca unless otherwise noted. The nonrandom sample included students at regional schools along the main road to the nearest city and also six schools outside the region for comparative purposes. I surveyed all students in each grade who were in attendance on the day of my visit. On many of my visits to regional schools, at the request of school officials, I made presentations to students about the lives of Mexican immigrants in the United States. They hoped my comments would quell students' desires to migrate and the problems with school retention they attributed to emigration. On a handful of occasions, I substituted for English teachers. Some schools I visited multiple times, learning about regional education politics. I took detailed field notes on these school visits. I also interviewed fifteen teachers and administrators on their views of the effects of international migration on education.

One of the limitations of my work in schools in the region was that the survey design required me to focus on children in grades six to twelve; younger children simply could not complete the surveys. In January 2006, I returned to Mexican schools, this time to the coastal region of Oaxaca and Guerrero, to expand the age range of data I collected from school students. I visited three primary schools to conduct a drawing project with students in the first through sixth grades. The goal was to match information collected in the earlier surveys with a younger population, as well as to learn more about how young Mexican children imagine their families and life in the United States. Each student was asked with minimal instruction to first draw a picture of his or her family and then a picture of how the child imagined the United States. From each of the 425 students, I collected two pictures and a family migration history.

The surveys and drawings offer a child-centered perspective on U.S. migration. They also provide the means for evaluating how the experiences of children with migrant parents may converge or diverge from those of other children in their respective communities. Although I did not conduct fieldwork with nonmigrant families in Mexico, the surveys and pictures allow for some comparisons between the perspectives of children in nonmigrant families and in transnational families. They help to illuminate the unique features of family life for parents and children divided by borders.

APPENDIX B Family Descriptions

Following are descriptions of the twelve families in my purposive sample whose members I interviewed both in the United States and in Mexico. I interviewed all members of the family listed except those listed without a proper name (e.g., "daughter"). I have changed some details to protect family members' identities. I list ages only for the children in each family.

Single-Mother Migrant Families

Migrant	*Children's Caregivers in Mexico*	*Children (Age at First Interview)*	*Migrant's Background*	*Additional Notes*
Paula	Her cousin Pedro and his wife, Blanca. They have two children: Lola (17) and Jessy (8)	Cindy (15), Mateo (18)	Paula was educated through the sixth grade. She worked in her cousin's home as a domestic after becoming a single mother at age 17.	At the age of 20, Mateo joined Paula in the United States.
Zelia	Zelia's mother, Doña Adelaida	Juan Luis (7)	Zelia studied through the ninth grade. She worked part time assisting a local physician before getting married. She migrated after her divorce.	During the study, Zelia went back to Mexico so she could take Juan Luis to the United States. He refused to go. She left without him.
Nicandra	Nicandra's mother, until she passed away. Later, the children were on their own with a cousin (24) and his wife, who rented a room in their apartment.	Miguel (16), Tony (19)	Nicandra had a high school diploma. She was working in a medical laboratory prior to migration.	I first met Nicandra a year after she had left her boys, ages 12 and 15, in Mexico. Tony and Miguel joined Nicandra in the United States when they were 18 and 21. They lived apart for 6 years.

Father-Only Migrant Families

Migrant	*Children's Caregivers in Mexico*	*Children (Age at First Interview)*	*Migrant's Background*	*Additional Notes*
Ángelo	His wife, Gabriela	Esmeralda (6), Lalo (8), Gilberto (10), Javier (11)	Ángelo had a ninth-grade education and was working for a governmental program prior to migration.	Ángelo migrated 4 years before we met, but he visited his family in Mexico twice during the course of this study.
Enrique	His wife, Laura	Trinidad (24), daughter (27), Paulo (30), Fernando (31), Cassandra (32)	Enrique was working as an accountant prior to migration.	Ten years prior to our interviews, Fernando (age 21) joined Enrique in New Jersey. Three years later, Laura and Trinidad (17) migrated legally to the United States through Enrique's family-based petitions.
Esteban	His wife, Yolanda	Hilda (12), Cynthia (16), son (18), daughter (20)	Esteban had a sixth-grade education. He was working for an agricultural program in town prior to migration.	Esteban had been in the U.S. for most of his children's lives, visiting twice in 12 years. I was not able to interview the couple's 18-year-old son, who migrated to join Esteban in New Jersey when he was 16. I also was not able to interview the couple's 20-year-old daughter, who had migrated at age 19 after marrying a return migrant.

Migrant Couple Families

Migrants	*Children's Caregivers in Mexico*	*Children (Age at First Interview)*	*Migrants' Background*	*Additional Notes*
Ofelia and Ricardo	Ofelia's mother and father, Doña María and Don Francisco	Germán (9), U.S-born daughter Stacy (3)	Ofelia and Ricardo had studied through the ninth grade. Ofelia did not work prior to migration. Ricardo worked in agriculture.	Ofelia left Germán when he was 2; Ricardo left when Germán was 1. A few months shy of his 14th birthday, Germán joined his parents in New Jersey. Ofelia and Germán lived apart for 11 years.
Nancy and Pablo	Nancy's mother, Doña Tricia, and a younger sister, Katrina (22)	Daughter (8)—speech impaired, U.S.-born daughter (5)	Nancy was college educated and worked in a laboratory prior to migration. Pablo had a high school diploma and was working as an accountant's assistant prior to migration.	I first met the family when their daughter was 4 years old and still in Mexico and their U.S.-born daughter was a newborn. Nancy and Pablo sent for their daughter in Mexico when she was 5. In total, they were separated for 4 years. During the course of the study, Nancy had another U.S.-born child.
Nydia and Carlos	Nydia's mother and father, Doña Ana and Don Mateo	Kevin (5)	Carlos had a high school education and was working in agriculture prior to migration. Nydia had a master's degree and was a high school teacher prior to migration.	Nydia left Kevin when he was 1. She returned to Mexico to live with Kevin during the course of the study, when he was 6. They were apart for 5 years. Nydia gave birth to a U.S.-born child months after we first met.

Families of Migrant Couples Who Divorced after Migrating

Migrants	*Children's Caregivers in Mexico*	*Children (Age at First Interview)*	*Migrants' Background*	*Additional Notes*
Elsa and José	Elsa's mother, Doña Ursula (both José's and Elsa's siblings live in the neighborhood)	Tina (13), Brian (15)	Both Elsa and José had a high school diploma. Elsa worked part time as a consultant prior to migration. José worked in a unionized factory prior to migration.	José left Tina and Brian when they were 9 and 12, respectively. Elsa migrated a year later, when they were 10 and 13. During the course of this study, José had a U.S.-born child with his new partner. Brian joined his parents in the U.S. in 2008.
Armando	Armando's mother, Doña Mica (also in the home, Mica's disabled son)	Lupe (4), Mary (6), Michael (9)	Armando had a high school diploma and trade school training. He was an electrician prior to migration.	Armando returned to Mexico during the course of the study. He had been away for 5 years. Also, during the course of the study, Doña Mica's two young nephews came to live with the family as well as her elderly mother.
Silvia and Daniel	Silvia's mother, Doña Beatriz, her husband, and their 7 children still at home, including Roberto (17)	Lourdes (6), Samuel (8), Jacinta (9)	Daniel and Silvia both had some college education. Daniel worked as a personal trainer prior to migration. Silvia was a student prior to migration.	All three children were born in the United States. When I met Silvia and Daniel, the children were living with Silvia's family in Mexico. After 3 years, the children returned to the United States to live with their mother.

Notes

ONE. SACRIFICE

1. All names are pseudonyms. For clarity of narrative, in all but a few cases I use names only to refer to the twelve families I followed over a period of four years. Their names and summaries of their family migration histories are listed in appendix B. In some cases, specific details about families have been modified to protect their identities. Many parents chose American names for their children, like Brandon. This is reflected in my choice of pseudonyms.

2. Cindy's routine varied throughout the course of the study. This vignette captures one moment in her overall experience. In contrast, Paula's routine remained fairly constant during the four years I was in contact with the family.

3. Pew Hispanic Center 2007. Please note that for references like this one that I have accessed via the Internet, the most recent link at the time of writing is provided in the references.

Jeffrey Passel and D'Vera Cohn (2008) found that 47 percent of the unauthorized population lives with spouses and children, and 35 percent of legal immigrants do. This compares to 21 percent of the U.S.-born population.

4. In a survey of Mexican immigrants at Mexican consulates throughout the United States, researchers at the Pew Hispanic Center found that 18 percent, and more than one in four parents, had one child or more in Mexico. See Suro 2005. Other, smaller-scale studies of Mexican migrants had similar findings. Adler (2004) found among her sample that 25 percent of parents had all of their children in Mexico, and 11 percent had some in Mexico and some in the United States. Hondagneu-Sotelo (2001) reports that of the Latina domestic workers interviewed in Los Angeles, 40 percent had children in their country of origin. Parreñas (2001b) found that of her sample of Filipina domestic migrant workers in Los Angeles and Rome, Italy, 54 percent were mothers with children in the Philippines. And, looking at the relationships from a different perspective, a longitudinal study of 407 immigrant children in Boston found that 79 percent had been separated from their fathers during migration, 55 percent had been separated from their mothers, and 42 percent of Mexican children had lived apart from their mothers prior to migration. See Suárez-Orozco, Todorova, and Louie 2002.

5. Of the nearly 10 million working mothers in the United States, 79 percent leave their children with someone besides a grandparent while they are at work (see Johnson 2005).

6. For descriptions of parents' struggles to achieve a work-family balance, see Edin and Lein 1997; Hochschild 1997; Schneider and Waite 2005; and Stone 2007.

7. Zolberg 2006: 11.

8. For more on immigration as a family affair, see Pessar 1999 and Rumbaut 1997.

9. Much ethnographic research analyzes social interactions in a public sphere. For examples of ethnographies of street life, see Duneier 2000; Liebow 1967; and Turnovsky 2006. For examples of classic ethnographies of workplaces, see Burawoy 1979; Fernández-Kelly 1983; and Kornblum 1975. For examples of classic neighborhood ethnographies, see Gans 1962; Horowitz 1983; Patillo-McCoy 2000; and Suttles 1968.

Arlie Hochschild's *The Second Shift* (1990) and *The Time Bind* (1997) are prime examples of "domestic ethnography," although they have not been termed as such. For other examples, see Lareau 2003 and Lewis 1959.

10. Robert Smith (2006: 123) refers to the expectations that children have of their migrant parents as the "immigrant bargain."

11. Massey et al. 1998.

12. Ibid.; Sassen 2001.

13. Foner 1997.

14. Fajnzylber and López 2008. Also see Suro 2003. For more on family dynamics in remittance economies, see Castañeda-Tinoco 2006.

15. See Bryceson and Vuorela 2002; Chavez 1992; Dreby 2006, 2007a; Glick-Schiller, Basch, and Blanc 1998; Glick-Schiller and Fouron 1999; Levitt 2001; Parreñas 2001a, 2001b, 2005; Schmalzbauer 2004, 2005a; Smith 2006; Zhou 1998.

16. What scholars often previously termed "split-family migration" was common a century ago for Chinese, Polish, Jewish, and Italian immigrants to the United States, among others. See Foner 2000; Gabaccia 2001; Nakano Glenn 1983; and Thomas and Znaniecki 1927. In the majority of cases, it was men who initially settled abroad. From 1870 to 1920, more than two-thirds of Italian migrants were men; the majority of them supported wives and children in Italy with remittances. See Gabaccia 2001. Male Chinese immigrants outnumbered women eighteen to one in 1860 and twenty-six to one in 1890, and more than half left wives at home in China. See Nakano Glenn 1983. Many men gradually brought their family members to the United States when possible, although return migration rates were also high; between 1900 and 1920, more than a third of immigrants to the United States returned home (Foner 2000: 172).

17. For more on migrating women and new dynamics in transnational families, see Ehrenreich and Hochschild 2002.

18. West Indian women, for example, have been leaving children with grandmothers to work in New York City since the 1920s (Soto 1987 and Watkins-Owens 2001). Carmen Sarasüa (2002) also found that wet nurses in eighteenth-century Spain left their infants with their husbands to work in the city of Madrid.

19. Robles and Watkins 1993.

20. Hondagneu-Sotelo 1994.

21. For a discussion of how gender relations shaped migration patterns from Italy to the United States in the early twentieth century, see Gabaccia 2001.

22. Bernhard, Landolt, and Goldring 2005; Chang 2000; Cohen 2000; Constable 1999; Dreby 2006; Erel 2002; Escrivá 2004; Gamburd 2000; Lan 2003; Parreñas 2001a, 2001b; Sørenson 2005.

23. Often women who obtain work visas in nursing or domestic service occupations migrate without or before their husbands (Gamburd 2008; George 2005; and Parreñas 2001b).

24. Pew Hispanic Center 2008; Suro 2005.

25. Chavez 1992; Donato 1993; Kanaiaupuni 2000. A number of journalists have recently reported on the plight of women migrating without their children. For examples, see Bernstein 2004; Flores 2006; García-Navarro 2006; Jones 2004; and Nazario 2006.

26. Ehrenreich and Hochschild 2002; Hondagneu-Sotelo and Avila 1997; Parreñas 2001b.

27. Hondagneu-Sotelo and Avila 1997: 549.

28. One primary focus of immigration scholarship has been on the factors, such as racial or ethnic identification, social capital, and ethnic economies, that assist or prevent immigrant and second-generation integration and adaptation in the United States. For examples of this approach, see Alba and Nee 2003; Kasinitz, Mollenkopf, and Waters 2004; Portes and Zhou 1993; Rumbaut and Portes 2001; Waters 1999; Waldinger and Bozorghehr 1996; Zhou and Bankston 1998. Over the past twenty years or so, migration scholars have been considering the impact of migration on the lives of community members in both home and host societies. For examples of studies adopting this transnational approach, see Grasmuck and Pessar 1991; Kyle 2001; Levitt 2001; Smith 2006; and Stephen 2007.

29. See Fouron and Glick Schiller 2001; Glick Schiller and Fouron 1999; Goldring 2001; Kearney 2000.

30. On migrants' ties to hometown development and community organizations, see Durand, Parrado, and Massey 1996; Fitzgerald 2008; and Smith 2006. On how national policies affect transnational migrants' activities, see Guarnizo 1998 and Waldinger and Fitzgerald 2004.

31. Smith 2006: 50.

32. On "social remittances," see Levitt 2001; Schmalzbauer 2008; and Stephen 2007. On changing gender dynamics in Mexican families, see D'Aubeterre 2000, 2002; González-López 2005; Hirsch 2003; Smith 2006; and Stephen 2007. On gender and transnational migration more broadly, see Pessar and Mahler 2003.

33. Sánchez 1993.

34. Hondagneu-Sotelo 1994; Sánchez 1993.

35. Martin 1998.

36. Massey et al. 1987.

37. On the effects of the debt crisis on migration rates, see Cornelius 1991; Escobar and González de la Rocha 1995; and Selby 1992. Migration rates specifically climbed in the Mixteca region of Puebla and Oaxaca after the Mexican debt crisis (Cortés Sanchez 2003).

38. Estimates from the Pew Hispanic Center (2008) show the Mexican foreign-born population in 2006 to be 11,534,972. The Census in Mexico placed the total population in 2005 at 103,263,388 (Instituto Nacional de Estadística y Geografía 2005). Updated information on the current Mexican population is available on the main Web site.

39. See Leite, Ramos, and Gaspar 2003; and Massey, Durand, and Malone 2002.

40. Cornelius 2001, 2004.

41. Ibid.

42. Ibid.

43. Massey, Durand, and Malone 2002.

44. See Durand, Massey, and Capoferro 2005; Millard and Chapa 2004; and Zuñiga and Hernández-Leon 2005.

45. See Chavez 1992 and Stephen 2007.

46. Data from the Pew Hispanic Survey of Mexican Migrants suggest that family separation may be higher among new destination populations. At the consulate in Fresno, California, only 9 percent of respondents indicated that none of their children lived in the United States; whereas in Raleigh, North Carolina, 26 percent of respondents indicated that all of their children live in Mexico (Suro 2005).

47. Thomas and Znaniecki 1927.

48. Conley 2004: 7, 16.

49. Immigration scholars describe these spaces as "transnational social fields" (Glick Schiller and Fouron 1999). For more on transnationalism as an analytic approach to the study of international migration, see Portes, Guarnizo, and Landolt 1999. For recent work on the divided lives of Honduran transnational families, see Schmalzbauer 2008.

50. Many scholars of transnational communities use multisited ethnographic techniques. On ethnographic methods in a global context, see Burawoy et al. 2000; Marcus 1998; and Nash 2006. In this project I use a multisited ethnographic approach that focuses on families rather than communities or social fields, what I term domestic ethnography. For more specific details on my method, see appendix A and Dreby 2007b.

51. See appendix A for a detailed account of the methods I used in this study.

52. U.S. Census Bureau 2000. I used the American FactFinder (http://factfinder.census.gov) using the site's zip code search for this information.

53. For scholars' descriptions of how parenting has facilitated research, see Adler and Adler 1998; Edin and Kefalas 2005; Mose Brown and de Casanova forthcoming; and Stack 1974.

54. Massey, Goldring, and Durand 1994.

55. According to surveys administered by the Pew Hispanic Center, 38 percent of Mexican mothers whose children live in the United States and 44 percent of transnational mothers have less than a primary school education. Twenty-nine percent of transnational mothers have no schooling whatsoever (Suro 2005).

56. On patterns of migration in the Mixteca, see Besserer 2004; Cortés Sánchez 2003; Smith 2001, 2006; Stephen 2007; and Velasco Ortiz 2005.

57. Ibarraran and Lubotsky 2005. For more on the educational background of migrants, see Hanson and Woodruff 2003.

58. Passel 2004, 2006; and Pew Hispanic Center 2009.

59. Chavez 1992. One Mexican immigrant in the New Jersey city where I conducted this study estimated that of every ten Mexicans he knew in town, seven had children in Mexico (see Sahn 2004a).

60. Sahn 2004b.

61. One interesting gender distinction is that Mexican men typically work in better-paying private restaurants, while women generally work in lower-paid jobs at fast-food restaurants (see Adler 2004: 97).

62. Diana Alarcon-Gonzalez and Terry McKinley (1999) have shown that structural adjustment programs in Mexico have adversely affected women's employment opportunities in Mexico.

63. Douglas Massey and his collaborators have shown that Mexican migration is a social process and that migration may alter individual motivations and household strategies in a way that further perpetuates migration north (see Massey et al. 1987: 6; Massey, Goldring, and Durand 1994).

64. See Ortega 2006.

65. Chavez 1992.

66. Pritchard 2004.

67. See also Bacallao and Smokowski 2007 and Malkin 2004.

68. See also Chavez 1992.

69. Overcrowded housing in central New Jersey is common. For a local report, see Peterson 2004. For overcrowded housing among immigrants more generally, see Capps 2001; Federation for American Immigration Reform 2003.

70. Hart 1979.

71. See Marizco 2004 and Nazario 2006. Note that even Enrique, the Honduran boy depicted in Sonia Nazario's *Enrique's Journey*, lived with family members who cared a great deal for him.

72. Stephanie Scott (2008) found that 6 percent of the sample reported leaving home because of gangs, violence, or abuse. The study also found that of those living with family, more than 80 percent reported feeling like they were treated the same as other children in the household.

73. Fletcher 1999.

74. Frank 2005a; Hildebrandt and McKenzie 2005; and Kanaiaupuni and Donato 1999.

75. Differences in the receipt of money are statistically significant ($p<.01$).

76. Differences in remittances are statistically significant ($p<.01$).

77. According to Leah Schmalzbauer (2005b), Honduran youth whose parents work in the United States adopt more consumerist attitudes than do their peers, owing to their access to parents' remittances (see also Castañeda-Tinoco 2006 and Schmalzbauer 2008).

78. See Schmalzbauer 2008 on the educational returns expected from migration in transnational families.

79. For more on the school situations of children in Mexico, see Bracho 2000; Muñiz 2000; and Muñoz Izquierdo and Ahuja Sánchez 2000.

80. For information on the 2006 teachers' strike in Oaxaca and the conditions

that led to the uprising, see Bacon 2007; Cohen 2007; Gibler 2006; and Roig-Franzia 2006.

81. See Smith 2006: 48.

82. Some men in San Ángel had worked as braceros during the mid-twentieth century. For an early account, see Romney and Romney 1966. Others in the region harvested sugar cane in Veracruz. Many migrated to Mexico City and Baja California. In the 1980s and 1990s, Mixtecans headed to the United States to work in agriculture. See Corbett 1992; Rivera-Salgado 1999; Stephen 2007; and Velasco Ortiz 1995, 2005.

83. Cohen 2004; Kandel and Massey 2002.

84. See Adler 2004: 81.

85. I conducted the drawing project at three primary schools located on the coast of Oaxaca and Guerrero. I collected two drawings each from 423 students: one of their family and one of how they imagine life in the United States.

86. On the significance of iconography in children's drawings, see Cowan 1999.

87. Leo Chavez (1992) describes a case in which a Mexican woman migrated to California before her husband, while Gail Mummert (2005) cites research on Mexican women recruited to work in the crab industry of North Carolina. This migration pattern, however, appears to be much more common in other parts of the world than in Mexico, particularly among women in the Philippines (Parreñas 2001a, 2001b, 2005).

88. The percentage of migrants who are single mothers appears to vary regionally. In a town on the coast of Oaxaca where I conducted surveys, 65 percent of children of migrants had just a father in the United States, 19 percent had both parents abroad, and 17 percent had single mothers abroad.

89. Lindstrom and Giorguli Saucedo 2007: 830.

90. See Hondagneu-Sotelo 1994 and Menjívar and Agadjanian 2007.

91. David Lindstrom and Silvia Gioguli Sacucedo (2007: 831) estimate that a pattern of migrating together to the United States accounts for 9 percent of migration events among Mexican couples, although their research looks at all couples, not just those who are parents.

92. For more on how Mexican women persuade their husbands to migrate, see Hondagneu-Sotelo 1994: 70.

93. Chavez 1992; Frank 2005b.

94. Boehm 2004; Fagetti 2000; Kanaiaupuni 2000; Mummert 1988.

95. D'Aubeterre 2002.

96. Dreby 2007b, 2009; Menjívar and Agadjanian 2007.

97. Dreby 2009; Menjívar and Agadjanian 2007.

98. See Dreby 2007b.

99. González-López 2005.

100. See also Chavez 1992.

101. Wayne Cornelius and Jessa Lewis (2007) found that people in central Mexico are aware of increases in border enforcement but that this does not dissuade them from migrating. Instead, awareness of increased border security affects the strategies Mexicans use to cross the border.

102. Elisabeth Valdez-Suiter, Nancy Rosas-Lopez, and Nayeli Pagaza (2007) found that women in central Mexico have a greater propensity than men to fear the border crossing. Interestingly, this appears to be a perceived fear. Among their sample, no gender differences were evident in reports of physical harm while crossing the border.

103. Amnesty International 1998.

104. For details on the harrowing journey children from Central America make through Mexico to the United States, see Nazario 2006. For descriptions of how Mexican parents smuggle their children across the border, see Adler 2004 and Marizco 2004.

105. National Public Radio 2005. See also Marizco 2004 for an in-depth report on the smuggling of children across the U.S.-Mexican border.

106. Hernández-Barajas 2008.

107. At the time of this writing, no conclusive statistics were available on the number of unaccompanied children crossing or being detained at the U.S.-Mexican border. Figures differ by source, but there appears to be a significant increase over the past few years. Ginger Thompson (2003) reports that in 2002, thirteen hundred unaccompanied minors were repatriated to Mexico. Socorro Hernández-Barajas (2008) reports that in 2006, forty-four thousand were detained, and an estimated fifty thousand were detained in 2007. For more on the risks Mexican children face at the border, see Hernández-Barajas 2008.

108. In the 1920s it would take four weeks or more to send remittances to Italy (Foner 2000: 171).

109. Mahler 2001.

110. For more on how new technologies transform family relationships in the transnational context, see Wilding 2006.

111. See Bernhard, Landolt, and Goldring 2005 on mothers' expectations that separations will be short.

112. Charles Tilly (1998) differentiates between categorical inequalities that are durable and those that fluctuate or are particular to social interactions. The inequalities I discuss here are related to the categories of gender, generation, and social location.

113. Hirsch 2003.

114. Leah Schmalzbauer (2008) paints this picture of Honduran transnational families, with migrant parents suffering to support the middle-class lifestyles of their children who have not migrated.

115. See Sánchez 1993 on patterns of migration to the United States from Mexico in the late nineteenth and early twentieth centuries.

116. Chavez 1992: 82.

TWO. OFELIA AND GERMÁN CRUZ: MIGRANT TIME VERSUS CHILD TIME

1. Zerubavel 1982: 4.

2. On the rhythm of parents' work in the United States, see Roy, Tubbs, and Burton 2004 and Thorpe and Daly 1999.

3. See Malkin 2004.

4. Daly 2001.

5. Malkin 2004: 80.

6. Parents and children in this study have remarkably less information about each other's lives than do other families who are separated because of parents' work. For example, in military families, children may live without a parent, but they know quite a bit about the structure of that parent's daily life (Black 2001 and Kelley 1994). Children of seafarers also seem knowledgeable about their parent's daily routines away from home (Sampson 2005).

7. Hochschild 1997.

8. Scholars assert that the dissonance between work time and family time causes tensions in families and that those with few resources experience different time pressures than do those with more resources (Hochschild 1997 and Roy, Tubbs, and Burton 2004). Research also suggests that children and adults have different perceptions of family time owing to their relative position in the family (Daly 2001 and Thorpe and Daly 1999). Parents and children divided by borders experience dissonance to a greater degree than any of these families because of the very few resources available to them, the socioeconomic differences between the geographic locations in which parents and children live, and the effects that physical distance may have on relationships.

THREE. GENDER AND PARENTING FROM AFAR

1. Please note that Efrén and Claudia's family are not listed in appendix B.

2. The percentages of women who have experienced physical assault resulting from intimate partner violence during their lifetime appear to be quite similar in the United States (20.4 percent) and Mexico (19.2 percent); however, Mexican women are about five times more likely to report victimization within the previous year than are U.S. women. For data on the prevalence of intimate

partner violence in the United States, see Tjaden and Thoennes 2000, and for Mexico, see Instituto Nacional de Estadística y Geografía 2006.

3. For more on how scholars have chosen to operationalize familism in studying Mexicans and Mexican Americans, see Behnke et al. 2008; Bean, Curtis, and Marcum 1977; Falicov 2001; Raley, Durden, and Wildsmith 2004; Suárez-Orozco and Suárez-Orozco 1995; and Tienda 1980. On gender roles and parenting in Mexican families, see Dreby 2006 and Oropesa 1997.

4. For examples of these negotiations among Mexican immigrant couples, see D'Aubeterre 2001; Fagetti 2000; Hirsch 2003; Mummert 1988; and Smith 2006. For an example of negotiations among Ecuadoran couples, see Pribilsky 2004.

5. Melhuus 1996 and Paz 1981 describe men's economic role in Mexican families. See also García and de Oliveira 2006.

6. On Mexican masculinity and machismo, see Lewis 1959; Melhuus and Stolen 1996; Paz 1981; Paredes 1993; and Prieur 1996. On masculinity in rural areas, or ranchero masculinity, see Smith 2006. On masculinity in urban areas, see Gutmann 1996.

7. Dreby 2006, 2007b.

8. On *marianismo,* see Melhuus 1996 and Stevens 1973. On expectations of Latina mothers, see Bernhard, Landolt, and Goldring 2005.

9. For more on "gender bargains" that Mexican men and women negotiate in the transnational context, see Smith 2006. On the "household realignments" that result from men's migrations, see Córdova Plaza 2007.

10. For more on gender and marital relationships among Mexican migrants, see Boehm 2004; Fagetti 2000; Frank 2005b; Hirsch 2003; Kanaiaupuni 2000; Mummert 1988; and Smith 2006.

11. On the construction of gender differences through child rearing, see Munch, McPherson, and Smith-Lovin 1997. Rhacel Salazar Parreñas's work (2005 and 2008) is one exception that does explore gendered expectations of transnational parents.

12. See Dreby 2006. Also, Rachel Adler (2004: 93) found more similarities between Mexican men and women migrants than the literature suggests.

13. On "doing gender," see West and Zimmerman 1987.

14. For descriptions of conventional gender roles in Mexican families, see Lewis 1959; Melhuus and Stolen 1996; and Paz 1981.

15. See Adler 2004 on Yucatan migrants' use of phone cards in Dallas.

16. Children of U.S. migrants in the Mixteca reported 4.93 phone calls to the United States per month, whereas children in the Mixteca with migrant relatives but nonmigrant parents reported 4.04 phone calls to the United States per month. This difference is statistically significant ($p<.01$).

17. A number of significance tests were used to check for differences in communication rates by family migration pattern. There was no significant differ-

ence in frequency of communication between students who have just a mother in the United States, just a father in the United States, or both parents in the United States. Among students with migrant parents, there was no significant difference in frequency of communication between students who have a mother in the United States and those who do not, or between students who have a father in the United States and those who do not. Finally, there are no significant differences in frequency of communication between those with just a mother in the United States and those with just a father in the United States.

18. Of children with migrant relatives other than parents, 70 percent reported receiving emotional gifts, 73 percent received basic necessities, and 50 percent received school supplies from the United States. The difference in receipt of emotional gifts from the United States between children of migrants and others is not significant. Differences in reported receipt of basic necessities are statistically significant ($p<.05$). Differences in the receipt of school supplies also are statistically significant ($p<.01$).

19. Various significance tests were performed to check for differences in types of gifts received by family migration pattern. The same procedures explained in note 17 were used to test for differences in receipt of four main types of gifts: emotional gifts, basic necessities, school supplies, and consumer goods. No significant differences in the receipt of gifts by family migration pattern were found.

20. Of girls in the Mixteca, 95 percent reported receiving gifts from their migrant parents, as did 87 percent of boys. This difference is statistically significant ($p<.05$). Of daughters, 84 percent reported receiving emotional gifts, 82 percent reported receiving basic necessities, 78 percent reported receiving consumer gifts, and 66 percent reported receiving school supplies. Of sons, 61 percent reported receiving emotional gifts, 77 percent reported receiving basic necessities, 69 percent reported receiving consumer gifts, and 52 percent reported receiving school supplies.

21. For the significance of gifts, see Mauss 1923.

22. Cornelius 1982.

23. Fernando Lozano Ascencio (2004) reported that 89 percent of Mexican remittance senders in the United States are men. Manuel Orozco (2007) found that Mexican men send more money home than do Mexican women. Elisabeth Valdez-Suiter, Nancy Rosas-Lopez, and Nayeli Pagaza (2007) found that amounts and frequency of remittances do not vary between male and female migrants but that since women earn less than men, their remittances represent a higher percentage of their income. See Abrego 2008 and Schmalzbauer 2004 on the gendered remittance patterns of Central Americans.

24. The mean amount of remittances per month in pesos was 2,598 for those

with just a father in the United States, 1,846 for those with a single mother abroad, and 2,482 for those with both parents in the United States.

25. Haugen 2005: 519. See Zelizer 1997 on the social significance of monetary transactions within families.

26. Reanne Frank (2005b) has shown rates of marital dissolution to be higher among Mexican migrants than their nonmigrant counterparts. See also Kibria 1993; Min 1998; Pribilsky 2004; and Smith 2006.

27. For more on transnational gossip, see Dreby 2009. Cecilia Menjívar and Victor Agadjanian (2007) describe similar dynamics in both Armenian and Guatemalan migrant families. For a historical example among Italian migrants, see Reeder 2001.

28. See Chinchilla and Zentgraf 2007.

29. See Hirsch 2003 and Smith 2006.

30. On Dominican men's participation in child rearing in the United States while their wives work, see Levitt 2001.

31. Furstenberg and Cherlin 1994; Jensen and McKee 2003.

32. Furstenberg and Cherlin 1994 and Haugen 2005.

33. See Smith 2006. Despite the popular belief that depression leads migrants in general, and Mexican men specifically, to drink, recent research suggests that alcoholism is less common among foreign-born Mexican Americans than their U.S.-born counterparts and Mexico-born nonimmigrants (see Borges et al. 2006 and Grant et al. 2004).

34. Frank Furstenberg and Andrew Cherlin (1994: 66) suggest that children need two things during the crisis period immediately following a divorce: an increase in emotional support and "structure provided by a reasonably predictable daily routine." International migration does not necessarily involve divorce, although it may, but it does entail the loss of one or both parents. As with children of divorce, structure and routine may help children in transnational families adjust to these changes.

35. Avila 2008.

36. Massey et al. 1987.

37. Maria Eugenia D'Aubeterre (2000, 2002) has found a consistent pattern in Puebla of women returning to their family homes when their husband migrates. I fully describe caregiving arrangements when women migrate in chapter 6.

38. Marjorie Faulstich Orellana et al. (2001) write about immigrant girls' participation in household labor (see also Orellana 2001).

39. For factors leading Mexican single mothers to migrate, see Chavez 1992; Fagetti 2000; and Kanaiaupuni 2000.

40. Coe 2008.

41. Parreñas 2005, 2008. Some researchers have also suggested that a father's

migration produces an ambivalent reaction among Mexican children (see Aguilera-Guzman et al. 2004).

42. A study conducted at a nearby school in San Ángel shows that a father's absence appears to negatively affect children's school performance (see Pérez López 2003).

43. This is in line with Ellen Galinsky's (1999) findings that taking into account children's perspectives on families shows fathers to be more important than adults give them credit for.

44. Of the children surveyed, 30 percent said it was better that neither parent migrate, 6 percent said that both parents should migrate, and less than 3 percent said that mothers should migrate.

45. "Qualities of father" and "relationship with mother" are not mutually exclusive categories. Some children cited both reasons.

46. This finding is interesting given that research among children in the United States suggests there has been a shift in the way children view parenting roles, with children today viewing fathers' roles as more recreational (see Milkie, Simon, and Powell 1997).

47. Aguilera-Guzman et al. 2004 and Heymann et al. 2009.

48. One primary goal for Mexican men during migration is financing the construction of a house with their remittances (see Fletcher 1999).

49. Riessman 1990: 155.

50. Cathy Schen (2005) describes the psychiatric symptoms women may experience when separated from their children.

51. On transnational mothers' feelings of guilt, see Avila 2008; Bernhard, Landolt, and Goldring 2005; and Parreñas 2001a.

52. West and Fenstermaker 1995: 9. See also West and Zimmerman 1987.

53. Specifically, research shows Puerto Rican women to be instrumental in maintaining transnational family networks (Alicea 1997; Aranda 2007; and Pérez 2004). Rhacel Parreñas (2005, 2008) also shows conventional gender roles to predominate in transnational households.

54. D'Aubeterre 2007; Hirsch 2003; González-López 2005; Levitt 2001.

55. Pierrette Hondagneu-Sotelo and Ernestine Avila (1997) suggest that migrating mothers challenge concepts of motherhood by migrating to work without their children. While on some level this is true, families' experiences suggest otherwise at the interpersonal level.

56. Research among families in the United States finds that mothers on the whole do more housework than fathers do, regardless of time available for such chores (see Bianchi et al. 2000; Kroska 2004; and Thompson and Walker 1989).

57. Hondagneu-Sotelo 1994: 67.

58. To get a divorce in Mexico, both husband and wife must sign the divorce papers. Thus when migrant men disappear in the United States, women in

Mexico often consider themselves abandoned. They are able to officially report this abandonment, as was the case for this mother, in order to protect themselves when their husbands return from the United States.

59. Hirsch 2003; Hondagneu-Sotelo 1994.

60. Parreñas's (2001b, 2005) work on gender expectations of transnational mothering of Filipina migrants also is relevant.

FOUR. ARMANDO LÓPEZ ON FATHERHOOD

1. Research shows historical changes in the expectations of fatherhood in the United States. Early in the twentieth century, fathers were expected to provide more guidance for their children (see Johansen 2001). Since industrialization, fatherhood has mostly been associated with providing children with economic and educational opportunities (see Marsiglio et al. 2000 and Thompson and Walker 1989). More recently, fathers' roles with children may be becoming more recreational (see Milkie, Simon, and Powell 1997). For an overview of masculinity in North America, see Kimmel 1996.

2. Gutmann 1996: 24. For more on concepts of masculinity in Latin America, see Lancaster 1992.

3. Esteinou 2004; García and de Oliveira 2006. See Gutmann 1996 on men's fathering activities in the *sectores populares* of Mexico City.

4. García and de Oliveira 2006.

5. Fox and Solís-Camara 1997.

6. Baca Zinn 1989: 95.

7. This finding corroborates research in the United States, which shows mothers as mediating children's relationships with nonresidential fathers. See, for example, Dunn et al. 2004; Edin and Lein 1997; and Furstenberg and Cherlin 1994.

8. For more on transnational gossip in Mexican families, see Dreby 2009.

9. In Mexico, people usually take two last names. The first last name is the father's, and the second is the mother's last name.

10. Stewart 1999: 894. See Ryan, Kalil, and Ziol-Guest 2008 on the association between parents' relationship status and their patterns of involvement.

11. See King and Heard 1999.

12. For descriptions of children's residence following their parents' divorce, see Amato and Booth 1996 and Furstenberg and Cherlin 1994.

13. See Esteinou 2004. Also, for more on child custody arrangements in Mexican families, see López 1999: 298.

14. Naomi Gerstel and Sally Gallagher (2001) theorize that men's caregiving is contingent on women's activities. They suggest two competing theories for

men's participation in housework that also hold true for caregiving: that there is a substitution effect, in which men do more caregiving when women are unavailable to do so, and that caregiving is complementary, in that men are more likely to engage in it if encouraged to do so by the women in their lives. Gerstel and Gallagher show men's caregiving to be complementary, with wives and daughters engaging them in caregiving activities. However, when men's extended family members are engaged in caregiving, they substitute for the care men give. In the transnational context, it appears that men's caregiving follows the substitution model, although—as Gerstel and Gallagher suggest—in both cases, men's roles in family caregiving are contingent on women's activities.

FIVE. CHILDREN AND POWER DURING SEPARATION

1. Smith 2006: 123.

2. Nazario 2006. Indeed, the number of minors illegally crossing the border appears to be rising. In 2002, border patrol officers arrested thirty-five thousand minors attempting to cross the border (Hansen 2003). Between October 1, 2003, and September 30, 2004, more than forty-three thousand minor children were detained while attempting illegal entry (Marizco 2004). Shelters have popped up along border communities to receive captured minors. In places where shelters do not exist, local authorities generally release minors to the streets since no legal guardians can claim them (Hansen 2003; Marizco 2004; and Nazario 2006).

3. Cati Coe (2008) found that children are more likely to describe feelings of emotional suffering due to family separation during migration than are their parents. Jason Pribilsky (2001) describes children of migrants living in the Ecuadoran Andes as frequently suffering from *nervios,* which is a culturally specific illness with depressive-like symptoms. Jodi Heymann and colleagues (2009) have shown that Mexican children with a caregiver in the United States are more likely to suffer from physical, emotional, and behavioral problems than are children with nonmigrant caregivers.

4. Kabeer 2000.

5. Ernesto Castañeda-Tinoco (2006) also writes of Mixteca migrants in Guerrero aspiring to retire in Mexico after investing some years working abroad (see also Massey et al. 1987 and Schmalzbauer 2008).

6. Corsaro 1997, 2003; Thorne 1987, 1993.

7. See Moran-Taylor 2008.

8. There is conflicting evidence on the educational outcomes of Mexican children of migrants. On the negative educational outcomes for children of migrants, see Aguilera Guzman et al. 2004; Giorguli Saucedo 2004; Hildebrandt

and McKenzie 2005; Kandel and Kao 2000; and Kandel and Massey 2002. On some of the educational benefits children accrue from having a migrant parent, see Hanson and Woodruff 2003 and Kandel and Kao 2001.

9. See Coe 2008.

10. Indeed, along with traditional gender roles, Mexican familism is characterized by the symbolic centrality of children to the family. For more on familism, see Raley, Durden, and Wildsmith 2004; Suárez-Orozco and Suárez-Orozco 1995; and Tienda 1980. For more on the centrality of children to mothers and fathers, see Esteinou 2004 and Gutmann 1996.

11. See Woodward, Fergusson, and Belsky 2000.

12. See also Dreby 2007a.

13. Leah Schmalzbauer (2004, 2005a) has similar findings in her study of Honduran transnational families.

14. Bowlby 1973, as cited in Smith, Lalonde, and Johnson 2004.

15. Research with adult children reminiscing about periods of separation from parents suggests that separation has some long-term effects on their lives. See Arnold 2006; Avila 2008; Olwig 1999; and Smith, Lalonde, and Johnson 2004.

16. On male prerogatives in families, see Esteinou 2004; Melhuus 1996; and Oropesa 1997.

17. Jeffrey Lewis (2000) describes parents in an upper Mixteca community as having a very standoffish approach to child rearing. For regional differences in parenting styles, see Esteinou 2004: 18.

18. See Artico 2003; Myers 1999; and Smith, Lalonde, and Johnson 2004.

19. I believe this is because the concept of migration for young children is more abstract. Children of migrants may like the idea of migration and report this in surveys, but when faced with the concrete possibility of joining their parents, they feel uncomfortable and resist joining them.

20. This difference is not statistically significant.

21. On parent-child relationships during adolescence, see Aquilino 1997 and Laursen, Coy, and Collins 1998.

22. Galambos and Almeida 1992.

23. On behavioral difficulties among children of migrants in Zacatecas, see Aguilera-Guzman et al. 2004; in Puebla, see Smith 2006; in the Dominican Republic, see Levitt 2001; in Honduras, see Nazario 2006.

24. Michelle Moran-Taylor (2008) writes that Guatemalans are most preoccupied with the behavior of girls during parental absences. As my examples show, I found complaints to be common about both girls and boys.

25. On educational indicators among children of migrants in Zacatecas, see Aguilera-Guzman et al. 2004 and Kandel and Kao 2001. See Giorguli Saucedo 2004 for national indicators. See Pérez López 2003 for a small-scale study of school performance among children of migrant men in the Mixteca.

26. On the depressive symptoms experienced by children of migrants in Ecuador, see Pribilsky 2001. On the negative health outcomes for Mexican children whose caregivers have migrated, see Heymann et al. 2009.

27. In Mexico, students are graded on a scale from 1 to 10. A 5 is generally considered a failing grade.

28. Patricia Adler and Peter Adler (1998) describe peer pressure in American schools from children's perspectives.

29. These data are from 1990 (Ham-Chande 1995: 35). The spread of literacy in Oaxaca has been uneven. Literacy rates appear to be higher in market-oriented economies and areas with well-developed transportation systems (Kowalewski and Saindon 1992). San Ángel has an agricultural base, and a paved road to the nearest large city was completed only in 1996. It is not surprising that literacy rates in San Ángel and nearby towns lag behind those in the state of Oaxaca and other areas of Mexico. A 2008 survey in a nearby town in the Mixteca of Oaxaca shows the illiteracy rate for those ages fifteen and older to be more than 32 percent (Sawyer et al. 2009).

30. The Orden Jurídico Nacional (n.d.) describes state laws pertaining to education and the vast importance of parents to regional schools.

31. Brett Laursen, Katherine Coy, and Andrew Collins (1998) describe typical conflicts among adolescents in American families.

32. A recent study shows that migration has no impact on the average educational attainment of residents in the Mixteca of Oaxaca (Sawyer et al. 2009).

33. Note that Rhacel Salazar Parreñas's (2008) finding that Filipino children are ambivalent about fathers' migrations may be explained by her method of interviewing young adult children, as I also find that as children age, they become more ambivalent about parental migrations.

34. Giorguli Saucedo 2004.

35. Pierrette Hondagneu-Sotelo (1994: 86) describes migration to the United States as part of the maturation process for young men. For more on migration and the life cycle, see also Massey et al. 1987: 197.

36. Among children over the age of eighteen, of those with migrant parents, 67 percent said they wanted to migrate to the United States, while 61 percent of those with nonmigrant parents did. This difference is not statistically significant.

37. Marcela Cerrutti and Douglas Massey (2001) found that women most often migrate following other family members, while men and unmarried young women more often migrate in search of employment opportunities.

38. Many scholars have written about Mexican women's migration via social networks and for family reasons. See Cerrutti and Massey 2001; Curran and Rivero-Fuentes 2003; and Goodson-Lawes 1993.

39. On the pattern of older children migrating north in other areas of Mexico, see Marroni 2000.

40. On the new sociology of childhood, see Corsaro 1997, 2003; James, Jenks, and Prout 1998; Thorne 1993; and Wrigley and Dreby 2005a.

41. Qvortrup 1999.

42. See Wrigley and Dreby 2005a.

43. Gry Mette Haugen (2005) describes children's perspectives on their roles in postdivorce families.

44. Esteinou 2004: 25.

45. For the emotional consequences of family separation on children, see Artico 2003; Giorguli Saucedo 2004; Kandel 1998; Kandel and Kao 2001; Levitt 2001; Menjívar 2000; Parreñas 2005; Smith 2006; Smith, Lalonde, and Johnson 2004; and Suárez-Orozco, Todorova, and Louie 2002.

46. For more on children's symbolic role in families, see Jensen 2003.

47. On health benefits of migration for children, see Frank 2005a; Hildebrandt and McKenzie 2005; and Kanaiaupuni and Donato 1999.

48. On migrant networks as a form of social capital, see Cohen 2004. Also see Leite, Ramos, and Gaspar 2003 and Santibáñez 2000 on the importance of social networks to current patterns in Mexican migration.

49. Kandel and Massey 2002.

50. Cohen 2004; Kandel and Massey 2002.

51. I do not believe that my findings contradict the patterns that Massey and colleagues have identified with regard to a "culture of migration"; rather, they complicate those findings. I suggest that, instead of parents passing on pro-migration attitudes to their children, the intergenerational transmission of migration is related to life course changes and resource availability (rather than culture or attitudes). My data demonstrate that children of migrants often have quite negative views about migration after a parent leaves. These children adopt pro-migration attitudes only over time, after their schooling is cut short and they have no resources for the future other than their parents' social capital. This distinction is important because of its implications. According to the "culture of migration" hypothesis, migration patterns will not change unless Mexican people change their attitudes about migration, or there is a cultural shift in Mexico. According to my findings, however, migration patterns could change if the children of migrants are given viable educational or work opportunities in Mexico.

52. Larson and Almeida 1999. See also Smith-Lovin 1989.

53. On stages in the transition to adulthood, see Hogan and Astone 1986 and Shanahan 2000.

54. On how the "culture of migration" affects youth in sending communities in Zacatecas, see Kandel and Massey 2002.

55. On how women bargain for family resources in their families, see Seltzer et al. 2005. Economists also have theorized how women's position in the family allows them to bargain for family resources. See Folbre 1986, 2001; Konrad and Lommerud 2000; Lundberg and Pollack 1996; and McElroy and Horney 1981.

SIX. MIDDLEWOMEN

1. The term "tangle of reciprocity" is from Hansen 2005.

2. In an issue of the *Journal of Marriage and Family*, Margaret Nelson (2006) wrote about how rural single mothers "do family," evoking responses about theorizing "doing family" from Suzanne Bianchi (2006) and Andrew Cherlin (2006).

3. Hansen 2005.

4. Ibid.

5. Stack 1974.

6. Andrea Hunter and Margaret Ensminger (1992) show that African American children's living arrangements are quite fluid and change over the life course.

7. Goody 1982.

8. See Alber 2003; Goody 1982; and Klomegah 2000.

9. Verhoef 2005.

10. For more on care networks in transnational families, see Reynolds and Zontini 2006; Zontini 2006.

11. Chamberlain 2003: 65. For more on fostering in families from the West Indies, see Watkins-Owens 2001.

12. Olwig 1999; Soto 1987.

13. Soto 1987: 134.

14. Moran-Taylor 2008; Parreñas 2005; Schmalzbauer 2005a.

15. See Anguiano Tellez 1992; Lomnitz 1977; Méndez Morales 2000; and Stephen 2007.

16. See Esteinou 2004; Raley, Durden, and Wildsmith 2004; and Tienda 1980.

17. See Bernhard, Landolt, and Goldring 2005.

18. In the Mixteca, of the eighteen children I surveyed whose mothers had migrated and who did not live with a grandparent, four lived with a father, twelve lived with a sibling, and two children, ages fifteen and nineteen, lived on their own.

19. This difference in living with grandparents is statistically significant ($p<.001$).

20. Fourteen percent of children reported living with both maternal and paternal grandparents. Note that there do appear to be some regional differences in these patterns. In the town on the coast of Oaxaca where I also distrib-

uted surveys, 48 percent of children of migrant mothers lived with their grandparents and 19 percent with fathers. This may be indicative of higher divorce rates on the coast of Oaxaca than in the Mixteca, with more fathers retaining custody of their children. The preference for maternal grandparents as caregivers, however, is consistent. Of those living with grandparents, only 7 percent lived exclusively with paternal grandparents.

21. Robichaux 1997. See also Mahler 1999 for descriptions of a similar pattern in El Salvador.

22. Anthropologists in Mexico have documented changes in family residential patterns resulting from migration (Cordova Plaza 2007; D'Aubeterre 2001; and Fagetti 2000).

23. These living patterns are not mutually exclusive. Sixteen percent of children reported living with both maternal and paternal grandparents.

24. For more on U.S. grandparents and child care, see Bowers and Myers 1999.

25. See Soto 1987.

26. See Moran-Taylor 2008, which found that men also often figure into caregiving relationships in Guatemala even though they are not actually involved in the daily care of children.

27. Regarding children as "women's wealth" in West Indian families, see Soto 1987: 134.

28. See Jendrek 1993.

29. See Wong, Palloni, and Soldo 2007 on how migration may help return-migrants in Mexico avoid economic hardship typical among older individuals in Mexico.

30. Ham-Chande 1995: 44.

31. Ibid.: 38.

32. Ibid.: 52. See also Wong, Palloni, and Soldo 2007 on the socioeconomic conditions elderly Mexicans face.

33. Schmalzbauer 2008: 344. Note that, drawing on Bryceson and Vuorela 2002, Schmalzbauer uses the concept of "relativizing" to describe the mechanism by which migrants in transnational families manage separation by selectively withholding the information they share with loved ones back home. She suggests that relativizing creates inequalities in families experiencing separation.

34. Michelle Moran-Taylor (2008) also found that relatives of migrants in Guatemala understand the economic difficulties migrants face working abroad.

35. See Bowers and Myers 1999.

36. See Cohen 2004 on the importance of social network ties to facilitating migration from Oaxaca to the United States.

37. See Moran-Taylor 2008 for a similar incident in a Guatemalan family.

38. Moran-Taylor 2008: 87.

39. Karen Fog Olwig (1999) found that adult children in the Caribbean reported economic difficulties as negatively impacting their relationships with caregivers, including with their own grandparents.

40. Margaret Platt Jendrek (1993) also found reports of family jealously between custodial parents and other family members when grandparents are the primary caregivers of their grandchildren.

41. This is also true in the United States. Bonita Bowers and Barbara Myers (1999) found that the greatest predictor of grandparent caregivers' feelings of burden and stress is children's bad behavior.

42. A UNICEF study comparing child death rates from maltreatment in industrialized nations in the 1990s finds death rates in both Mexico and the United States to be 2.2 per 100,000 children (United Nations Children's Fund 2003).

43. Marizco 2004; Nazario 2006.

44. For information on perpetrators of child maltreatment and neglect in the United States, see Administration for Children and Families 2006.

45. See Hayslip and Kaminski 2005; Hughes et al. 2007; and Minkler and Fuller-Thompson 1999.

46. Hughes et al. 2007: 112.

47. According to Rhacel Salazar Parreñas, who has studied Filipino transnational families extensively, "Much academic and newspaper writing on transnational families assumes that children growing up in the Philippines without their parents, particularly their mothers, are prone to delinquency and declining moral values, particularly materialism" (2005: 39).

48. Hansen 2005: 157.

49. Goody 1982.

50. Jessaca Leinaweaver (forthcoming) also suggests that transnational migration in the case of Peruvians transforms the ways both children and the elderly are cared for.

51. For more on reciprocity, see Gouldner 1960 and Hansen 2005.

52. Bryceson and Vuorela 2002: 10.

53. Goody 1982.

54. Ibid.

55. Nelson 2006.

56. Velasco Ortiz 2005: 146. On the importance of extended family for Mexicans, see Esteinou 2004; Raley, Durden, and Wildsmith 2004; and Tienda 1980.

57. Weston 1991. See also Stacey 1998.

58. Nelson 2006: 783.

59. Schneider 1968.

SEVEN. CINDY RODRÍGUEZ BETWEEN TWO WORLDS

1. Schneider 1968.

2. It is common practice in rural areas of Oaxaca for teachers who retire to pass on their employment contract to another member of the family.

3. One study on children in long-term foster care arrangements in Australia found that children describe foster care parents as more centrally part of their families than their biological parents (Gardner 1996). See also Fox and Berrick 2007.

4. Schneider 1968.

5. Ibid: 7.

6. On cultural constructs of Mexican families and Mexican familism, see Esteinou 2004; Raley, Durden, and Wildsmith 2004; Tienda 1980; and Velasco Ortiz 2005.

EIGHT. DIVIDED BY BORDERS

1. Amayo 2005.

2. Rhacel Salazar Parreñas (2005) reported similar findings in the Philippines, although she found that much of the negative sentiment was directed at migrant mothers. See also Gamburd 2008.

3. Moen and Wethington 1992. Economists have argued that families are cooperative units and that ventures like international migration are examples of "joint-utility functions" that benefit all members of the family (Becker 1991; Folbre 1986, 2001; and Fomby 2006). The analytical focus on family adaptive strategies is similar in that these strategies highlight how family members exhibit "social solidarity and income pooling among members" (Grasmuck and Pessar 1991: 133). However, studies of family adaptive strategies also acknowledge and seek to highlight how family members have different stakes in migration. For examples of social historians' analyses of families' adaptive strategies, see Bras 2003; Paping 2004; Ryan 2004; and Vencent 2000.

4. For an earlier version of women's employment as a family adaptive strategy, see Tilly and Scott 1978.

5. Manuel Orozco (2007) reports that Mexican migrants tend to send the most money when they have been away between four and six years, at which point the amounts of remittances begin to decline. Although this may contradict my point, all migrants are included. It is possible that selecting for those with family commitments in the United States would show different results. Indeed, Orozco also shows that U.S. citizens remit less money than do noncitizens, suggesting that those with more substantial ties in the United States remit less money to relatives in Mexico.

6. Suárez-Orozco, Todorova, and Louie 2002. Thirty-three percent of children were reunited with fathers after two to five years apart, and 33 percent joined fathers in the United States after more than five years of separation.

7. King and Heard 1999; Stewart 1999.

8. Marjorie Faulstich Orellana et al. (2001) also suggest that migration affords children power in their relationships with adults in their lives after migration.

9. Research suggests that Mexican women rely more on social networks to arrive in the United States than men do (Curran and Rivero-Fuentes 2003).

10. Children with both parents in the United States are significantly more likely to draw both parents in their pictures than are children actually living with both parents ($p<.05$).

11. Students living with a parent who is single because of migration are significantly more likely to draw both parents than are those living with a parent who is single because of divorce, separation, or death ($p<.01$). This same pattern is repeated between students living with neither parent because both parents have migrated and those living with neither parent owing to causes other than migration ($p<.001$).

12. On foster-care children's perceptions of their families, see Fox and Berrick 2007; Gardner 1996; and Kufeldt, Armstrong, and Dorosh 1995.

13. For the effects of separation on family relationships after reunification, see Artico 2003; Avila 2008; Menjívar 2006; Mitrani, Santisteban, and Muir 2004; Smith, Lalonde, and Johnson 2004; and Suárez-Orozco, Todorova, and Louie 2002.

14. Artico 2003; Mitrani, Santisteban, and Muir 2004.

15. Elder and Kirkpatrick Johnson 2002: 52.

16. Elder 1998.

17. Families' decisions about migration also shape controversy over U.S. immigration policy and the structure of the U.S. economy. This other side of the coin, however, is not the topic of this study. See Chang 2000 for an example of work that traces the impact that families' decisions have on policy.

18. On the new destinations of Mexican migrants, see Durand, Massey, and Capoffero 2005; Millard and Chapa 2004; Passel 2006; and Zúñiga and Hernández-León 2005.

19. On female migration rates in Mexico, see Cerutti and Massey 2002; Donato 1993; and Kanaiaupuni 2000.

20. Cornelius 2001 and Massey, Durand, and Malone 2002.

21. Passel 2005.

22. In Canada, for example, Filipina domestic workers endure a long process to legally sponsor their children's immigration (Cohen 2000).

23. For more on the culture of migration, see Kandel and Massey 2002.

24. Kandel 1998. A smaller sample of sixth graders also surveyed in Zacate-

cas ($N = 310$) found that at any given time, 34 percent of students had one or both of their parents working in the United States (Aguilera-Guzman et al. 2004).

25. Of children in the Mixteca, 81 percent of those with migrant parents reported that they wanted to migrate, compared to 82 percent of those with non-migrant parents.

26. In an OLS regression model, both of these family migration patterns significantly affect educational aspirations ($p<.05$). This model includes controls for who in the family has migrated (aside from parents), if the respondent has been to the United States, if the respondent receives money from the United States, and parents' marital status.

27. Elder 1998: 3.

28. Bernhard, Landolt, and Goldring 2005; Chang 2000; Cohen 2000; Constable 1999; Erel 2002; Escrivá 2004; Lan 2003; Parreñas 2001a, 2005; Sørenson 2005.

29. For a comprehensive discussion of U.S. immigration policy, see Zolberg 2006.

30. Department of Homeland Security 2008. Note that increases in spending on border control and enforcement began in the 1980s and grew significantly in the late 1990s. Deborah Waller Meyers (2006) reports that the number of border patrol agents deployed at the U.S.-Mexican border grew from 2,580 in 1978, to 5,000 in 1992, and to 9,000 in 2000. The budget for border patrol activities grew from $325 million in 1992 to $1 billion in 2000. For more on earlier trends, see also Dunn 1996.

31. Cornelius 2001, 2004, 2007.

32. See Massey 2006 and Massey, Durand, and Malone 2002.

33. Menjívar 2006. See also Nazario 2006.

34. This estimate of the undocumented Mexican population is based on 2008 data (Passel and Cohn 2008).

35. On how immigrants can become prey to unscrupulous lawyers, see Rivlan 2006.

36. Passel and Cohn 2008.

37. U.S. Citizenship and Immigration Services 2009 and U.S. Department of the State 2009.

38. For more on Mexicans' employment in new destinations of settlement throughout the United States, see Zúñiga and Hernández-León 2005.

39. U.S. Department of State 2009. The U.S. Department of State publishes a visa bulletin every month with the current wait times for each category of visa. The numbers I report here are from the most recent visa bulletin for May 2009.

40. Zolberg 2006.

41. Vivian Garrison and Carol Weiss (1979) make the point that U.S. immigration policy trumps family reunification, but the definition of family used in

policy does not match families' lived experiences and, in particular, members' mechanisms of cooperation.

42. Menjívar 2006.

43. The total Mexican population is estimated at 11,534,972 for 2006. In the same year, the Salvadoran population was 1,042,218; the Guatemalan population was 740,986; and the Honduran population was 2,182,572. See Pew Hispanic Center 2008.

44. Urban Institute 2006. For more on mixed-status families, see Boehm 2008 and Romero 2008.

45. Foner 2000: 16. Indeed, until the 1920s, there were no numerical limits on European migrants coming through Ellis Island; those denied entry primarily had communicable diseases, had questionable political views, or were deemed physically or mentally unfit. Chinese immigrants, however, were excluded starting in 1882.

46. Rumbaut et al. 2006.

47. Although at the time of this study I found that many of those detained for criminal activity were referred to immigration officials, by 2007 this practice had expanded significantly. After an undocumented immigrant was involved in a murder in Newark, New Jersey, in August 2007, statewide referrals to immigration have doubled. Immigrants describe being asked about their immigration status even when not involved in criminal activities (Fahim 2008).

48. See Llorente 2008.

49. Hazelton, Pennsylvania, drew national attention by trying to adopt an ordinance that penalized renting to undocumented immigrants in 2006, which was struck down by a federal judge in 2007. Riverside, New Jersey, adopted a similar ordinance in 2006. The controversy led to an exodus from the old industrial town that had been in decline prior to the arrival of immigrants, many from Brazil, and the economic consequences led the town to rescind the ordinance in 2007 (Belson and Capuzzo 2007). Nonetheless, Bound Brook and Middletown, New Jersey, attempted to pass similar ordinances in 2008 (Penton 2008).

50. In 2007, prior to resigning after getting caught up in a prostitution scandal, Attorney General Elliot Spitzer announced that he would no longer restrict driver's licenses to those with legal documentation in New York, only to drop his plan after a month of facing widespread controversy over the proposal (Bernstein 2007 and Confessore 2007).

51. On the 2008 incident on Long Island, see Semple 2008. In 2001, two Mexican day laborers in Farmingville, Long Island, were victims of a hate crime, the aftermath of which is documented in the film *Farmingville.* During the spring and summer of 2004, seventeen Latino men in Plainfield, New Jersey, were victims of crimes mostly committed by African Americans. There is debate over

whether the men were targeted because they were Latino or because they typically were paid in cash by their employers (Cave 2004).

52. For more on local responses to immigration nationwide, see Migration Policy Source 2007.

53. Capps et al. 2007.

54. See Larini 2008 and Mandell 2008. Nationally, deportations increased by 20 percent between 2007 and 2008.

55. Preston 2007. See also Capps et al. 2007 and Romero 2008.

56. Preston 2007.

57. Thank you to Rubén Rumbaut for pointing out the impact that forced separation may have on second-generation children.

58. On the price of motherhood, see Crittenden 2001. On how professional women are pushed out of their high-level jobs, see Stone 2007.

59. There is no federally funded program for child care until children are age three, at which point safety risks of child care greatly diminish. For more on the types of child care available to U.S. parents, see Wrigley and Dreby 2005b.

60. Indeed, since 1996, family-based petitions require the sponsoring U.S. citizen or resident family member to sign an affidavit of support for the intended immigrant. This affidavit of support obligates the sponsoring family member to be financially responsible for the immigrant and liable for any public welfare benefits the immigrant many use. The purpose of this requirement is to prevent immigrants from becoming public charges of the U.S. government.

61. Cornelius 2004, 2007; Massey 2006; Massey, Durand, and Malone 2002.

62. Despite the economic crisis of 2008 and 2009, as of this writing the Obama administration had announced that immigration reform would be part of the new administration's agenda during the coming years (Preston 2009).

63. For concrete examples of how to support domestic workers, see Chang 2000 and Hondagneu-Sotelo 2001.

64. See Smith 2006 and Stephen 2007.

65. Raelene Wilding (2006) shows that while immigrants to Australia reported phone calls to be their primary means of communicating with family members in other countries during the early 1990s, by the late 1990s, e-mail became the primary mode of communication. Parreñas (2005) describes Filipina migrant mothers communicating with their children repeatedly during the day via text-messaging on mobile phones.

66. León-García 2008.

67. Ten states have awarded in-state tuition benefits for undocumented immigrants who have attended high school for between one and three years in that state. As of April 2009, New Jersey was not one of them (Donaldson James 2005 and Morse and Speasmaker 2006).

68. Ehrenreich and Hochschild 2002; Parreñas 2001b; Sassen 2002.

APPENDIX A. RESEARCH DESIGN

1. Marcus 1998: 90. See also Burawoy et al. 2000 and Nash 2006.

2. Since the 1990s, transnational scholars have employed multisited ethnographic methods to study migrant communities. For examples, see Grasmuck and Pessar 1991; Levitt 2001; Mahler 1999; and Smith 2006.

3. For research on domestic workers, see Hondagneu-Sotelo and Avila 1997; Hondagneu-Sotelo 2001; Parreñas 2001a, 2001b; and Wrigley 1995.

4. A table that summarizes specific details on each individual interviewed is purposively excluded from this study in order to protect the privacy of these individuals.

5. Malkin 2004.

6. See Gutmann 1996.

7. Mose Brown and de Casanova forthcoming: 17.

8. Instituto Mexicano de Seguro Social 2004.

9. In fact, in the early 1980s, it was estimated that of every ten Mixtecans, three permanently left the region, four were temporary migrants, and only three stayed in the area (Velasco Ortiz 1995). High emigration rates have been attributed to poor land quality (Anguiano Tellez 1992). In the 1980s, 30 percent of land in the region was estimated to have no practical use for human, vegetable, or animal life (Velasco Ortiz 1995). It was during these years that migrants from the Mixteca region of Puebla headed to New York City in unprecedented numbers (Cortés Sánchez 2003 and Smith 2001). Research on Oaxacan migration describes waves of Mixtec migration to Oregon and California in the 1980s and 1990s, with most migrants working in U.S. agriculture as their fathers and grandfathers had done in years past (Besserer 2004; Corbett 1992; Rivera-Salgado 1999; Smith 2001; and Stephen 2002).

10. Romney and Romney 1966.

11. Instituto Mexicano de Seguro Social 2004.

12. On talking to children, see Corsaro 2003. On local ranchero culture, see Smith 2006.

13. Lareau 2003.

14. Hansen 2005; Lareau 2003.

15. For prior research on transnational migration, see Grasmuck and Pessar 1991; Hirsch 2003; Levitt 2001; and Smith 2006. For detailed documentation of the dispersed patterns of migration from the Mixteca, see Besserer 2004.

16. For half the year, a family friend of Raúl's from Veracruz came with me to Oaxaca.

References

Abrego, Leisy. 2008. "Barely Subsisting, Surviving, or Thriving: How Parents' Legal Status and Gender Shape the Economic and Emotional Well-Being of Salvadoran Transnational Families." Ph.D. dissertation, Department of Sociology, University of California, Los Angeles.

Adler, Patricia, and Peter Adler. 1998. *Peer Power: Preadolescent Culture and Identity.* New Brunswick, NJ: Rutgers University Press.

Adler, Rachel H. 2004. *Yucatecans in Dallas, Texas: Breaching the Border, Bridging the Distance.* Boston: Pearson, Allyn, and Bacon.

Administration for Children and Families. 2006. "Chapter 5 Perpetrators." *Child Maltreatment 2006.* Washington, DC: U.S. Department of Health and Human Services. Retrieved April 27, 2009 (http://www.acf.hhs.gov/programs/cb/pubs/cm06/chapter5.htm#character).

Aguilera-Guzman, Rosa Maria, V. Nelly Salgado de Snyder, Martha Romero, and Maria Elena Medina-Mora. 2004. "Paternal Absence and International

Migration: Stressors and Compensators Associated with the Mental Health of Mexican Teenagers of Rural Origin." *Adolescence* 39: 711–723.

Alarcón-González, Diana, and Terry McKinley. 1999. "The Adverse Effects of Structural Adjustment on Working Women in Mexico." *Latin American Perspectives* 26: 103–117.

Alba, Richard, and Victor Nee. 2003. *Remaking the American Mainstream: Assimilation and Contemporary Immigration.* Cambridge, MA: Harvard University Press.

Alber, Erdmute. 2003. "Denying Biological Parenthood: Fosterage in Northern Benin." *Ethos* 68: 487–506.

Alicea, Marixsa. 1997. "A Chambered Nautilus: The Contradictory Nature of Puerto Rican Women's Role in the Social Construction of Transnational Community." *Gender and Society* 11: 597–626.

Amato, Paul R., and Alan Booth. 1996. "A Prospective Study of Divorce and Parent-Children Relationships." *Journal of Marriage and Family* 58: 356–365.

Amayo, Apolonia. 2005. "Preocupa desintegración familiar." *El Sol de Tehuacan,* April 10, A1.

Amnesty International. 1998. "Human Rights Concerns in the Border Region with Mexico." AMR 51/03/98, May 20. Retrieved April 27, 2009 (http://web.amnesty.org/library/Index/engAMR510031998).

Anguiano Tellez, Maria Eugenia. 1992. "Migrantes agrícolas en la Frontera Norte: el caso de los Mixtecos." Pp. 105–115 in *Migración e etnicidad en Oaxaca,* edited by J. Corbett. Nashville, TN: Vanderbilt University Publications in Anthropology.

Aquilino, William S. 1997. "From Adolescent to Young Adult: A Prospective Study of Parent-Child Relations During the Transition to Adulthood." *Journal of Marriage and Family* 59: 670–686.

Aranda, Elizabeth. 2007. *Emotional Bridges to Puerto Rico: Migration, Return Migration, and the Struggles of Incorporation.* Lanham, MD: Rowman and Littlefield Publishers.

Arnold, Elaine. 2006. "Separation and Loss through Immigration of African Caribbean Women to the UK." *Attachment and Human Development* 8: 159–174.

Artico, Ceres I. 2003. *Latino Families Broken by Immigration.* New York: LFB Scholarly Publishing LLC.

Avila, Ernestine M. 2008. "Transnational Motherhood and Fatherhood: Gendered Challenges and Coping." Ph.D. dissertation, Department of Sociology, University of Southern California, Los Angeles.

Baca Zinn, Maxine. 1989. "Chicano Men and Masculinity." Pp. 87–97 in *Men's Lives,* edited by M. S. Kimmel and M. A. Messner. New York: Macmillan Publishing Company.

Bacallao, Martica L., and Paul R. Smokowski. 2007. "The Costs of Getting Ahead: Mexican Family System Changes After Immigration." *Family Relations* 56: 52–66.

Bacon, David. 2007. "Teachers in Oaxaca Face Repression and Violence." Znet. Retrieved January 22, 2008 (http://www.zmag.org/content/showarticle.cfm?ItemID=11914).

Bean, Frank D., Russell L. Curtis Jr., and John P. Marcum. 1977. "Familism and Marital Satisfaction Among Mexican Americans: The Effects of Family Size, Wife's Labor Force Participation, and Conjugal Power." *Journal of Marriage and Family* 39: 759–767.

Becker, Gary. 1991. *A Treatise on the Family*. Cambridge, MA: Harvard University Press.

Behnke, Andre O., Shelly M. MacDermid, Scott L. Coltrane, Ross D. Parke, Sharon Duffy, and Keith F. Widaman. 2008. "Family Cohesion in the Lives of Mexican American and European American Parents." *Journal of Marriage and Family* 70: 1045–1059.

Belson, Ken, and Jill Capuzzo. 2007. "Town Rethinks Laws Against Illegal Immigrants." *New York Times*, September 26. Retrieved April 27, 2009 (http://www.nytimes.com/2007/09/26/nyregion/26riverside.html).

Bernhard, Judith, Patricia Landolt, and Luin Goldring. 2005. "Transnational, Multi-Local Motherhood: Experiences of Separation and Reunification among Latin American Families in Canada." Latin American Research Group, May 15. Retrieved April 27, 2009 (http://www.yorku.ca/cohesion/LARG/PDF/Transantional_Families_LARG_May_05.pdf).

Bernstein, Nina. 2004. "A Mother Deported, and a Child Left Behind." *New York Times*, November 24, A1.

———. 2007. "Spitzer Grants Illegal Immigrants Easier Access to Driver's Licenses." *New York Times*, September 22. Retrieved April 27, 2009 (http://www.nytimes.com/2007/09/22/nyregion/22licenses.html?scp=19&sq=immigration%20fraud%20lawyer&st=cse).

Besserer, Federico. 2004. *Topografías transnacionales: Hacia una geografía de la vida transnacional*. Mexico DF: Universidad Autónoma Metropolitana.

Bianchi, Suzanne M. 2006. "Mothers and Daughters 'Do,' Fathers 'Don't Do' Family: Gender and Generational Bonds." *Journal of Marriage and Family* 68: 812–816.

Bianchi, Suzanne M., Melissa A. Milkie, Liana C. Sayer, and John P. Robinson. 2000. "Is Anyone Doing the Housework? Trends in the Gender Division of Household Labor." *Social Forces* 79: 191–228.

Black, William G. 2001. "Military-Induced Family Separation: A Stress Reduction Intervention." *Social Work* 38: 273–280.

Boehm, Deborah. 2004. "Gender(ed) Migrations: Shifting Gender Subjectivities in a Transnational Mexican Community." Working Paper No. 100, Center for Comparative Immigration Studies. Retrieved April 27, 2009 (http://ccis.ucsd.edu/PUBLICATIONS/wrkg100.pdf).

———. 2008. "'For My Children': Constructing Family and Navigating the State in the U.S.-Mexico Transnation." *Anthropological Quarterly* 81: 777–802.

Borges, Guilherme, Maria Elena Medina-Mora, Anne Lown, Ye Yu, Marjorie J. Robertson, Cheryl Cherpitel, and Tom Greenfield. 2006. "Alcohol Use Disorders in National Samples of Mexicans and Mexican-Americans." *Hispanic Journal of Behavioral Sciences* 28: 425–449.

Bowers, Bonita F., and Barbara J. Myers. 1999. "Grandmothers Providing Care for Grandchildren: Consequences of Various Levels of Caregiving." *Family Relations* 48: 303–311.

Bracho, Teresa. 2000. "Poverty and Education in Mexico, 1984–1996." Pp. 248–284 in *Unequal Schools, Unequal Chances: The Challenges of Equal Opportunity in the Americas,* edited by F. Reimers. Boston: Harvard University David Rockefeller Center for Latin American Studies.

Bras, Hilde. 2003. "Maids to the City: Migration Patterns of Female Domestic Servants from the Province of Zeeland, the Netherlands (1850–1950)." *History of the Family* 8: 217–247.

Bryceson, Deborah, and Ulla Vuorela. 2002. *The Transnational Family: New European Frontiers and Global Networks.* Oxford and New York: Berg Books.

Burawoy, Michael. 1979. *Manufacturing Consent.* Chicago: University of Chicago Press.

Burawoy, Michael, et al. 2000. *Global Ethnography: Forces, Connections, and Imaginations in a Postmodern World.* Berkeley and Los Angeles: University of California Press.

Capps, Randy. 2001. "Hardship among Children of Immigrants: Findings from the 1999 National Survey of America's Families." New York: Urban Institute. Retrieved April 27, 2009 (http://www.urban.org/uploadedPDF/411566_immigration_raids.pdf).

Capps, Randy, Rosa Maria Castañeda, Ajay Chaudry, and Robert Santos. 2007. "Paying the Price: The Impact of Immigration Raids on America's Children." Washington, DC, and New York: National Council of La Raza and the Urban Institute. Retrieved August 8, 2008 (http://www.nclr.org/content/publications/download/49166).

Castañeda-Tinoco, Ernesto. 2006. "Living in Limbo: The Social Context and Developmental Impact of Migrant Remittances." Master's thesis, Department of Sociology, Columbia University, New York.

Cave, Damien. 2004. "In a Divided Town, A Question of Hate or Cash?" *New York Times,* October 24. Retrieved April 27, 2009 (http://www.nytimes.com/2004/10/24/nyregion/24bias.html).

Cerrutti, Marcela, and Douglas Massey. 2001. "On the Auspices of Female Migration from Mexico to the United States." *Demography* 38: 187–200.

Chamberlain, Mary. 2003. "Rethinking Caribbean Families: Extending the Links." *Community, Work, and Family* 6: 63–76.

Chang, Grace. 2000. *Disposable Domestics: Immigrant Women Workers in the Global Economy.* Cambridge, MA: South End Press.

Chavez, Leo. 1992. *Shadowed Lives: Undocumented Immigrants in American Society.* Fort Worth, TX: Harcourt Brace Jovanovich.

Cherlin, Andrew J. 2006. "On Single Mothers 'Doing' Family." *Journal of Marriage and Family* 68: 796–799.

Chinchilla, Norma, and Kristine Zentgraf. 2007. "Immigrant Children's Views of Family Separation and Reunification." Paper presented at the Latin American Studies Conference. Montreal, Canada (September).

Coe, Cati. 2008. "The Structuring of Feeling in Ghanaian Transnational Families." *City and Society* 20: 222–250.

Cohen, Jeffrey H. 2004. *The Culture of Migration in Southern Mexico.* Austin: University of Texas Press.

———. 2007. "The Effects of Political Unrest on Migration Decisions: New Evidence and Preliminary Findings from Oaxaca, Mexico." Working Paper 154, Center for Comparative Immigration Studies. Retrieved April 27, 2009 (http://www.ccis-ucsd.org/PUBLICATIONS/wrkg154.pdf).

Cohen, Rina. 2000. "'Mom Is a Stranger': The Negative Impact of Immigration Policies on the Family Life of Filipina Domestic Workers." *Canadian Ethnic Studies* 32: 76–89.

Confessore, Nicolas. 2007. "Spitzer Drops Bid to Offer Licenses More Widely." *New York Times,* November 14. Retrieved April 27, 2009 (http://www.nytimes.com/2007/11/14/nyregion/14cnd-spitzer.html?hp).

Conley, Dalton. 2004. *The Pecking Order.* New York: Vintage Books.

Constable, Nicole. 1999. "At Home but Not at Home: Filipina Narratives of Ambivalent Returns." *Cultural Anthropology* 14: 203–228.

Corbett, Jack. 1992. "El contexto de la migración temporal Oaxaca-Oregon: elementos del mercado de empleo en el estado receptor." In *Migración e etnicidad en Oaxaca,* vol. 43. Nashville, TN: Vanderbilt University Publications in Anthropology.

Córdova Plaza, Rosio. 2007. "Sexuality and Gender in Transnational Spaces: Ralignments in Rural Veracruz Families due to International Migration." *Social Text* 25: 37–55.

Cornelius, Wayne. 1982. "Interviewing Undocumented Immigrants: Methodological Reflections Based on Fieldwork in Mexico and the U.S." *International Migration Review* 16: 378–411.

———. 1991. "Los Migrantes de la Crisis: The Changing Profile of Mexican

Migration to the United States." Pp. 155–194 in *Social Responses to Mexico's Economic Crisis of the 1980s,* edited by M. Gonzalez de la Rocha and A. Escobar Latapi. San Diego: University of California, Center for U.S. Mexican Studies.

———. 2001. "Death at the Border: Efficacy and Unintended Consequences of U.S. Immigration Control Policy." *Population and Development Review* 27: 661–685.

———. 2004. "Evaluating Enhanced U.S. Border Enforcement." Migration Information Source. Retrieved April 27, 2009 (http://www.migrationinformation.org/feature/print.cfm?ID=223).

———. 2007. "Introduction: Does Border Enforcement Deter Unauthorized Immigration?" Pp. 1–15 in *Impacts of Border Enforcement on Mexican Migration: The View from Sending Communities,* edited by W. A. Cornelius and J. M. Lewis. La Jolla, CA: Center for Comparative Immigration Studies, UCSD.

Cornelius, Wayne, and Jessa M. Lewis. 2007. *Impacts of Border Enforcement on Mexican Migration: The View from Sending Communities.* La Jolla, CA: Center for Comparative Immigration Studies.

Corsaro, William. 1997. *The Sociology of Childhood.* Thousand Oaks, CA: Pine Forge Press.

———. 2003. *We're Friends, Right? Inside Kids' Culture.* Washington, DC: National Academy Press.

Cortés Sánchez, Sergio. 2003. "Migration by Residents of the State of Puebla in the Decade of the 1990s." Pp. 183–202 in *Immigrants and Schooling Mexicans in New York,* edited by R. Cortina and M. Gendreau. New York: Center for Migration Studies.

Cowan, Peter. 1999. "'Drawn' into the Community: Re-Considering the Artwork of Latino Adolescents." *Visual Sociology* 14: 91–107.

Crittenden, Ann. 2001. *The Price of Motherhood.* New York: Owl Books.

Curran, Sara R., and Estela Rivero-Fuentes. 2003. "Engendering Migrant Networks: The Case of Mexican Migration." *Demography* 40: 289–307.

Daly, Kerry J. 2001. "Deconstructing Family Time: From Ideology to Lived Experience." *Journal of Marriage and Family* 63: 283–294.

D'Aubeterre, Maria Eugenia. 2000. "Mujeres y espacio social transnacional: maniobras para renegociar el vínculo conyugal." Pp. 63–85 in *Migración y relaciones de género en México,* edited by D. Barrera and C. Oehmichen. Ciudad de México: GIMTRAP and UNAM, Instituto de Investigaciones Antropológicas.

———. 2001. "¿Todos estamos bien? Género y parentesco en familias de transmigrantes poblanos." Paper presented at the Latin American Studies Association. Washington, DC.

———. 2002. "Genero, parentesco y redes migratorias femeninas." *Alteridades* 12: 51–60.

———. 2007. "Género, prácticas matrimoniales y comunidad reterritorializada." Paper presented at the Latin American Studies Association. Montreal, Canada.

Department of Homeland Security. 2008. "DHS Announces $12.4 Billion for Border Security and Immigration Enforcement Efforts." Press Release, January 31. Retrieved April 27, 2009 (http://www.dhs.gov/xnews/releases/pr_1201803940204.shtm).

Donaldson James, Susan. 2005. "For Illegal Immigrants, a Harsh Lesson." *New York Times,* June 19. Retrieved April 27, 2009 (http://www.nytimes.com/2005/06/19/nyregion/19njCOVER.html?pagewanted=print).

Donato, Catherine M. 1993. "Current Trends and Patterns of Female Migration: Evidence from Mexico." *International Migration Review* 27: 748–768.

Dreby, Joanna. 2006. "Honor and Virtue: Mexican Parenting in the Transnational Context." *Gender and Society* 20: 32–60.

———. 2007a. "Children and Power in Mexican Transnational Families." *Journal of Marriage and Family* 69: 1050–1064.

———. 2007b. "Parent-Child Separation in Mexican Transnational Families." Ph.D. dissertation, Department of Sociology, Graduate Center, City University of New York, New York.

———. 2009. "Gender and Transnational Gossip." *Qualitative Sociology* 32: 733–752.

Duneier, Mitchel. 2000. *Sidewalk.* New York: Farrar, Straus, and Giroux.

Dunn, Judy, Helen Cheng, Thomas G. O'Connor, and Laura Bridges. 2004. "Children's Perspectives on Their Relationships with Their Nonresident Fathers: Influences, Outcomes, and Implications." *Journal of Child Psychology and Psychiatry* 45: 553–566.

Dunn, Timothy. 1996. *The Militarization of the U.S.-Mexico Border, 1978–1992: Low-Intensity Conflict Doctrine Comes Home.* Austin: Center for Mexican American Studies, University of Texas.

Durand, Jorge, Douglas S. Massey, and Chiara Capoferro. 2005. "The New Geography of Mexican Immigration." Pp. 1–20 in *New Destinations: Mexican Immigration in the United States,* edited by Víctor Zúñiga and Rubén Hernández-León. New York: Russell Sage Foundation.

Durand, Jorge, Emilio Parrado, and Douglas Massey. 1996. "Migradollars and Development: A Reconsideration of the Mexican Case." *International Migration Review* 30: 423–444.

Edin, Kathryn, and Maria Kefalas. 2005. *Promises I Can Keep: Why Poor Women Put Motherhood before Marriage.* Berkeley and Los Angeles: University of California Press.

Edin, Kathryn, and Laura Lein. 1997. *Making Ends Meet: How Single Mothers Survive Welfare and Low-Wage Work.* New York: Russell Sage Foundation.

Ehrenreich, Barbara, and Arlie R. Hochschild. 2002. *Global Woman: Nannies, Maids, and Sex Workers in the New Economy.* New York: Henry Holt.

Elder, Glen H., Jr. 1998. "The Life Course as Developmental Theory." *Child Development* 69: 1–12.

Elder, Glen H., Jr., and Monica Kirkpatrick Johnson. 2002. "The Life Course and Aging: Challenges, Lessons, and New Directions." Pp. 49–84 in *Invitation to the Life Course: Toward New Understandings of Later Life.* Edited by R. A. Settersten. Amityville, NY: Baywood Publishing.

Erel, Umet. 2002. "Reconceptualizing Motherhood: Experiences of Migrant Women from Turkey Living in Germany." Pp. 127–145 in *The Transnational Family: New European Frontiers and Global Networks,* edited by D. Bryceson and U. Vuorela. Oxford and New York: Berg.

Escobar Latapi, Agustin, and Mercedes González de la Rocha. 1995. "Crisis, Restructuring and Urban Poverty in Mexico." *Environment and Urbanization* 7: 57–76.

Escrivá, Angeles. 2004. "Securing Care and Welfare of Dependents Transnationally: Peruvians and Spaniards in Spain." Working Paper No. WP404. Oxford: Oxford Institute of Ageing. Retrieved April 27, 2009 (http://www.ageing.ox.ac.uk/files/workingpaper_404.pdf).

Esteinou, Rosario. 2004. "Parenting in Mexican Society." *Marriage and Family Review* 36: 7–29.

Fagetti, Antonella. 2000. "Mujeres abandonadas: Desafíos y vivencias." Pp. 119–134 in *Migración y Relaciones de Género en México,* edited by D. Barrera and C. Oehmichen. Ciudad de México: GIMTRAP and UNAM, Instituto de Investigaciones Antropológicas.

Fahim, Kareem. 2008. "Immigration Referrals by Police Draw Scrutiny." *New York Times,* March 23. Retrieved April 27, 2009 (http://www.nytimes.com/2008/03/23/nyregion/23immig.html).

Fajnzylber, Pablo, and J. Humberto López. 2008. "The Development Impact of Remittances in Latin America." Pp. 1–19 in *Remittances and Development: Lessons from Latin America.* Washington, DC: World Bank. Retrieved September 11, 2008 (http://siteresources.worldbank.org/INTLAC/Resources/Remittances_and_Development_Ch_1_Eng.pdf).

Falicov, Celia J. 2001. "The Cultural Meanings of Money: The Case of Latinos and Anglo-Americans." *American Behavioral Scientist* 45: 313–328.

Federation for American Immigration Reform (FAIR). 2003. "Immigration and Crowded Housing." *Immigration and Society.* Retrieved April 27, 2009 (http://www.fairus.org/site/PageServer?pagename=iic_immigrationissuecentersbfob).

Fernández-Kelly, Patricia. 1983. *For We Are Sold, I and My People: Women and Industry in Mexico's Frontier.* Albany: State University of New York Press.

Fitzgerald, David. 2008. "Colonies of the Little Motherland: Membership, Space, and Time in Mexican Migrant Hometown Associations." *Comparative Studies in Society and History* 50: 145–169.

Fletcher, Peri. 1999. *La Casa de Mis Sueños: Dreams of Home in a Mexican Transnational Community.* Boulder, CO: Westview Press.

Flores, Emilio. 2006. "More and More, Women Risk All to Enter U.S." *New York Times,* January 10.

Folbre, Nancy. 1986. "Hearts and Spades: Paradigms of Household Economics." *World Development* 14: 245–255.

———. 2001. *The Invisible Heart: Economics and Family Values.* New York: The New York Press.

Fomby, Paula. 2006. *Mexican Migrants and Their Parental Households in Mexico.* New York: LFB Scholarly Publishing.

Foner, Nancy. 1997. "The Immigrant Family: Cultural Legacies and Cultural Changes." *International Migration Review* 31: 961–974.

———. 2000. *From Ellis Island to JFK: New York's Two Great Waves of Immigration.* New Haven, CT, and London: Yale University Press.

Fouron, Georges, and Nina Glick Schiller. 2001. "All in the Family: Gender, Transnational Migration, and the Nation-State." *Identities* 7: 539–582.

Fox, Adair, and Jill Duerr Berrick. 2007. "A Response to No One Ever Asked Us: A Review of Children's Experiences in Out-of-Home Care." *Child and Adolescent Social Work Journal* 24: 23–51.

Fox, Robert, and Pedro Solís-Cámara. 1997. "Parenting of Young Children of Fathers in Mexico and the United States." *Journal of Social Psychology* 137: 489–495.

Frank, Reanne. 2005a. "International Migration and Infant Health in Mexico." *Journal of Immigrant Health* 7: 11–22.

———. 2005b. "The Grass Widows of Mexico: Migration and Union Dissolution in a Binational Context." *Social Forces* 83: 919–947.

Furstenberg, Frank, and Andrew J. Cherlin. 1994. *Divided Families: What Happens to Children When Parents Part.* Cambridge, MA: Harvard University Press.

Gabaccia, Donna. 2001. "When the Migrants Are Men: Italy's Women and Transnationalism as a Working Class Way of Life." Pp. 190–208 in *Women, Gender, and Labour Migration: Historical and Global Perspectives,* edited by P. Sharpe. London and New York: Routledge.

Galambos, Nancy L., and David M. Almeida. 1992. "Does Parent-Adolescent Conflict Increase in Early Adolescence?" *Journal of Marriage and Family* 54: 737–747.

Galinsky, Ellen. 1999. *Ask the Children: What America's Children Really Think About Working Parents.* New York: William Morrow.

Gamburd, Michele R. 2000. *The Kitchen's Spoonhandle: Transnationalism and Sri Lanka's Migrant Housemaids.* Cornell, NY: Cornell University Press.

———. 2008. "Milk Teeth and Jet Planes: Kin Relations in Families of Sri Lanka's Transnational Domestic Servants." *City and Society* 20: 5–31.

Gans, Herbert. 1962. *The Urban Villagers.* New York: The Free Press.

García, Brígida, and Orlandina de Oliveira. 2006. *Las familias en el México metropolitano: visiones femeninas y masculinas.* Mexico, DF: El Colegio de Mexico.

García-Navarro, Lourdes. 2006. "Mexican Migrants Leave Kids, Problems Back Home." *Morning Edition,* National Public Radio, May 9, 2006. Retrieved April 27, 2009 (http://www.npr.org/templates/story/story.php?storyId=5392227).

Gardner, Helen. 1996. "The Concept of Family: Perceptions of Children in Family Foster Care." *Child Welfare* 75: 161–182.

Garrison, Vivian, and Carol Weiss. 1979. "Dominican Family Networks and United States Immigration Policy." *International Migration Review* 13: 264–283.

George, Sheba. 2005. *When Women Come First: Gender and Class in Transnational Migration.* Berkeley and Los Angeles: University of California Press.

Gerstel, Naomi, and Sally K. Gallagher. 2001. "Men's Caregiving: Gender and the Contingent Character of Care." *Gender and Society* 15: 197–217.

Gibler, John. 2006. "Teacher Rebellion in Oaxaca." *In These Times.* Retrieved April 29, 2009 (http://www.inthesetimes.com/article/2795/).

Giorguli Saucedo, Silvia. 2004. "To Study or Not to Study: The Influence of Family Migration on School Enrollment among Mexican Adolescents." Paper presented at the Annual Meeting of the Population Association of America. Boston.

Glick Schiller, Nina, Linda Basch, and Cristina Szanton Blanc. 1998. "Transnationalism: A New Analytic Framework for Understanding Migration." Pp. 26–59 in *Migration, Diasporas, and Transnationalism,* edited by Steven Vertovec. Gloucester, UK: Edward Elgar.

Glick Schiller, Nina, and Georges Fouron. 1999. "Terrains of Blood and Nation: Haitians' Transnational Social Fields." *Ethnic and Racial Studies* 22: 340–366.

Goldring, Luin. 2001. "The Gender and Geography of Citizenship in Mexico-U.S. Transnational Spaces." *Identities* 7: 501–537.

González-López, Gloria. 2005. *Erotic Journeys: Mexican Immigrants and Their Sex Lives.* Berkeley and Los Angeles: University of California Press.

Goodson-Lawes, Julie. 1993. "Feminine Authority and Migration: The Case of One Family from Mexico." *Urban Anthropologist* 22: 277–297.

Goody, Esther. 1982. *Parenthood and Social Reproduction.* Cambridge, London, and New York: Cambridge University Press.

Gouldner, Alvin W. 1960. "The Norm of Reciprocity: A Preliminary Statement." *American Sociological Review* 25: 161–178.

Grant, Bridget J., Frederick S. Stinson, Deborah S. Hansin, Deborah A. Dawson, S. Patricia Chou, and Karyn Anderson. 2004. "Immigration and Lifetime Prevalence of DSM-IV Psychiatric Disorders Among Mexican Americans and Non-Hispanic Whites in the United States." *Archives of General Psychiatry* 61: 1226–1233.

Grasmuck, Sherri, and Patricia Pessar. 1991. *Between Two Islands: Dominican International Migration.* Berkeley and Los Angeles: University of California Press.

Guarnizo, Luis. 1998. "The Rise of Transnational Social Formations: Mexican and Dominican State Responses to Transnational Migration." *Political Power and Social Theory* 12: 45–94.

Gutmann, Matthew C. 1996. *The Meanings of Macho: Being a Man in Mexico City.* Berkeley and Los Angeles: University of California Press.

Ham-Chande, Roberto. 1995. *The Elderly in Mexico: Another Challenge for a Middle-Income Country.* United Nations-Malta: INIA/CICRED.

Hansen, Gerry. 2003. "Number of Children Crossing U.S.-Mexico Border Rises." *Morning Edition*, National Public Radio, June 23. Retrieved April 27, 2009 (http://www.npr.org/templates/story/story.php?storyId=1307611).

Hansen, Karen V. 2005. *Not-So-Nuclear Families: Class, Gender, and Networks of Care.* New Brunswick, NJ: Rutgers University Press.

Hanson, Gordon H., and Christopher Woodruff. 2003. "Emigration and Education Attainment in Mexico." National Bureau of Economic Research. Retrieved April 27, 2009 (http://www.economics.ucr.edu/seminars/winter04/03-05-04 Gordon%20Hanson.pdf).

Hart, Roger. 1979. *Children's Experience of Place.* New York: Irvington Publishers.

Haugen, Gry Mette D. 2005. "Relations between Money and Love in Postdivorce Families: Children's Perspectives." *Childhood* 12: 507–526.

Hayslip, Bert, Jr., and Patricia L. Kaminski. 2005. "Grandparents Raising Their Grandchildren." *Marriage and Family Review* 37: 147–169.

Hernández-Barajas, Socorro. 2008. "The Vulnerability and Risk of Unaccompanied Mexican Children Crossing the U.S. Border." Paper presented at the Childhood and Migration Interdisciplinary Conference. Philadelphia (June).

Heymann, Jody, Francisco Flores-Macias, Jeffrey A. Hayes, Malinda Kennedy, Claudia Lahaie, and Alison Earle. 2009. "The Impact of Migration on the Well-Being of Transnational Families: New Data from Sending Communities in Mexico." *Community, Work and Family* 12: 91–103.

Hildebrandt, Nicole, and David Joan McKenzie. 2005. "The Effects of Migration on Child Health in Mexico." Working Paper No. 3573. Washington, DC, World Bank Policy Research. Retrieved April 29, 2009 (http://www-wds.worldbank.org/external/default/WDSContentServer/WDSP/IB/2005/04/29/000012009_20050429125802/Rendered/PDF/wps3573.pdf).

Hirsch, Jennifer S. 2003. *A Courtship after Marriage: Sexuality and Love in Mexican Transnational Families.* Berkeley and Los Angeles: University of California Press.

Hochschild, Arlie R. 1990. *The Second Shift: Working Parents and the Revolution at Home.* New York: Viking Penguin.

———. 1997. *The Time Bind: When Work Becomes Home and Home Becomes Work.* New York: Metropolitan Books.

Hogan, Dennis P., and Nan Marie Astone. 1986. "The Transition to Adulthood." *Annual Review of Sociology* 12: 109–130.

Hondagneu-Sotelo, Pierrette. 1994. *Gendered Transitions: Mexican Experiences of Immigration.* Berkeley and Los Angeles: University of California Press.

———. 2001. *Doméstica: Immigrant Workers Cleaning and Caring in the Shadows of Affluence.* Berkeley and Los Angeles: University of California Press.

Hondagneu-Sotelo, Pierrette, and Ernestine Avila. 1997. "'I'm Here but I'm There': The Meanings of Latina Transnational Motherhood." *Gender and Society* 11: 548–560.

Horowitz, Ruth. 1983. *Honor and the American Dream: Culture and Identity in a Chicano Community.* New Brunswick, NJ: Rutgers University Press.

Hughes, Mary Elizabeth, Linda J. Waite, Tracey A. LaPierre, and Ye Luo. 2007. "All in the Family: The Impact of Caring for Grandchildren on Grandparents' Health." *Journals of Gerontology Series B: Psychological Sciences and Social Sciences* 62B: S108–S119.

Hunter, Andrea G., and Margaret E. Ensminger. 1992. "Diversity and Fluidity in Children's Living Arrangements: Family Transitions in an Urban Afro-American Community." *Journal of Marriage and Family* 54: 418–426.

Ibarraran, Pablo, and Darren Lubotsky. 2005. "Mexican Immigration and Self-Selection: New Evidence from the 2000 Mexican Census." Working Paper No. 11456, National Bureau of Economic Research. Retrieved April 27, 2009 (http://www.internationalpolicy.umich.edu/edts/pdfs/Ibarraran_Lubotsky.pdf).

Instituto Mexicano de Seguro Social. 2004. "Actualización del Censo Universo de Trabajo 2002–2003. Región 1 Mixteca-Cañada." Acción Comunitaria.

Instituto Nacional de Estadística y Geografía. 2005. "Población Total." México DF: Sistemas Nacionales Estadístico y de Información Geográfica. Retrieved July 10, 2008 (http://www.inegi.gob.mx/lib/olap/general_ver4/MDXQueryDatos.asp).

———. 2006. "Encuesta Nacional sobre la Dinámica de las Relaciones en los

Hogares 2006. ENDIREH. Tabulados." México DF: Sistemas Nacionales Estadístico y de Información Geográfica. Retrieved April 27, 2009 (http://www.inegi.org.mx/prod_serv/contenidos/espanol/biblioteca/Default.asp?accion=4&UPC=702825001348&c=13213).

James, Allison, Chris Jenks, and Alan Prout. 1998. *Theorizing Childhood*. New York: Teachers College Press.

Jendrek, Margaret Platt. 1993. "Grandparents Who Parent Their Grandchildren: Effects on Lifestyle." *Journal of Marriage and the Family* 55: 609–621.

Jensen, An-Magritt. 2003. "For the Children's Sake: Symbolic Power Lost?" Pp. 134–148 in *Children and the Changing Family*, edited by A. M. Jensen and L. McKee. London and New York: Routledge Falmer.

Jensen, An-Margritt, and Lorna McKee. 2003. *Children and the Changing Family: Between Transformation and Negotiation*. London and New York: Routledge Falmer.

Johansen, Shawn. 2001. *Family Men: Middle Class Fatherhood in Early Industrializing America*. New York: Routledge.

Johnson, Julia Overturf. 2005. "Who's Minding the Kids? Child Care Arrangements: Winter 2002." Washington, DC: U.S. Census Bureau. Retrieved April 27, 2009 (http://www.census.gov/prod/2005pubs/p70–101.pdf).

Jones, Bart. 2004. "Haunted by a Desperate Sacrifice." *Newsday*. Retrieved July 5, 2004 (http://www.newsday.com/news/local/longisland/ny-momo704,0,7557405.story?coll=ny- topstories-headlines).

Kabeer, Naila. 2000. "Inter-generational Contracts, Demographic Transitions and the 'Quantity-Quality' Tradeoff: Parents, Children and Investing in the Future." *Journal of International Development* 12: 463–482.

Kanaiaupuni, Shawn Malia. 2000. "Reframing the Migration Question: An Analysis of Men, Women and Gender in Mexico." *Social Forces* 78: 1311–1342.

Kanaiaupuni, Shawn Malia, and Katherine Donato. 1999. "Migradollars and Mortality: The Effects of Migration on Infant Survival in Mexico." *Demography* 36: 339–353.

Kandel, William. 1998. "Temporary U.S. Migration and Educational Outcomes in Three Mexican Communities." Ph.D. dissertation, Department of Sociology, University of Chicago.

Kandel, William, and Grace Kao. 2000. "How U.S. Labor Migration Affects Children's Aspirations in Mexican Migrant Communities." *Social Science Quarterly* 81: 16–32.

———. 2001. "The Impact of Temporary Labor Migration on Mexican Children's Educational Aspirations and Performance." *International Migration Review* 35: 1205–1231.

Kandel, William, and Douglas S. Massey. 2002. "The Culture of Mexican Migration: A Theoretical and Empirical Analysis." *Social Forces* 80: 981–1005.

Kasinitz, Philip, John H. Mollenkopf, and Mary C. Waters. 2004. *Becoming New Yorkers: Ethnographies of the New Second Generation*. New York: Russell Sage Foundation.

Kearney, Michael. 2000. "Transnational Oaxacan Indigenous Identity: The Case of Mixtecas and Zapotecs." *Identities* 7: 173–195.

Kelley, Michelle L. 1994. "Military-Induced Separation in Relation to Maternal Adjustment and Children's Behaviors." *Military Psychology* 6: 163–176.

Kibria, Nazli. 1993. *Family Tightrope: The Changing Lives of Vietnamese Americans*. Princeton, NJ: Princeton University Press.

Kimmel, Michael. 1996. *Manhood in America: A Cultural History*. New York: Free Press.

King, Valerie, and Holly Heard. 1999. "Nonresident Father Visitation, Parental Conflict, and Mother's Satisfaction: What's Best for Child Well-Being." *Journal of Marriage and Family* 61: 385–396.

Klomegah, Roger. 2000. "Child Fostering and Fertility: Some Evidence from Ghana." *Journal of Comparative Family Studies* 31: 107–115.

Konrad, Kai A., and Kjell Erik Lommerud. 2000. "The Bargaining Family Revisited." *Canadian Journal of Economics* 33: 471–487.

Kornblum, William. 1975. *Blue Collar Community*. Chicago: University of Chicago Press.

Kowalewski, Stephen A., and Jacqueline J. Saindon. 1992. "The Spread of Literacy in a Latin American Peasant Society: Oaxaca, Mexico, 1890 to 1980." *Comparative Studies in Society and History* 34: 110–140.

Kroska, Amy. 2004. "Divisions of Domestic Work: Revising and Expanding the Theoretical Explanations." *Journal of Family Issues* 25: 900–932.

Kufeldt, Kathleen, James Armstrong, and Marshall Dorosh. 1995. "How Children in Care View Their Own and Their Foster Families: A Research Study." *Child Welfare* 74: 695–715.

Kyle, David. 2001. *Transnational Peasants: Migration, Networks and Ethnicity in Andean Ecuador*. Baltimore: Johns Hopkins University Press.

Lan, Pei-Chia. 2003. "Maid or Madam? Filipina Migrant Workers and the Continuity of Domestic Labor." *Gender and Society* 17: 187–208.

Lancaster, Roger N. 1992. *Life Is Hard: Machismo, Danger, and the Intimacy of Power in Nicaragua*. Berkeley and Los Angeles: University of California Press.

Lareau, Annette. 2003. *Unequal Childhoods: Class, Race, and Family Life*. Berkeley and Los Angeles: University of California Press.

Larini, Rudy. 2008. "Migrants Deported in Record Numbers: Federal Enforcement Stepped Up in New Jersey." *The Star Ledger*, November 7. Retrieved April 27, 2009 (http://www.nj.com/news/ledger/jersey/index.ssf?/base/news-11/1226035564320550.xml&coll=1).

Larson, Reed W., and David M. Almeida. 1999. "Emotional Transmission in the Daily Lives of Families: A New Paradigm for Studying Family Process." *Journal of Marriage and Family* 61: 5–20.

Laursen, Brett, Katherine C. Coy, and W. Andrew Collins. 1998. "Reconsidering Parent-Child Conflict across Adolescence: A Meta-analysis." *Child Development* 69: 817–832.

Leinaweaver, Jessaca B. Forthcoming. "Outsourcing Care: How Peruvian Migrants Meet Transnational Family Obligations." *Latin American Perspectives,* special issue, "Peruvian Migration in a Global Context," coordinated by Karsten Pærregaard, Ayumi Takenaka, and Ulla Berg. Projected publication date: 2010.

Leite, Paula, Luis Felipe Ramos, and Selene Gaspar. 2003. "Tendencias recientes de la migración México-Estados Unidos." CONAPO. Retrieved April 27, 2009 (http://www.conapo.gob.mx/publicaciones/sdm/sdm2003/07.pdf).

León-García, Maria Alejandra. 2008. "Mexican Educational Policy Implementation: A Focus on Outward Migration as a Social Influence in the Primary Classroom." Paper presented at the Childhood and Migration Interdisciplinary Conference. Philadelphia (June).

Levitt, Peggy. 2001. *The Transnational Villagers.* Berkeley and Los Angeles: University of California Press.

Lewis, Jeffrey. 2000. "The Social Construction of Childhood in a Mixtec Community." Ph.D. dissertation, Department of Education and Sociocultural Studies, University of California, Davis.

Lewis, Oscar. 1959. *Five Families: Mexican Case Studies in the Culture of Poverty.* New York: Basic Books.

Liebow, Elliot. 1967. *Tally's Corner.* Boston and Toronto: Little, Brown and Company.

Lindstrom, David P., and Silvia Giorguli Saucedo. 2007. "The Interrelationship Between Fertility, Family Maintenance, and Mexico-U.S. Migration." *Demographic Research* 17: 821–858.

Llorente, Elizabeth. 2008. "Morris Rejects Jail Wing for Illegals." *The Record,* February 22. Retrieved April 27, 2009 (http://www.northjersey.com/news/immigration/15865522.html).

Lomnitz, Larissa. 1977. *Networks and Marginality: Life in a Mexican Shantytown.* New York: Academic Press.

López, Antoinette Sedillo. 1999. "International Law—U.S./Mexico Cross-Border Child Abduction—The Need for Cooperation." University of New Mexico. Retrieved April 27, 2009 (https://repository.unm.edu/dspace/bitstream/1928/3582/1/US%20Mexico%20Cross%20Border%20Child%20Abduction.pdf).

Lozano Ascencio, Fernando. 2004. "Tendencias recientes de las remesas de los migrantes mexicanos en Estados Unidos." Working paper 99, Center for Comparative Immigration Studies. Retrieved April 27, 2009 (http://www.ccis- ucsd.org/PUBLICATIONS/wrkg99.pdf).

Lundberg, Shelly, and Robert A. Pollak. 1996. "Bargaining and Distribution in Marriage." *Journal of Economic Perspectives* 10: 139–158.

Mahler, Sarah. 1999. "Engendering Transnational Migration: A Case Study of Salvadorans." *American Behavioral Scientist* 42: 690–719.

———. 2001. "Transnational Relationships: The Struggle to Communicate Across Borders." *Identities* 7: 583–619.

Malkin, Victoria. 2004. "We Go to Get Ahead: Gender and Status in Two Mexican Migrant Communities." *Latin American Perspectives* 31: 75–99.

Mandell, Meredith. 2008. "Immigration Raid Raises Questions about Passaic's 'Safe Haven' Status." *Herald News*, March 9.

Marcus, George E. 1998. *Ethnography through Thick and Thin*. Princeton, NJ: Princeton University Press.

Marizco, Michael. 2004. "Smuggling Children." *Arizona Daily Star*, November 21.

Marroni, Maria da Gloria. 2000. "'El siempre me ha dejado con los chiquitos y se ha llevado a los grandes . . . ' Ajustes y desbarajustes familiares de la migración." Pp. 87–118 in *Migración y relaciones de género en México*, edited by D. Barrera and C. Oehmichen. Ciudad de México: GIMTRAP and UNAM, Instituto de Investigaciones Antropológicas.

Marsiglio, William, Paul Amato, Randal Day, and Michael Lamb. 2000. "Scholarship on Fatherhood in the 1990s and Beyond." *Journal of Marriage and Family* 62: 1173–1191.

Martin, Philip. 1998. "Guest Workers: Past and Present." Mexico-United States Binational Study volume 3. Retrieved September 21, 2005 (www.utexas.edu/lbj/uscir/binpapers/v3a- 3martin.pdf).

Massey, Douglas. 2006. "Borderline Madness." *Chronicle of Higher Education*, June 30, B11.

Massey, Douglas, Rafael Alarcon, Jorge Durand, and Humberto González. 1987. *Return to Aztlan: The Social Process of International Migration from Western Mexico*. Berkeley and Los Angeles: University of California Press.

Massey, Douglas S., Joaquin Arango, Graeme Hugo, Ali Kouaouci, Adela Pellegrino, and J. Edward Taylor. 1998. *Worlds in Motion: Understanding International Migration at the End of the Millennium*. Oxford, UK: Clarendon Press.

Massey, Douglas, Jorge Durand, and Nolan Malone. 2002. *Beyond Smoke and Mirrors: Mexican Immigration in the Era of Economic Integration*. New York: Russell Sage Foundation.

Massey, Douglas, Luin Goldring, and Jorge Durand. 1994. "Continuities in Transnational Migration: An Analysis of Nineteen Mexican Communities." *American Journal of Sociology* 99: 1492–1533.

Mauss, Marcel. 1923. *The Gift: The Form and Reason for Exchange in Archaic Societies.* London: Routledge.

McElroy, Marjorie B., and Mary Jean Horney. 1981. "Nash-Bargained Household Decisions: Toward a Generalization of the Theory of Demand." *International Economic Review* 22: 333–349.

Melhuus, Marit. 1996. "Power, Value and the Ambiguous Meanings of Gender." Pp. 230–259 in *Machos, Mistresses, Madonnas: Contesting the Power of Latin American Gender Imagery,* edited by M. Melhuus and K. A. Stolen. London and New York: Verso.

Melhuus, Marit, and Kristi Anne Stolen. 1996. "Introduction." Pp. 1–33 in *Machos, Mistresses, Madonnas: Contesting the Power of Latin American Gender Imagery,* edited by M. Melhuus and K. A. Stolen. London and New York: Verso.

Méndez Morales, Sara. 2000. "Características de la migración femenina temporal en la mixteca oaxaqueña." Pp. 251–280 in *Migración y relaciones de género en México,* edited by D. Barrera and C. Oehmichen. Ciudad de México: GIMTRAP and UNAM, Instituto de Investigaciones Antropológicas.

Menjívar, Cecilia. 2000. *Fragmented Ties: Salvadoran Immigrant Networks in America.* Berkeley and Los Angeles: University of California Press.

———. 2006. "Liminal Legality: Salvadoran and Guatemalan Immigrants' Lives in the United States." *American Journal of Sociology* 111: 999–1037.

Menjívar, Cecilia, and Victor Agadjanian. 2007. "Men's Migration and Women's Lives: Views from Rural Armenia and Guatemala." *Social Science Quarterly* 88: 1243–1262.

Meyers, Deborah Waller. 2006. "From Horseback to High-Tech: U.S. Border Enforcement." Migration Information Source. Washington, DC: Migration Policy Institute. Retrieved April 29, 2009 (http://www.migrationinformation.org/USfocus/display.cfm?ID=370).

Migration Policy Source. 2007. "U.S. Cities Face Legal Challenges, and All 50 States Try Their Hand at Making Immigration-related Laws." Washington, DC: Migration Policy Institute. December 3.

Milkie, Melissa A., Robin W. Simon, and Brian Powell. 1997. "Through the Eyes of Children: Youths' Perceptions and Evaluations of Maternal and Paternal Roles." *Social Psychology Quarterly* 60: 218–237.

Millard, Ann V., and Jorge Chapa. 2004. *Apple Pie and Enchiladas, Latino Newcomers in the Rural Midwest.* Austin, TX: University of Texas Press.

Min, Pyong Gap. 1998. *Changes and Conflicts: Korean Immigrant Families in New York.* Boston: Allyn and Bacon.

Minkler, Meredith, and E. Fuller-Thompson. 1999. "The Health of Grandparents Raising Grandchildren: Results of a National Study." *American Journal of Public Health* 89: 1384–1389.

Mitrani, Victoria B., Daniel A. Santisteban, and Joan A. Muir. 2004. "Addressing Immigration-Related Separations in Hispanic Families with a Behavior-Problem Adolescent." *American Journal of Orthopsychiatry* 74: 219–229.

Moen, Phyllis, and Elaine Wethington. 1992. "The Concept of Family Adaptive Strategies." *Annual Review of Sociology* 18: 233–251.

Moran-Taylor, Michelle J. 2008. "When Mothers and Fathers Migrate North: Caretakers, Children and Child Rearing in Guatemala." *Latin American Perspectives* 35: 79–95.

Morse, Ann, and Leya Speasmaker. 2006. "In-State Tuition and Unauthorized Immigrant Students." Washington, DC: National Conference of State Legislators, July 26. Retrieved April 29, 2009 (http://www.ncsl.org/programs/immig/immig_InStateTuition0706.htm).

Mose Brown, Tamara, and Erynn Masi de Casanova. Forthcoming. "Mothers in the Field: How Motherhood Shapes Fieldwork and Researcher-Subject Relations." *Women's Studies Quarterly.*

Mummert, Gail. 1988. "Mujeres de migrantes y mujeres migrantes de Michoacon: Nuevo papeles para las que se quedan y las que se van." Pp. 281–295 in *Movimientos de población en el occidente de México,* edited by T. Calvo and G. Lopez. Mexico, DF and Zamora Michoacán: Centre d'Estudes Mexicaines et Centroamericaines and El Colegio de México.

———. 2005. "Transnational Parenting in Mexican Migrant Communities: Redefining Fatherhood, Motherhood, and Caregiving." Presented at the Mexican International Family Strengths Conference. Cuernavaca, Mexico (June).

Munch, Allison, J. Miller McPherson, and Lynn Smith-Lovin. 1997. "Gender, Children, and Social Contact: The Effects of Childrearing for Men and Women." *American Sociological Review* 62: 509–520.

Muñiz, Patricia E. 2000. "The Schooling Situation of Children in Highly Underprivileged Rural Localities in Mexico." Pp. 290–314 in *Unequal Schools, Unequal Chances: The Challenges of Equal Opportunity in the Americas,* edited by F. Reimers. Boston: Harvard University David Rockefeller Center for Latin American Studies.

Muñoz Izquierda, Carlos, and Raquel Ahuja Sánchez. 2000. "Function and Evaluation of a Compensatory Program Directed at the Poorest Mexican States: Chuipas, Guerrero, Hidalgo and Oaxaca." Pp. 340–373 in *Unequal Schools, Unequal Chances: The Challenges of Equal Opportunity in the Americas,* edited by F. Reimers. Boston: Harvard University David Rockefeller Center for Latin American Studies.

Myers, Scott. 1999. "Childhood Migration and Social Integration in Adulthood." *Journal of Marriage and Family* 61: 774–789.

Nakano Glenn, Evelyn. 1983. "Split Household, Small Producer, and Dual Wage

Earner: An Analysis of Chinese-American Family Strategies." *Journal of Marriage and Family* 45: 35–46.

Nash, June. 2006. *Practicing Ethnography in a Globalizing World: An Anthropological Odyssey.* New York: Rowman and Littlefield.

National Public Radio. 2005. "Profile: Increasing Numbers of Children Being Smuggled into the U.S. through the Border between San Diego and Tijuana." Transcript. February 24, 2005.

Nazario, Sonia. 2006. *La Travesía de Enrique.* New York: Random House Trade Paperbacks.

Nelson, Margaret K. 2006. "Single Mothers 'Do Family.'" *Journal of Marriage and Family* 68: 781–795.

Olwig, Karen Fog. 1999. "Narratives of the Children Left Behind: Home and Identity in Globalised Caribbean Families." *Journal of Ethnic and Migration Studies* 25: 267–284.

Orden Jurídico Nacional. N.d. "Ley Estatal de Educación [State Education Law]." Retrieved April 29, 2009 (http://www.ordenjuridico.gob.mx/Estatal/OAXACA/Leyes/OAXLEY055.pdf).

Orellana, Marjorie Faulstich. 2001. "The Work Kids Do: Mexican and Central American Children's Contributions to Households and Schools in California." *Harvard Educational Review* 71: 366–390.

Orellana, Marjorie Faulstich, Barrie Thorne, Anne Chee, and Wan Shun Eva Lam. 2001. "Transnational Childhoods: The Participation of Children in Processes of Family Migration." *Social Problems* 48: 572–591.

Oropesa, R.S. 1997. "Development and Marital Power in Mexico." *Social Forces* 75: 1291–1318.

Orozco, Manuel. 2007. "Connecting the Dots: Demographic and Labor Trends' Impact on Remittances." Inter-American Development Bank. Retrieved April 29, 2009 (http://idbdocs.iadb.org/wsdocs/getdocument.aspx?docnum=980587#509,1,).

Ortega, Ralph R. 2006. "No Papers? No Problem." *The Star Ledger,* July 23.

Paping, Richard. 2004. "Family Strategies Concerning Migration and Occupations of Children in a Market-Oriented Agricultural Economy." *History of the Family* 9: 159–192.

Paredes, Américo. 1993. "The United States, Mexico and Machismo." Pp. 215–234 in *Folklore and Culture on the Texas-Mexican Border,* edited by R. Bauman. Austin, TX: Center for Mexican American Studies Books, University of Texas at Austin.

Parreñas, Rhacel Salazar. 2001a. "Mothering from a Distance: Emotions, Gender, and Intergenerational Relations in Filipino Transnational Families." *Feminist Studies* 27: 361–384.

———. 2001b. *Servants of Globalization: Women, Migration, and Domestic Work.* Stanford, CA: Stanford University Press.

———. 2005. *Children of Global Migration: Transnational Families and Gender Woes.* Stanford, CA: Stanford University Press.

———. 2008. "Transnational Fathering: Gendered Conflicts, Distant Disciplining, and Emotional Gaps." *Ethnic and Migration Studies* 34: 1057–1072.

Passel, Jeffrey. 2004. "Mexican Immigration to the U.S.: The Latest Estimates." Mexican Information Source. Retrieved April 29, 2009 (http://www.migrationinformation.org/Feature/display.cfm?ID=208).

———. 2005. "Unauthorized Migrants: Size and Characteristics." Pew Hispanic Center, Washington, DC. Retrieved April 29, 2009 (http://pewhispanic.org/files/reports/44.pdf).

———. 2006. "The Size and Characteristics of the Unauthorized Migrant Population in the U.S." Pew Hispanic Center, Washington, DC. Retrieved April 29, 2009 (http://pewhispanic.org/files/reports/61.pdf).

Passel, Jeffrey, and D'Vera Cohn. 2008. "Trends in Unauthorized Immigration: Undocumented Inflow Now Trails Legal Inflow." Pew Hispanic Center, Washington, DC. Retrieved April 27, 2009 (http://pewhispanic.org/files/reports/94.pdf).

Patillo-McCoy, Mary. 2000. *Black Picket Fences: Privilege and Peril among the Black Middle Class.* Chicago: University of Chicago Press.

Paz, Octavio. 1981. *El laberinto de la soledad.* México DF: Fondo de Cultura Económica.

Penton, Kevin. 2008. "Plan: Punish Illegal Immigrants' Landlords." Asbury Park Press, July 8. Retrieved July 21, 2008 (http://www.app.com/apps/pbcs.dll/article?AID=/20080708/NEWS01/807080374/1004).

Pérez, Gina M. 2004. *The Near Northwest Side Story: Migration, Displacement, and Puerto Rican Families.* Berkeley and Los Angeles: University of California Press.

Pérez López, Ángel. 2003. "Ausencia del padre emigrante en el rendimiento académico del Bachiller del Plantel 14 'Mariscala', Oaxaca, México." Tesis para Licenciado, Facultad de Psicología, Universidad Regional del Sureste.

Pessar, Patricia. 1999. "The Role of Gender, Households, and Social Networks in the Migration Process: A Review and Appraisal." Pp. 53–70 in *The Handbook of International Migration: The American Experience,* edited by C. Hirschman, P. Kasinitz, and J. DeWind. New York: Russell Sage Foundation.

Pessar, Patricia, and Sarah Mahler. 2003. "Transnational Migration: Bringing Gender Back In." *International Migration Review* 37: 812–46.

Peterson, Iver. 2004, "A New Jersey Deputy Chief Is Killed Fighting a Fire." *New York Times,* September 4. Retrieved January 22, 2008 (http://www.nytimes.com/2004/09/04/ nyregion/04fire.html).

Pew Hispanic Center. 2007. "Fact Sheet: Indicators of Recent Migration Flows from Mexico." Pew Hispanic Center, Washington, DC. Retrieved April 29, 2009 (http://pewhispanic.org/files/factsheets/33.pdf).

———. 2008. "Statistical Portrait of the Foreign-Born Population in the United States, 2006." Pew Hispanic Center, Washington, DC. Retrieved April 29, 2009 (http://pewhispanic.org/files/factsheets/foreignborn2006/Table-5.pdf).

———. 2009. "Fact Sheet: Mexican Immigrants in the United States, 2008." Pew Hispanic Center, Washington D.C. Retrieved April 29, 2009 (http://pewhispanic.org/files/factsheets/47.pdf).

Portes, Alejandro, Luis Guarnizo, and Patricia Landolt. 1999. "The Study of Transnationalism: Pitfalls and Promise of an Emergent Research Field." *Ethnic and Racial Studies* 22: 217–237.

Portes, Alejandro, and Min Zhou. 1993. "The New Second Generation: Segmented Assimilation and Its Variants." *Annals of the American Academy of Political and Social Science* 22: 217–238.

Preston, Julia. 2007. "Immigration Quandary: A Mother Torn from her Baby." *New York Times.* November 17. Retrieved April 29, 2009 (http://www.nytimes.com/2007/11/17/us/17citizen.html?_r=1&oref=slogin).

———. 2009. "Obama to Push Immigration Reform Bill Despite Risks." *New York Times,* April 9. Retrieved April 27, 2009 (http://www.nytimes.com/2009/04/09/us/politics/09immig.html?_r=1andhp).

Pribilsky, Jason. 2001. "Nervios and 'Modern Childhood': Migration and Shifting Contexts of Child Life in the Ecuadorian Andes." *Childhood* 8: 251–273.

———. 2004. "'Aprendemos a Convivir': Conjugal Relations, Co-Parenting, and Family Life among Ecuadorian Transnational Migrants in New York City and the Ecuadorian Andes." *Global Networks* 4: 313.

Prieur, Annick. 1996. "Domination and Desire: Male Homosexuality and the Construction of Masculinity in Mexico." Pp. 83–107 in *Machos, Mistresses, Madonnas: Contesting the Power of Latin American Gender Imagery,* edited by M. Melhuus and K. A. Stolen. London and New York: Verso.

Pritchard, Justin. 2004, "AP Investigation: Mexican Worker Deaths Rise Sharply Even as Overall U.S. Job Safety Improves." *Associated Press,* March 13. Retrieved April 29, 2009 (http://fmmac2.mm.ap.org/polk_awards_dying_to_work_html/DyingtoWork.html).

Qvortrup, Jens. 1999. "Childhood and Societal Macrostructures: Childhood Exclusion by Default." Working Paper No. 9, Odense: Department of Contemporary Cultural Studies, University of Southern Denmark. Retrieved April 29, 2009 (http://www.sdu.dk/~/media/Files/Information_til/Studerende_ved_SDU/Din_uddannelse/Kultur_og_formidling/WorkingPapers/09_ChildhoodAndSocietalMacrostructures%20pdf.ashx).

Raley, R. Kelly, T. Elizabeth Durden, and Elizabeth Wildsmith. 2004. "Understanding Mexican American Marriage Patterns Using a Life Course Approach." *Social Science Quarterly* 85: 872–890.

Reeder, Linda. 2001. "Conflict Across the Atlantic: Women, Family and Mass Male Migration in Sicily, 1880–1920."*International Review of Social History* 46: 371–391.

Reynolds, Tracey, and Elisabetta Zontini. 2006. "A Comparative Study of Care and Provision Across Caribbean and Italian Transnational Families." Working Paper No. 16, Families and Social Capital ESRC Research Group: London South Bank University. Retrieved April 29, 2009 (http://www.lsbu.ac.uk/families/workingpapers/familieswp16.pdf).

Riessman, Catherine Kohler. 1990. *Divorce Talk: Women and Men Make Sense of Personal Relationships.* New Brunswick, NJ, and London: Rutgers University Press.

Rivera-Salgado, Gaspar. 1999. "Mixtec Activism in Oaxacalifornia: Transborder Grassroots Political Strategies." *American Behavioral Scientist* 42: 1439–1458.

Rivlan, Gary. 2006. "Dollars and Dreams: Immigrants as Prey." *New York Times,* June 11. Retrieved April 29, 2009 (http://www.nytimes.com/2006/06/11/business/yourmoney/11migrate.html?_r=1&scp=1&sq=notarios&st=nyt&oref=slogin).

Robichaux, D. 1997. "Un modelo de familia para el 'Mexico profundo.'" Pp. 187–213 in *Espacios familiares: Ámbitos de sobrevivencia y solidaridad.* Programa Universitaria de Estudios de Género/Consejo Nacional de Población/DIF/Universidad Autónoma Metropolitana-Azcapotzalco, Mexico.

Robles, Arodys, and Susan Cott Watkins. 1993. "Immigration and Family Separation in the U.S. at the Turn of the Twentieth Century." *Journal of Family History* 18: 191–211.

Roig-Franzia, Manuel. 2006. "Police Ordered to Oaxaca After 3 Killings in Strike." *Washington Post,* October 29.

Romero, Mary. 2008. "The Inclusion of Citizenship Status in Intersectionality: What Immigration Raids Tells Us about Mixed-Status Families, the State and Assimilation." *International Journal of Sociology of the Family* 34: 131–152.

Romney, Kimball, and Romaine Romney. 1966. *The Mixtecans of Juxtlahuaca, Mexico.* Huntington, NY: Robert E. Krieger Publishing Company.

Roy, Kevin M., Carolyn Y. Tubbs, and Linda M. Burton. 2004. "Don't Have No Time: Daily Rhythms and the Organization of Time for Low-Income Families." *Family Relations* 53: 168–178.

Rumbaut, Rubén. 1997. "Ties that Bind: Immigration and Immigrant Families in the United States." Pp. 3–46 in *Immigration and the Family: Research and Policies on U.S. Immigrants,* edited by A. Booth, A.C. Crouter, and N. Landale. Mahwah, NJ: Lawrence Erlbaum Associates.

Rumbaut, Rubén, Roberto G. Gonzales, Golnaz Komaie, and Charlie V. Morgan. 2006. "Debunking the Myth of Immigrant Criminality: Imprisonment among First and Second Generation Young Men." Migration Information Source. Retrieved April 29, 2009 (http://www.migrationinformation.org/USFocus/display.cfm?ID=403).

Rumbaut, Rubén G., and Alejandro Portes, eds. 2001. *Ethnicities: Children of Immigrants in America.* Berkeley and Los Angeles: University of California Press; New York: Russell Sage Foundation.

Ryan, Louise. 2004. "Family Matters: (E)Migration, Familial Networks, and Irish Women in Britain." *Sociological Review* 52: 351–371.

Ryan, Rebecca M., Ariel Kalil, and Kathleen M. Ziol-Guest. 2008. "Longitudinal Patterns of Nonresident Fathers' Involvement: The Role of Resources and Relations." *Journal of Marriage and Family* 70: 962–977.

Sahn, Michelle. 2004a. "For Immigrant Dads, Father's Day Holds Bittersweet Times." *Home News Tribune,* June 21.

———. 2004b. "Program Speaks Their Language." *Home News Tribune,* June 13.

Sampson, Helen. 2005. "Left High and Dry? The Lives of Women Married to Seafarers in Goa and Mumbai." *Ethnography* 6: 61–85.

Sánchez, George J. 1993. *Becoming Mexican American: Ethnicity, Culture, and Identity in Chicano Los Angeles, 1900–1945.* New York and Oxford: Oxford University Press.

Santibáñez, Jorge. 2000. "Características recientes de la migración mexicana a Estados Unidos." CONAPO. Retrieved April 29, 2009 (http://www.conapo.gob.mx/publicaciones/ migra3/06.pdf).

Sarasüa, Carmen. 2002. "Leaving Home to Help the Family? Male and Female Temporary Migrants in Eighteenth and Nineteenth Century Spain." Pp. 29–59 in *Women, Gender, and Labour Migration: Historical and Global Perspectives,* edited by P. Sharpe. London and New York: Routledge.

Sassen, Saskia. 2001. *The Global City: New York, London, Tokyo,* 2nd ed. Princeton, NJ: Princeton University Press.

———. 2002. "Global Cities and Survival Circuits." Pp. 254–274 in *Global Woman: Nannies, Maids, and Sex Workers in the New Economy,* edited by B. Ehrenreich and A. R. Hoschschild. New York: Henry Holt.

Sawyer, Adam, David Keyes, C. Velasquez, G. Lima, and M. Bautista. 2009. "Going to School, Going to el Norte: The Impact of Migration on Education." In *Migration from the Mixteca: A Transnational Community in Oaxaca and California,* edited by W. Cornelius, D. Fitzgerald, J. Hernandez-Diaz, and S. Borger. Boulder, CO: Lynne Rienner.

Schen, Cathy R. 2005. "When Mothers Leave Their Children Behind." *Harvard Review of Psychiatry* 13: 233–243.

Schmalzbauer, Leah. 2004. "Striving and Surviving: A Daily Life Analysis of

Honduran Transnational Families." Ph.D. dissertation, Department of Sociology, Boston College.

———. 2005a. "Searching for Wages and Mothering from Afar: The Case of Honduran Transnational Families." *Journal of Marriage and Family* 66: 1317–1331.

———. 2005b. "Transamerican Dreamers: The Relationship of Honduran Transmigrants to the Ideology of the American Dream and Consumer Society." *Berkeley Journal of Sociology* 49: 3–31.

———. 2008. "Family Divided: The Class Formation of Honduran Transnational Families." *Global Networks* 8: 329–346.

Schneider, Barbara, and Linda J. Waite. 2005. *Being Together, Working Apart: Dual-Career Families and the Work-Life Balance.* Cambridge and New York: Cambridge University Press.

Schneider, David M. 1968. *American Kinship.* Chicago: University of Chicago Press.

Scott, Stephanie. 2008. "Unaccompanied, Undocumented Children in Federal Custody: How Are They Faring?" Paper presented at the Childhood and Migration Interdisciplinary Conference. Philadelphia (June).

Selby, Henry. 1992. "The Economic and Social Effects of the Crisis on Mexican Urban Households: 1978–1990." *The Sociodemographic Effects of the Crisis in Mexico,* edited by H. A. Selby and H. Browning. Austin: University of Texas.

Seltzer, Judith A., Christina A. Bachrach, Suzanne M. Bianchi, Caroline H. Bledsoe, Lynne M. Caspar, P. Lindsay Chase-Lansdale, Thomas D. DiPrete, V. Joseph Hotz, S. Philip Morgan, Seth G. Sanders, and Duncan Thomas. 2005. "Explaining Family Change and Variation: Challenges for Family Demographers." *Journal of Marriage and Family* 67: 908–925.

Semple, Kirk. 2008. "A Killing in a Town Where Latinos Sense Hate." *New York Times,* November 13. Retrieved April 29, 2009 (http://www.nytimes.com/2008/11/14/nyregion/14immigrant.html?pagewanted=1&_r=1&emc=eta1).

Shanahan, Michael J. 2000. "Pathways to Adulthood in Changing Societies: Variability and Mechanisms in Life Course Perspective." *Annual Review of Sociology* 26: 667–692.

Smith, Andrea, Richard N. Lalonde, and Simone Johnson. 2004. "Serial Migration and Its Implications for the Parent-Child Relationship: A Retrospective Analysis of the Experiences of the Children of Caribbean Immigrants." *Cultural Diversity and Ethnic Minority Psychology* 10: 107–122.

Smith, Robert C. 2001. "Mexicans: Social, Educational, Economic, and Political Problems and Prospects in New York." Pp. 275–300 in *New Immigration in New York,* edited by N. Foner. New York: Columbia University Press.

———. 2006. *Mexican New York: Transnational Lives of New Immigrants.* Berkeley and Los Angeles: University of California Press.

Smith-Lovin, Lynn. 1989. "Sentiments, Affect and Emotion." *Social Psychology Quarterly* 52: v–xii.

Sørenson, Ninna Nyberg. 2005. "Transnational Family Life across the Atlantic: The Experience of Colombian and Dominican Migrants in Europe." Paper presented at the International Conference on Migration and Domestic Work in a Global Perspective. Wassenar, Netherlands.

Soto, Isa Maria. 1987. "West Indian Child Fostering: Its Role in Migrant Exchanges." Pp. 131–149 in *Caribbean Life in New York City: Sociocultural Dimensions,* edited by C. R. Sutton and E. M. Chaney. New York: Center for Migration Studies of New York.

Stacey, Judith. 1998. *Brave New Families: Stories of Domestic Upheaval in Late-Twentieth-Century America.* Berkeley and Los Angeles: University of California Press.

Stack, Carol. 1974. *All Our Kin: Strategies for Survival in a Black Community.* New York: Harper and Row.

Stephen, Lynn. 2002. "Globalización, El Estado y la creación de trabajadores indígenas 'Flexible': trabajadores agrícolas Mixtecos en Oregon." *Relacciones* 90: 87–114.

———. 2007. *Transborder Lives.* Durham, NC, and London: Duke University Press.

Stevens, Evelyn P. 1973. "Marianismo: The Other Face of Machismo." Pp. 90–101 in *Female and Male in Latin America: Essays,* edited by A. Pescatello. Pittsburgh: University of Pittsburgh Press.

Stewart, Susan D. 1999. "Nonresident Mothers' and Fathers' Social Contact with Children." *Journal of Marriage and the Family* 61: 894–907.

Stone, Pamela. 2007. *Opting Out? Why Women Really Quit Careers and Head Home.* Berkeley and Los Angeles: University of California Press.

Suárez-Orozco, Carola, and Marcelo Suárez-Orozco. 1995. *Transformations: Immigration, Family Life, and Achievement Motivation among Latino Adolescents.* Stanford, CA: Stanford University Press.

Suárez-Orozco, Carola, Irina Todorova, and Josephine Louie. 2002. "Making Up for Lost Time: The Experience of Separation and Reunification among Immigrant Families." *Family Processes* 41: 625–643.

Suro, Roberto. 2003. "Remittance Senders and Receivers: Tracking the Transnational Channels." Pew Hispanic Center. Retrieved April 29, 2009 (http://pewhispanic.org/reports/report.php?ReportID=23).

———. 2005. "Survey of Mexican Migrants Part I: Attitudes about Immigration and Major Demographic Characteristics." Pew Hispanic Center. Retrieved April 29, 2009 (http://pewhispanic.org/files/reports/41.pdf).

Suttles, Gerald D. 1968. *The Social Order of the Slum: Ethnicity and Territory in the Inner City.* Chicago: University of Chicago Press.

Thomas, William I., and Florian Znaniecki. 1927. *The Polish Peasant in Europe and America.* New York: Alfred A. Knopf.

Thompson, Ginger. 2003. "Crossing with Strangers: Children at the Border; Littlest Immigrants, Left in Hands of Smugglers." *New York Times,* November 3. Retrieved April 29, 2009 (http://query.nytimes.com/gst/fullpage.html?res=9A03EEDA1130F930A35752C1A9659C8B63).

Thompson, Linda, and Alexis Walker. 1989. "Gender in Families: Women and Men in Marriage, Work, and Parenthood." *Journal of Marriage and the Family* 51: 845–871.

Thorne, Barrie. 1987. "Re-visioning Women and Social Change: Where Are the Children?" *Gender and Society* 1: 85–109.

———. 1993. *Gender Play: Girls and Boys in School.* New Brunswick, NJ: Rutgers University Press.

Thorpe, Kate, and Kerry Daly. 1999. "Children, Parents, and Time: The Dialectics of Control." *Contemporary Perspectives on Family Research* 1: 199–223.

Tienda, Marta. 1980. "Familism and Structural Assimilation of Mexican Immigrants in the United States." *International Migration Review* 14: 383–408.

Tilly, Charles. 1998. *Durable Inequality.* Berkeley and Los Angeles: University of California Press.

Tilly, Louise A., and Joan W. Scott. 1978. *Women, Work, and Family.* New York and London: Methuen.

Tjaden, Patricia, and Nancy Thoennes. 2000. "Prevalence and Consequences of Male-to-Female and Female-to-Male Intimate Partner Violence as Measured by the National Violence against Women Survey." *Violence against Women* 6: 142–161.

Turnovsky, Carolyn. 2006. "A la Parada: The Social Practices of Men on a Street Corner." *Social Text* 88: 55–72.

United Nations Children's Fund. 2003. "Child Maltreatment Deaths in Rich Nations." *UNICEF Innocenti Report Card no. 5.* Florence, Italy: UNICEF Innocenti Research Centre. Retrieved April 29, 2009 (http://www.unicef.at/fileadmin/medien/pdf/repcard5e.pdf).

Urban Institute. 2006. The Children of Immigrants: Facts and Figures. Washington, DC: Office of Public Affairs. Retrieved April 29, 2009 (http://www.urban.org/UploadedPDF/900955_children_of_immigrants.pdf).

U.S. Census Bureau. 2000. "Census of Population and Housing Summary File 3." Retrieved May 2, 2005 (http://www.factfinder.census.gov).

U.S. Citizenship and Immigration Services. 2009. "Cap Count for H-1B and H-1B Workers for Fiscal Year 2010." Retrieved April 29, 2009 (http://www.uscis.gov/portal/site/uscis/menuitem.5af9bb95919f35e66f614176543f6d1a/?vgnextoid=138b6138f898d010VgnVCM10000048f3d6a1RCRD&vgnextchannel=e7d696cfcd6ff110VgnVCM1000004718190aRCRD).

U.S. Department of State. 2009. Visa Bulletin for May 2009. Washington, DC. Department of State Publication 9514. Retrieved April 29, 2009 (http://travel.state.gov/visa/frvi/bulletin/bulletin_4454.html).

Valdez-Suiter, Elisabeth, Nancy Rosas-Lopez, and Nayeli Pagaza. 2007. "Gender Differences." Pp. 97–114 in *Impacts of Border Enforcement on Mexican Migration: The View from Sending Communities,* edited by W. A. Cornelius and J. M. Lewis. La Jolla, CA: Center for Comparative Immigration Studies, UCSD.

Velasco Ortiz, Laura. 1995. "Migración femenina y estrategias de sobrevivencia de la unidad domestica: un caso de estudio de mujeres Mixtecas en Tijuana." Pp. 37–64 in *Mujeres, migración y maquila en la frontera norte,* edited by S. González, O. Ruiz, L. Velasco, and O. Woo. Mexico, DF, and Tijuana: El Colegio de la Frontera Norte and El Colegio de Mexico.

———. 2005. *Mixtec Transnational Identity.* Tucson: University of Arizona Press.

Verhoef, Heidi. 2005. "A Child Has Many Mothers: Views on Child Fostering in Northwestern Cameroon." *Childhood* 12: 369–390.

Vincent, Susan. 2000. "Flexible Families: Capitalist Development and Crisis in Rural Peru." *Journal of Comparative Family Studies* 31: 155–170.

Waldinger, Roger, and Medhi Bozorghehr. 1996. *Ethnic Los Angeles.* New York: Russell Sage Foundation.

Waldinger, Roger, and David Fitzgerald. 2004. "Transnationalism in Question." *American Journal of Sociology* 109: 1177–1195.

Waters, Mary. 1999. *Black Identities: West Indian Immigrant Dreams and American Realities.* New York: Russell Sage Foundation.

Watkins-Owens, Irma. 2001. "Early Twentieth-Century Caribbean Women: Migration and Social Networks in New York City." Pp. 25–51 in *Islands in the City: West Indian Migration to New York,* edited by N. Foner. Berkeley and Los Angeles: University of California Press.

West, Candace, and Sarah Fenstermaker. 1995. "Doing Difference." *Gender and Society* 9: 8–37.

West, Candace, and Don Zimmerman. 1987. "Doing Gender." *Gender and Society* 1: 125–151.

Weston, Kath. 1991. *The Families We Choose.* New York: Columbia University Press.

Wilding, Raelene. 2006. "'Virtual' Intimacies? Families Communicating across Transnational Contexts." *Global Networks* 6: 125–142.

Wong, Rebeca, Alberto Palloni, and Beth J. Soldo. 2007. "Wealth in Middle and Old Age in Mexico: The Role of International Migration." *International Migration Review* 41: 127–151.

Woodward, Lianne, David Fergusson, and Jay Belsky. 2000. "Timing of Parental

Separation and Attachment to Parents in Adolescence: Results of a Prospective Study from Birth to Age 16." *Journal of Marriage and Family* 62: 162–174.

Wrigley, Julia. 1995. *Other People's Children*. New York: Basic Books.

Wrigley, Julia, and Joanna Dreby. 2005a. "Children and Inequality." Pp. 213–237 in *Blackwell's Companion to Social Inequality*, edited by M. Romero and E. Margolis. Malden, MA, Oxford, and Victoria, Australia: Blackwell Publishing.

———. 2005b. "Fatalities and the Organization of U.S. Child Care 1985–2003." *American Sociological Review* 70: 729–757.

Zelizer, Vivian A. 1997. *The Social Meaning of Money: Pin Money, Paychecks, Poor Relief and Other Currencies*. Princeton, NJ: Princeton University Press.

Zerubavel, Eviatar. 1982. "The Standardization of Time: A Sociohistorical Perspective." *American Journal of Sociology* 88: 1–23.

Zhou, Min. 1998. "'Parachute Kids' in Southern California: The Educational Experience of Chinese Children in Transnational Families." *Educational Policy* 12: 682–702.

Zhou, Min, and Carl Bankston III. 1998. *Growing Up American*. New York: Russell Sage Foundation.

Zolberg, Aristide. 2006. *A Nation by Design: Immigration Policy in the Fashioning of America*. New York: Russell Sage Foundation; Cambridge, MA: Harvard University Press.

Zontini, Elisabetta. 2006. "Italian Families and Social Capital: Care Provision in a Transnational World." *Community, Work and Family* 9: 325–345.

Zúñiga, Víctor, and Rubén Hernández-León, eds. 2005. *New Destinations: Mexican Immigration in the United States*. New York: Russell Sage Foundation.

Index

Pseudonyms of study subjects are listed by given name.

Text: 10/14 Palatino
Display: Univers Condensed Light 47, Bauer Bodoni
Compositor: BookMatters, Berkeley
Printer and binder: Maple-Vail Book Manufacturing Group